Revised 2024 edition

ROCK YOUR STRIPES

JILINDA LEE

ENDORSEMENTS

'I've had the great pleasure of working with Jilinda in various capacities over the past few years, and *Rock Your Stripes* is without a doubt the summary of how she lives her life, how she leads and how she influences others. In a world that is becoming increasingly beige, it's such a relief to read a book from someone encouraging high-level integrity while maintaining individuality. I have enormous respect for Jilinda. I know that those who read *Rock Your Stripes*, or get to experience a workshop or event of some sort where Jilinda is presenting, will quickly see all of the good that she brings to the table, with a wonderful combination of down-to-earth wisdom and high-level knowledge. So sit back, grab a big cup of coffee and go on the journey that *Rock Your Stripes* is bound to take you on.'

Andrew Griffiths
International Bestselling Author and Global Speaker

'For me, this book is a journey through a process of realisation in both personal and career. It made me laugh many times, at myself and at the author's experiences, as I related so many instances to my own life; being female, adopted, qualifying as a mature student, being a similar age and hitting the glass ceiling on many occasions. How many "if only I had done ..." moments.

'It is inspirational, challenges you and makes you reflect. I have never regarded myself as the "F word" but certainly want equality, consistency and fairness. This is not a "let's hate men" book, it is a book that reasons with why women have not succeeded; some through entrenched views and others through stereotypes, but many through inequality.

'One sentence sums it up for me: "If this book helps just one woman to step up, stand out, speak up and lead positive change ... then sharing my stories and experiences here will be worth it.'"

Jackie Paterson BA (Hons) MCIPD CMgr FCMI
Educational Practitioner & Consultant

'As the head of one of the oldest and most respected leadership institutes in the world, I consider myself extremely fortunate that I am frequently asked to read and review books about management and leadership. Few that I have read are as practical and as "different" as *Rock Your Stripes*. And I say "different" in a very positive way! Jilinda's perspective on – and approach to – leadership is unique. As is *Rock Your Stripes*. It's a fast-moving, sweeping journey across the modern leadership landscape told from the perspective of a leader who has certainly "earned her stripes" in the world of management. What hits you right between the eyes about Jilinda is that she doesn't mince her words or beat around the bush! *Rock Your Stripes* is crammed full of practical tips to help you lead better and, more importantly, be better.

'There's no gentle lead in! The first chapter implores us to Disrupt the Status Quo ... and the rest of the book continues in the same bold vein. And rightly so. As Jilinda states, "I believe the most important single thing .. is daring to dare".

'*Rock Your Stripes* is a bold, brave and long overdue book about putting your fear aside and jumping in; in to life and in to leadership. Jilinda is an out and proud zebra, and after reading *Rock Your Stripes* I reckon there's a bit of zebra in all of us, waiting to be put proudly on display.'

David Pich MA (Cantab) FIML
Chief Executive

'Straight forward and straight from the heart, this is a very accessible read. It just might make you reflect, re-frame and re-envision your opportunities for making a difference.

'Jilinda encourages women to lead with authenticity, find better ways of solving problems and build positive change in workplace culture.'

Vivienne Tippett PhD OAM
Professor

'*Rock Your Stripes* is everything I expected from the dynamic individual that is Jilinda. Her desire to stand out as an accomplished professional and individual thinker is well charted in her first foray into the world of publishing.

'Focused, gutsy and relentless are all virtues that she expresses well in writing, and a very logical and convincing argument accompanies every motivating chapter of her book.

'While she professes to be a feminist, she has, throughout her life and in this book, maintained her respect for women and men, a respect that is clearly evident as she charts the steps of her self-help program.'

Errol R J Morrison
Media Creative

'What a privilege to be asked to review *Rock Your Stripes*. I have been waiting in anticipation for this book to be written and printed. From the first chapter it's *kapow*, *wow*, then so many *ah-ha moments* woven throughout the book.

'Jilinda shares her life experiences, her rawness, honesty and vulnerability, through every chapter – there's no fluffing of words. What has always struck me about Jilinda is how incredibly passionate she is about leadership, speaking out, questioning, disrupting the status quo. She encourages you to do the same.

'This is a book that you can read, absorb the message, take action, then re-read it. A manual to pour through, to inspire you to BE more, DO more, or pick you up during the challenges of life.

'Jilinda not only encourages you to rock your stripes your way – she boldly leads by walking her talk and rocking her stripes!'

Leonie Lomax
Intuitive Leadership Mentor

ABOUT JILINDA

Known for her vibrant, passionate personality, and straight-shooting commentary, Jilinda Lee is not afraid to challenge the status quo. She doesn't try to blend in with the ordinary and is not inspired by the average, nor does she believe in playing small to suit others. Instead, she purposefully rocks individuality, espouses authenticity, and dares to disrupt irrelevant social norms for greater-good outcomes.

After three decades of richly diverse leadership experiences in both the private and public sectors, Jilinda made the courageous jump to establish a consulting and coaching practice, its core mission to develop dynamic leaders, diverse and engaged teams, and vibrant cultures.

An internationally accredited leadership expert, 'Change Champion' facilitator and go-to leadership coach for government agencies, industry groups and communities across Australia, Jilinda is driven to help others be authentic, genuine, emotionally intelligent, inclusive and engaging leaders. Leaders many wish they had. Leaders the world needs more than ever.

She regularly connects with a growing community through her on-point posts, articles, panel commentary and videos, featured across a range of media platforms, and her energetic keynote presentations are packed with real and raw stories that provoke thought and inspire change.

Jilinda values knowledge and embraces life-long learning, both formal and informal through varied experiences. She holds a Master's degree in management (people and leadership majors), the globally recognised Chartered Managers designation, as well as accreditations in behavioural science analysis, coaching, and facilitation. To quench her 'need to know' thirst, she constantly researches and reads.

As a proud feminist and passionate advocate for greater equality and diversity, Jilinda established the ElevateHER Leadership Community in

2014, facilitated Lean In coaching circles (part of the global foundation LeanIn.org), and in 2020 founded the not-for-profit enterprise ElevateHER Australia, to support circle networks and their leaders nationally, provide education, and partner with other gender equality agencies in advocacy initiatives. She is a member and supporter of numerous women's groups, agencies and forums, including the Australian Gender Equality Council – AGEC, Australian Local Government Women's Association – ALGWA, UN Women Australia – UNWA, Women and Leadership Australia – WLA, and Women for Election – WFE, and active in advocacy initiatives such as #100daysforchange, #honourawoman, #ItsTime, #EqualPayDay, #IWD, and #UNWomen. In 2021, Jilinda was elected to the national Australian Gender Equality Council as a Board Director.

There is no doubt that Jilinda's high-energy sweet spot is fuelled and fired up when combining her two great passions: leadership and gender equality.

Shortly after Jilinda first published *Rock Your Stripes* (mid-2019), the world experienced a widespread global pandemic that particularly impacted women, initially with reduced choices and chances to focus on their own career goals, and subsequent heightened awareness of gendered role imbalances in homes, companies and communities. Being acutely conscious of these impacts, Jilinda embraced this crisis as a potential catalyst for accelerating changes to entrenched systemic gendered barriers.

Jilinda's ongoing research, writing and commentary is focused on addressing women's critical needs in areas of flexible career opportunities, creating life by design – not default – affordable housing and financial security, and abolishing ageism bias that compounds with other gender biases women are impacted by at every age, stage and phase of their lives.

When not travelling to deliver projects and presentations, Jilinda re-energises by rising early to watch the sun rise over the ocean, soaking up warm tropical sunshine, breathing in sea breezes, taking beach walks with her dog, and swimming laps, from her home base at Cairns Northern Beaches, Australia. She is an avid believer in daily meditation and journalling, flexible work practices and healthy lifestyle choices.

Jilinda's personal mission is to help women create life on their own terms, rock their stripes, raise their voice, rock the world, and change the game.

DEDICATION

To Chloe and Beau, my independent children – deep pride and gratitude

You are undoubtedly the protégés of a strong, feminist
mother. May you keep rocking your individual stripes.

To Saffron and George, my grand-children – deep bond

Your arrival sparked an urgency in me to write this book and
deepened my resolve to keep advocating for a more equal world.
May your lives be full of exciting choices, chances and changes.

To Gary, my Change Champion partner and side-line supporter – deep love

You got me from the start. Our Yin & Yang traits
balance and complement each other, while navigating
the swings and shifts that is life and love.
May we continue to rock our zigzag journey together.

To ALL the awesome women, who hold up half the world

You are the reason for this book. May more of you step
into lead roles, sit at the decision-making tables, rock
your unique feminine stripes and change the world.

First published in 2019 by Jilinda Lee
This edition published in 2024

A catalogue entry for this book is available from the National Library of Australia.

ISBN: 978-1-923007-73-4

Project management and text design by Publish Central
Cover design by Maria Biaggini (Independent Ink), Jilinda Lee and Peter Reardon

The paper this book is printed on is certified as environmentally friendly.

Disclaimer

CONTENTS

PART II: F.A.V.E. 5 FORMULA

INTRODUCTION

Let's start with the glaringly obvious. One of the strongest messages we receive is from what we see. It can have a huge impact on us. We form a view from a visual message in a nanosecond. Contrary to the adage *you can't judge a book by its cover*, most people do. At least initially. One thing I know from decades of personal experience in service-orientated industries: first impressions *really do count*. So, might as well stand out.

Yes … my book cover is deliberately bold, bright and brave. The stark contrasts of black-and-white zebra stripes mixed with my signature colour – bold orange – and the splashes of strong, vibrant colours; it all fits well with my personality, my purpose, and the personal stories I share within these pages. Perhaps that's what led you to pick this book up at a bookstore or online. I hope it grabbed your attention among the millions of marketing messages that get thrown at you each day. Uniqueness rocks!

Whatever the reason you are now reading this, it is my genuine intention to inspire and encourage you to make positive changes and bold decisions about your life. To make your unique mark. Let me explain why …

'SO .... WHAT'S WITH THE ZEBRA THEME?'

I'm a *name-the-elephant-in-the-room* kind of person. From many years of honing my communication skills from initial quiet questioning to a frustrated *WTF* judgement tone, to now one of genuine curiosity that feeds my need to know *why it is so*, I've learned the value in addressing the obvious questions up front. It distracts focus and flow when big questions are left unanswered.

So, as it makes no sense to tiptoe around this; here goes …

Elephant #1 … ironically, turns out — it's a ZEBRA! Yes, you ask, 'What's with the zebra theme?'

Here's the thing; I *love* zebras. For a very long time, I have been drawn to anything with strikingly bold zebra print or the stark contrast of black-and-white striping – clothing, bags, shoes, rugs, feature walls, and most recently – an awesome zebra-print couch for my reading nook. And, when I say *'very long time'*, I mean V E R Y long time. I designed my 21st-birthday party outfit: a black pantsuit with white inverted panels in the sleeves and pant legs, big white buttons and wide, white collar features. You get the picture; so '80s but oh so individual.

Decades later, it's become my signature style – no, not the '80s pantsuit … zebra print. It's part of my personal brand. In fact, my absolute favourite presentation outfits are either zebra print (#1 fave – sequin-embellished zebra-print kaftan) or variations of black-and-white striping with a splash of unexpected bright colour added (I'll explain the colourful splashes later).

A few years ago, I met a wonderful, intuitive coaching colleague (now one of my 'besties') who introduced me to the world of African animal spiritual meanings, initially sending me a short paragraph about the zebra. It was one of those OMG moments. If ever I was going to be likened to an animal or take on a symbolic animal, it would have to be the zebra.

Here's why:

The zebra is a powerful animal,
a symbol of individuality and balance

Rock Your Stripes

When you study the zebra, of course the first thing that stands out is its bold, high-contrast striping; each animal with its own unique design. Just like human fingerprints. No two zebras are alike. They have an extraordinary ability to survive and flourish in a harsh land. They enjoy and thrive on a challenge, like they know it's a chance for growth and strength. They don't give up, they step up – rising to confront obstacles. They are extremely resilient, resourceful and adaptable.

African animal researchers have observed that it's the zebra who is most situationally aware. They are always scanning the horizon, on high alert and the first to notice slight changes and potential threats. It is said that when the zebra stops, raises its head and starts twitching, all the surrounding animals watch the zebra; when it starts to move, the others follow. Therefore, it's often the zebra that influences and drives change.

Interesting? Most people think of the lion as being king of the prairie, but in fact it's the zebra who is often leader of the masses … the game-changing influencer.

Those who know me would recognise that the zebra symbolism sits well with me. My friends often say: *'That's SO YOU, Jilinda.'* Yes, it is – but it is not *exclusively* mine …

My hope, as you read through this book, is that you will not just recognise the quirky synergies between my shared personal stories and learnings and that of the zebra's characteristics – you will also embrace the self-confidence and powerful courage that comes from fully embracing your unique self. *Your* unique stripes. Your stark black-and-white contrasts, and your bright splashes of brilliant colour.

So get ready to ROCK YOUR STRIPES.

You'll find the zebra theme peppered throughout the pages following, to illustrate my overall intentional purpose and passionate drive to help women:

- **STEP UP** … to be brave

- **STAND OUT** … to be bold

- **SPEAK UP** … to brilliantly influence, drive and lead change.

IT'S TIME FOR FUNDAMENTAL CHANGE

Why do I think women need to do that? Aahh, it's time to reveal the second rather large elephant in the room:

> Elephant #2 ... the F word. No, not **that** one. I've made sure it doesn't pop up in print, although the same surety is not given at my presentations (I like to splash a little colour across all areas of my life). I'm talking about the **other** F word: yes, I'm a proud FEMINIST. Always have been, always will be.

Born in the '60s, my generation fought hard to ensure the 1940s–50s submissive housewife model was shown for what it was: unequal, unfair, uninspiring, undermining, and just plan unacceptable. Frankly, a set of man-made rules, conceived by men for the benefit of men.

'Oh, please no; not 1960s feminism again.'

I hear your screams.

'I don't want to be like one of them.'

I know. Surely we've progressed enough for there to be no need to rehash the outdated feminist movement, right? After all, as the Canadian Prime Minister Justin Trudeau so famously responded to questions regarding the number of females he appointed to his first cabinet: *'It's 2015'* – delivered with a good dose of unapologetic WTF tone of: *'How is that even a relevant question in today's world?'* Good on him for being a gender-equality role model; he's right. But sadly, years later – where are all the other notable global examples?

I hear it in the ladies' circles I mentor, the numerous international women's movements I belong to, and the many thousands of women all over the world who have recently rallied to send a clear message about unacceptable misogynistic, unequal views espoused by some of our elected 'leaders'.

Who could possibly ignore that?

Rock Your Stripes

In recent years, the global *#metoo* uprising has flushed out sexual abuse and gender discrimination that those in power (particularly in male-led industries) have been dishing out for centuries to women who felt they had no choice but to tolerate it. How great it is to now see women all over the world standing side by side, stating clearly: NO, NOT ACCEPTABLE!

Wrong is always wrong, even if some think they have the power to get away with it.

Yes, it's time for fundamental change. Women are sick of waiting for the game to change; for real equality of choices. It's time we stop hoping that 'one day, someone will do something'. It is my long-held, passionate hope that each of our lives be filled with more choices, chances and game-changing opportunities than those who walked the path before us.

May we be forever grateful to those brave, bold women of past eras who cleared and widened the path, reducing the obstacles to equal rights and choices in such things as voting, education, birth control, divorce settlements, child support, financial independence and career options. May we continue to draw strength from those radically disruptive women who dare to proudly wear the 'feminist' badge; still today. May we continue to strive for equality in our own circles and in our own lives.

However, despite all that – hope, gratitude, and acknowledgement of our sister placard-bearers – these are not personal action strategies. If you are feeling stuck, or belittled, or held back, and are ready to raise the bar, you will need to action your own game-changing plan.

Whether you are comfortable personally using the F-word (feminism) or not really doesn't matter. Whatever meaning you take from past eras and events, the true meaning of feminism is simply gender equality – that's *it*. Equal choices. Equal opportunities. Regardless of what different jiggly bits we possess below the neck. It's simply about fairness.

Frankly, from my observations, I believe in the last few decades we have dropped the ball on this issue, especially in my homeland, Australia. Research stats confirm this. To be up there at the top of global comparisons for the number of Australian women per capita who hold university-level degrees, and in the same report be ranked as low as 50th in the world for the number of women participating in the workforce, is astonishingly concerning.

Surely, most of us – men and women alike – would see these results as totally unacceptable, even shameful. While it's easy to point the finger at far-right conservative political parties, or blame that all-male corporate leadership team, or our own personal circumstances, I believe each one of us needs to act to ensure gender equality remains high on the agenda. Your agenda, my agenda, women's worldwide agenda, the agenda of our daughters, and most importantly, the agenda of our male partners and our sons.

But let's not just make it an agenda item or an aspirational quota goal; I believe it's time for more women to **step up**, **stand out** and **speak up**; to demand and drive much-needed change. It's also time for our men to help drive this change and support women to do that. We ALL need to pick up that ball, run with it and collectively slam-dunk it. The right time is NOW.

Okay ... so you're probably thinking that's all very inspirational, but your life is a little more complicated than most. Perhaps you are already juggling enough balls and are not sure you want to be a game-changing leader or sitting in a C-suite chair – even if it was offered to you on a platter. Besides, what would I know about your life or what you've already tried? Who am I to suggest it's now time for you to step up, right?

Yes, I get that stepping up into a leadership role in your chosen career might not be your thing, but there may be other areas in your life where you could drive some much-needed changes. Perhaps your role in addressing the equality challenge is to influence and support other women to step up, stand out, and speak up, or your daughters, granddaughters, and sons.

I certainly don't profess to have all the answers, and I'm not saying ALL women need to be sitting at the decision-making tables, but what I do know is that many hold themselves back from all sorts of opportunities and chances. I observe this continuously, and it concerns me greatly.

After years of coaching and mentoring others, I know the core reason for holding back is generally found in their crippling fears. The three most universally common fears of all are:

- **fear of failure (mistakes and losses)**

- **fear of rejection (not belonging)**

- **fear of not being good enough (expectations and judgements).**

… and then there's the main fear that halts progress on gender equality matters:

- **fear of the unknown (uncertainty and change)**

… and another one that's a massive fear for many women, and relates to the fear of rejection:

- **fear of what others will think (how others will talk about and treat them).**

I experienced all those fears very early on in life, and spent much of my first three decades striving to overcome them. Smashing through those fears. Unlearning old programming and relearning new ways to think and feel. I gradually grew and changed into the person I was meant to be. The real me – Ms Change Champion … with a voice and mission that mattered.

OOOOOPS

In fact, I started life a little differently to most, embracing change from day one. So … here comes the third elephant in the room:

Elephant #3 ... I was an accidental baby, given up for adoption by my teenage mother at birth.

Some may choose stronger emotive words like 'unwanted', 'abandoned' or 'discarded', but I don't see the point in dramatising what was the commonly accepted solution to 'the shame' of unplanned teenage pregnancies in the 1960s. The circumstances are not important; it is what it is.

I have no judgement and hold no malice for my birth mother, who has no doubt had to live with what would have been a very difficult decision at a time when there were far fewer choices, and to this day, still chooses to keep it a secret from her family. I respect her wishes.

That said, I spent the early formative years of my life trying to feel 'good enough', and to find some sense of belonging with my adopted family and their chosen circles, the hordes of relatives (big families), and their narrow-minded religious sect.

From an epiphany moment at age seven, I started my own journey of letting go of the need to fit in. Discovering that it was way more exciting to creatively explore and embrace my own individuality, I began to design my own reality. (You'll have to flip forward to read more about that moment, one of my earliest memories of awakening the 'real' me.)

Throughout my life, rather than ever thinking 'woe is me', I gradually built immense personal power and a positive attitude of: 'WOW, is me'. I learned from very early on the self-confident power that uniqueness and individuality gives; of being deliberately different, of standing out from the ordinary, of not trying to Compare, Compete, Copy or Conform. Individuality absolutely rocks!

EMBRACE THE ZIGZAGS

One more 'C' word I should mention at this point: I love CHANGE. Some would say I embraced it from birth. Zigzags are so much more fun than straight lines. I have a 'what's next' thirst, and enjoy the excitement and new opportunities that change brings. It makes no sense to keep doing stuff that's not working or is no longer relevant. For me, there is far more fear in being stuck with limited choices than in making changes. I think of change as simply turning the page to start another new chapter, and it's fair to say my personal book is thick from creating a life of interesting chapters.

As I wrote the chapters in this book, I'd lived in 11 regional locations, experienced two very different marriages, raised two individual, independent-thinking children, welcomed two adult step-sons and their families, had three very different career paths (more to come), and stepped up into various leadership roles (private business, partnerships, public sector, corporate and community) – driving change in all of them. No wonder I'm known as a Change Champion in my professional circles. Change is so exciting ☺.

Writing this book is another change for me; a challenging one. Fully embracing my vulnerability. Putting my thoughts, personal stories and learnings out into the world with no guarantee it will be accepted or even appreciated; well, that's kind of scary, and somewhat risky. I spent hours (read: years of procrastinating) mulling over what to include, how much to tell, and the real biggy: how to share my stories while respecting others who have been directly involved in my journey.

Real stories are not always pretty or comfortable for others.

In 2012, I built greater courage while making a life-changing career decision, and around the same time I read Brené Brown's book *Daring Greatly* about how the courage to be vulnerable transforms us. Like taking off a mask or standing naked on a stage, I learned that vulnerability – in all its uncomfortableness – is a strength. It takes courage to put it out there.

Three things I know for sure:

1. We have no control over how others will think or respond, nor do we own their shit ... so worrying about that is a waste of time and energy.

2. We learn more from doing the uncomfortable, uncertain, scary things that challenge us ... to become wiser, stronger, more resilient, and to grow and evolve.

3. I'm okay with not being perfect ... no-one is. There's no such thing.

My life has certainly not been perfect or particularly remarkable, and I would never have achieved all I have done, or experienced all that I have, without making mistakes along the way. Having a go, stuffing up, and learning from that is how we grow stronger and achieve more. I'm planning a few more zigzags; some will work, some will be another lesson, and I will be wiser for all of it.

So, with all that said, I courageously present to you my warts-and-all version. My who, why, what and how. My learnings, my opinion rants, my personal stories, snippets from those I admire, my passionate messages of encouragement, and proven tips to help you create your own stripes and boldly *rock* them.

My hope is, as you work your way through this book, you will be inspired to raise your own bar and design a life full of the opportunities you deserve to experience. May you add some excitement to your life and embrace the challenging zigzag pathways.

May you be one of those awesome women willing to step up, stand out, speak up, and be the change our world is so desperately needing.

INTRODUCTION

HOW TO GET THE MOST OUT OF THIS BOOK ...

Firstly, the intended outcome of this book is to inspire more women to step up, stand out and speak up, and to encourage more women to sit at the decision-making tables. I have deliberately repeated this theme throughout the parts and chapters, as it is the fundamental purpose for my writing this book, and is an extension of the women's support circles, programs, retreats and coaching services I offer.

The book is divided into two parts.

Part I is my inspirational call-out challenge to you.

By sharing my personal stories with you, I dare you to play a bigger game of life ... your full-arse, colourful, zebra version ☺.

I DARE you to:

DISRUPT the status quo ...

ASPIRE to be your greatest version ...

REACH for your goals ...

EVOLVE and keep growing ...

Inspiration is one thing, but it's your changes of behaviour and observable actions that will make the biggest difference. That's why I've included Part II.

Part II is about making those changes: doing it. From my own learnings and experience as a leadership mentor, I have developed a formula of five core igniters and strengtheners of personal power. I now boldly refer to this as the FAVE 5 Formula: five 'I's for HOW to be a brave, bold, and brilliant game-changing woman:

Fuchsia	**Be an INDIVIDUAL**
Red	**Be INDEPENDENT**
Yellow	**Be an INITIATOR**
Orange	**Be an INFLUENCER**
Teal	**Be INVOLVED**

Although I colour-code these five sections in presentations and programs, the colour printing costs would potentially have made the book less accessible to all. So, instead: grab some colouring pencils or highlighters and add your own splashes of colour. I've given you suggestions of the colours I associate with each chapter, but I encourage you to be creative. Personalise it. Make this book your own unique copy. Rock your own colours.

Colouring the chapter title pages in Part II will make it easier to find and go to any section of interest, whenever you feel the need to build more muscle around that behaviour. While these sections are not an ordered process, the first two are foundational as they build your personal power that fuels the confidence needed to propel your progress. They are the strong central core of the FAVE 5 Formula.

It is my aim for this book to be a useful reflection tool and a go-to reference source. For that reason, I have included some key points and checklists as simple reminders, and a few reflective exercises and questions for you to ponder. Oh, and when you flip to the very back, you'll find a thought-bubble section for you to easily record your ideas and take-away actions in one easy location.

One more thing: I'm a bit of a quote queen. I personally find inspirational quotes to be a wonderful way to motivate positive actions. Peppered throughout the book, please take a moment to pause and reflect on the meaning you take from these quotes.

Embrace the journey … it's time to change the game … shake it up a bit … be bolder, braver and brighter … and make a bigger difference.

WHAT A WONDERFUL TIME TO BE A WOMAN

Are you ready to elevate your goals? …

To fuel your inner power and boost your confidence? …

To change how you play your game of life? …

To stride out in your unique, colourful stripes? …

To be a game-changing woman? …

To make a bigger difference?

I DARE you to turn the pages, embrace the learnings, and then bravely step up, boldly stand out and brilliantly speak up. The world is waiting for you to ROCK YOUR STRIPES.

THE STARFISH STORY

Original story by Loren Eisley.

One day a man was walking along the beach, when he noticed a boy hurriedly picking up and gently throwing things into the ocean.

Approaching the boy, he asked, 'Young man, what are you doing?'

The boy replied, 'Throwing starfish back into the ocean. The surf is up and the tide is going out. If I don't throw them back, they'll die.'

The man laughed to himself and said, 'Don't you realise there are miles and miles of beach and hundreds of starfish? You can't make any difference!'

After listening politely, the boy bent down, picked up another starfish, and threw it into the surf. Then, smiling at the man, he said,

'I made a difference to that one.'

This story, originally written by Loren Eisley as part of an essay in 1969, has been retold and used by many motivational speakers to illustrate the point that ONE motivated individual CAN make a difference – even if the effort is just one touch point, or one chunk of work at a time. It all counts.

Likewise, if this book helps just one woman to step up, stand out, speak up and lead positive change … then sharing my stories and experiences here will be worth it. Like waves leaving a mark on the sand, I believe the ripple effect that starts from just one person leading change can be powerful beyond measure.

I believe that the most important single thing, beyond discipline and creativity, is daring to **DARE.**

Maya Angelou

PART I

D.A.R.E.

DISRUPT ... the status quo

ASPIRE ... to be your
greatest version

REACH ... for your goals

EVOLVE ... keep learning
and growing

Rock Your Stripes

What a wonderful time to be a woman.

Now, more than any time in the past six decades I have lived through, there is immense opportunity for you to reach your greatest potential … ready right now for you to grasp hold of.

> **WARNING: I passionately write this section like an obsessed woman on an urgent mission to influence change at the deepest level — to challenge core beliefs, entrenched habits, and our perceived role in society as women. To open our eyes to choices and chances.**

This is a call to action for my own daughter, my beautiful granddaughter, my niece and grand-niece, the young women in my partner's family, the women in circles I've facilitated, and all those I've met at networking events and in client organisations, and those I'm yet to meet; especially to those who have been holding back, blending in or keeping quiet.

> **I urge you … now is the time to step up, stand out and speak up.**
>
> **I DARE you to be all you can be … to play your game of life at 100%.**
>
> **Become your full-arse version … don't settle for half-arse.**

NOW IS THE TIME TO …

- **DISRUPT** the status quo …
  It's madness to keep doing the same things and hope for a better result. Hope is not a strategy … it's a fantasy.

- **ASPIRE** to be your greatest version …

   Why would you want to be or do less than you are capable of? Playing small is not a predetermined destiny … it's a choice.

- **REACH** for your goals …

   Success happens to those who make it happen, rather than those who wait for it to be offered. Reach wider and higher than you think will be possible.

- **EVOLVE** and keep evolving …

   Life is a journey of continual learning and growth. Like filling up your wisdom bucket; you are never 'there yet'.

I hope this section will inspire you to DARE to dream, DARE to explore, DARE to plan and – most of all – DARE to take that first step … and the second … and keep climbing that staircase towards your biggest goals.

FIRST UP …

There are two words I want you to delete from your thinking and your responses – verbal and written. They are *'SHOULD'* and *'WISH'*.

   Write them in big letters, put them up on your wall, and draw a thick red line through them.

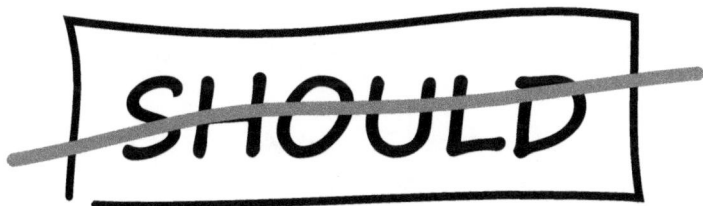

'SHOULD' is a judgemental expectation based on comparing your life with others, and is driven by one of the most universally common and most debilitating FEARS:

The fear of not being good enough.

Smash that! Leave perfectionism where it belongs – perfection is an illusion. Focus on your current skills and your ability to learn new things and new ways of doing the things you are passionate about. You have everything you need inside you to take hold of this journey called *life*.

Your journey – your life.

You have the right to make your own decisions and do whatever you want, without going on a 'shoulding' guilt trip. So, stop *shoulding* on yourself, stop listening to the *should-ers*, and simply be the person you want to be – your unique version.

WISH ~~WISH~~

A 'WISH', like hope, is not a strategy. It belongs only in fairy tales and birthday cards. The problem with wishing stuff for ourselves is it's often just a whimsical thought that our over-protective, risk-averse, internal BS voice immediately blows away with, *'But, I can't'*, or, *'But, that won't happen because …'*, or some other slap-down response. Turn your wishes into real actions. You CAN (or you can't), you WILL (or you won't), you ARE already starting to act with this first step: you've picked up this book for a reason. Well done.

**You ARE enough … you ARE capable …
you CAN change … you CAN do this.**

Keep reading … go ahead. Highlight sections and add your scribbled thoughts and ideas. This is your book to play with. Go nuts with colour and sticky notes … or not – it's your journey.

Now … let's be DARING, and begin with a little DISRUPTION ☺.

CHAPTER 1

DISRUPT ...
the status quo

Here's to the **CRAZY ONES.** Because it's the people who are crazy enough to think they can **CHANGE THE WORLD** who do exactly that.

DISRUPTION IS NOT A DIRTY WORD

DISRUPTION – like all behaviours – can be used for good or for evil intent. The disruption I'm referring to means deliberately driving change or stopping something to reassess better options. Disruption that intentionally shakes things up to make a positive difference. Not disruption just to be disruptive or a trouble-maker. That's a selfish, ego-based, attention-seeking intent.

I deliberately use the word *disrupt* because it's strong. It suggests that what's needed is more than just a minor change or a tweak. It is a heavy-duty interruption to the status quo, a notable change in direction, with deliberate intention of gaining a very different result.

So, I'm encouraging you to get comfortable with the word *disrupt*.

You don't have to be loud, aggressive and obnoxious to be disruptive.

In my young childhood years (up until my teens), most people we associated with (protectively restricted to family and church friends) thought I was a quiet child, often referred to as shy.

My older sister was more of the openly inquisitive one, and I tended to sit back, observe, and say very little. But, I assure you, my thoughts ran wild and deep. My mind was constantly questioning and assessing. Sorting out the manipulative crap from the truth; actively forming my own strong beliefs and values. I became very astute at observing others' behaviours and understanding what drives their actions.

Most would say I was a quiet achiever. I did well academically with little effort or fuss. Although I did make a minor fuss when the year 10 English teacher marked down my frank book review of a Shakespearian story. Apparently, my 1970s realist, feminist-leaning dismissal of 'helpless women needing rescuing' was missing the point. Personally, I think my overall review that the book sent the wrong message to women was VERY on point. Maybe I was a little ahead of my time (again!) for the conservative country town where I grew up – Toowoomba, Queensland.

So, while I pretty much did as I was told so as not to rock the boat, I certainly wasn't a 'goody two-shoes'. Come on – I grew up in the '70s, the era that questioned everything 'traditional'. I asked my fair share of 'why' and 'why not' questions and pushed a few envelopes – just quietly.

Of course, there were some indiscretions that I hid from my strict parents and the 'always watching' eyes of their narrow circle of church friends; those other 'perfect Christians' who were ready to judge and point fingers at the drop of a hat. At least, that was until my late teens, when my determined inner voice could no longer be contained and I unleashed a strong, determined outer voice.

I was becoming the REAL ME ☻.

Now, on reflection, I know I was continually observing and assessing each situation, working out what stories I was going to take away from every experience, often deliberately choosing NOT to follow the crowd or NOT to 'be like that'. Psychologists would probably say I was actively trying to discover WHO the real me was, and WHAT I wanted to be like … knowing deep down that I didn't quite fit or belong with my childhood scene.

Oh, and that's how I developed a strong dislike for the word *'should'* … more on that later.

By my early teens I had basically switched off from the surrounding 'white noise'. I was no longer fully present or invested in what was going on around me; like I was physically there but my mind had already left the building. My adventurous, excitingly independent plans were starting to form in my head. I was eager to start MY life.

By age 14, what I knew clearly was that I would leave school at the end of junior high school, year 10 (at 15 years of age), and start a career. Teachers tried to talk me out of that and encouraged me to go on to do senior high and university. I certainly had the grades, but I had a different goal in mind. Apart from not wanting to be a nurse or a teacher (the main reasons girls did senior schooling and university studies back then), I knew I needed to become financially independent, so I could leave home as soon as I turned 18. Going to university would not provide that option.

That was my plan, and that's exactly what I did.

Rock Your Stripes

Looking back is something I've deliberately not wasted much time doing, but writing this book forced me to dig around on the back shelves of my memories and reflect. What I think is quite amazing is that I had worked out what I needed to do in the next chapter of my life (my early adult years) by age 14.

I also understood it would be disruptive and disappointing for my parents, who held very traditional views about their role of raising a respectable young woman. A good girl. The ideal, quietly spoken teenager who blossomed into a demure woman, got decent grades at school, took a secretarial job for a few years, dated a nice boy from a Christian family (preferably the same religion), married a few months later (as a virgin, of course), then stayed home to cook, clean, copulate and care … becoming the perfect housewife and mother (aka: servant).

Frankly, I could not think of anything worse. I imagine you are all laughing at this point; it's not something young women today would subscribe to, so at least we've evolved from such subservient models. Right? Hmmm, but maybe not as far as we could?

I became determined to forge a career that could take me places, in which I could continue to learn, grow and achieve. One where I could creatively do things 'my way' – add that individual touch. One where I could create my own career path, perhaps my own business, which would all lead to personal and financial independence.

So, at age 15, I was offered a hairdressing apprenticeship with the top salon in Toowoomba, known for their excellent training and creating individualistic, avant-garde, high-fashion styles. I jumped at the chance. Two weeks later, I had my long school-girl hair cut to collar length. With my first pay packet I had my ears double-pierced, and a few months later I was wearing the latest super-short asymmetric-with-attitude hair, in rich mahogany red … topped off with super-hoop earrings, tight jeans and towering platform shoes. Oh … the joy of individual expression! The good girl just found her authentic attitude!

Uniquely me

Disruption at its finest! From then on I fell in love with the excitement of creative expression, the ability to continually change, reinvent and individualise, and subsequently I developed a distaste of anything normal, mediocre, average, bland or same-same. Unafraid to disrupt the status quo, I discovered the thrill of individualism, independence and initiating change.

> **People should stop expecting
> normal from me ... we all know
> it's never going to happen.**

DISRUPT THE STATUS QUO

Fast forward a few years to NOW ...

If ever there was a time for women to shine, for women to be front and centre in leading and driving much-needed change, for women to join as a formidable force to purposefully disrupt entrenched, ineffective practices ...

> **... that time is now.**

Why do I say that? Well, if you take a broader look at the current leadership status quo across the world, many things are clearly not working well, and they haven't been for some time. You don't have to scratch the surface very deeply to see poor leadership models, unethical decision-making, underhanded dealings, inequality, unfair treatment, lots of back scratching and C-seat swapping, lots of MDBTY (*my dick's bigger than yours*) powerplays, corruption coverups, and a whole lot of self-preservation strategising.

Woah! Steady on Jilinda, you say. That's a whole barrel full of below-the-line negative behaviours there. Sure is. But let's take off the rose-coloured glasses and the good-girl smiley-face masks for a moment: it IS really that bad. It IS really unacceptable.

Rock Your Stripes

As I write this:

- there are seriously concerning powerplay decisions being made by influential global leaders, whose emotional intelligence levels, morals and motives are questionable at best

- an increasing number of Commission-led investigations are uncovering some very disturbing, unethical practices

- our politicians often finger-point, deflect, and spin the same parroted spiels focused on denigrating their opponents

- some local government organisations are in damage control over growing investigations into crime, corruption and poor governance behaviours from their elected and senior leaders.

I've personally observed, experienced, and had to coach people who think that behaviours like that are simply 'how it is' or 'how to play a politically savvy game'. Sadly, there are both men and women who subscribe to that thinking. I know; I've felt their pushback, and a few knives in the back from questioning such practices. These passed-down unacceptable behaviours that survive year to year, generation to generation, board to board and CEO to CEO continue because not enough is being done to change things.

In fact, despite the entire world watching these days through online connectedness and global communication, I find the blatant lack of appetite from many of the power players to change what is increasingly showcased as unacceptable behaviour quite remarkable and, frankly, just arrogant.

Ignorance is no longer an acceptable excuse, nor should it be tolerated. Information, research and data are broadly shared; knowledge and understanding are readily available. You'd have to be choosing to keep your head in the sand to not notice what's really going on, or a self-absorbed narcissist with no care factor for others. Most people I speak with are increasingly concerned with the way things are.

But, thankfully, there is some good news: glimmers of hope, ripples of dissent and courageous questioning. It's a good thing that these major enquiries are now occurring, but my point is this: there is not yet enough game-changing, positive action happening at the root of the cause.

Real change, systemic and sustainable, will require fundamental change to entrenched and widely accepted societal norms; changes in the way we think, in what we value and believe, which will then drive better behaviours and new actions, the greater-good goal being more inclusive, equal and fairer cultures and more collaborative communities. That's going to take a bucket load of disruption, right?

Deliberate and daring disruption is necessary.

Okay, so the world is not *all* doom and gloom. I definitely swing more towards the optimist side of the scale than pessimist. You know the saying: *focus on the glass half full rather than the glass half empty.* Actually, I'm probably more of an opportunistic realist. I'm less interested in labelling something, more focused on changing it for the better. To me, if the glass is half full, it provides opportunity to explore solutions; like how to fill it to the top, perhaps adding a more interesting and refreshing mix. Then, let's shake it up for an even better result. Celebratory cocktail, anyone?

What I'm saying is: why accept and try to describe the status quo when you can change it?

I love that Millennials (those born from 1980 to 1995 – yes, my kids) are seriously questioning the status quo, and rightly so. Previous generations have not got this right or done nearly enough to fix the obvious issues. We've been accepting the status quo and traditions that no longer make sense for way too long now. Yes, I'm talking about my generation, although I do consider myself a 'Millennial thinker' – a 'BT Millennial-Xer' perhaps?[1]

Reflecting on all those WTF, head-shaking moments I've experienced over the years – I'm sure many of you have them too – there's been too much politicking and posturing and not nearly enough

---

1   BT: before time 😊.

problem solving. There's just so much apathy towards changing entrenched practices. Way too much protectionism of the status quo, mostly for the benefit of the powerful; not for the greater good of society in general.

ONE SUCH HAUNTING IMAGE

In a world so rich in resources and highly successful companies, why do we still have such enormous amounts of poverty?

Back in 2007, while exploring Italy, I took a tour through the Vatican. The tour guide was well versed in providing details about the amount of gold inlaid in the marble tiles, etched into the walls and columns, woven into the huge tapestry wall hangings. There was gold everywhere, from the door handles to the statues, the thrones, and even the robes worn by the highest-level priests – the gold drippings certainly showcased a sense of prosperity, power, pompousness and pride.

Even though I had been brought up in a highly religious family, and my parents gave much of their time and money towards the growth and prosperity of their church, I remember being immensely overwhelmed by what I saw at the Vatican. I was moved to tears. Not because of its beauty, but because of such a blatant waste of resources that, if redirected, could profoundly and positively change the world in so many ways.

I recall fleeing across St Peter's Square to a coffee shop on the opposite corner, where I waited until the tour group finished viewing the last section inside the holy Basilica. I just couldn't take any more of it; such wasted opulence felt so wrong on so many levels.

Likewise, in our own countries and local communities some things are very obviously wrong, and yet many of us struggle to challenge them, much less drive changes to them. We continue to downplay and accept entrenched practices, sometimes as hallowed traditions (just the way it's always been), sometimes it's become a political football (just game playing), and sometimes as hopeless cases (just too hard to address).

Often, things stay the way they are because we tell ourselves:

- *'Who am I to speak up and be listened to?'*
- *'What difference can I make … I'm just one voice?'*
- *'Hopefully someone will do something, sometime soon … but not me … that's not my role.'*

Like the way-too-often touted Polish proverb:

Not my circus, not my monkeys.

The easiest thing is to walk past, look away, or hope someone else will deal with it. Except, it IS our circus. We are *all* in the big tent. The big tent of global, national and community responsibility.

Are you sitting on the sidelines, or perhaps in the very back row, content to just observe?

We live in a world where many people who already have a good life with everything they realistically need think it's okay to shut the doors on those who are just striving for the basic things, like a safe place to live, a roof over their head, a warm bed, a few clothes, a chance for an education, a job to pay their way, and at least one decent meal a day.

It's not okay.

It's not okay that in 2017 just NINE of the richest men in the world (yes, they were all men) had more combined wealth than the poorest 4 billion people. It's not okay that in some countries where many thousands of people are dying from hunger, their leaders are living in palaces with private jets and designer-clad families. It's not okay that those who make the designer clothes are often women in the poorest countries working 12-hour days, earning less per year than the company's CEO earns in one day.

Rock Your Stripes

A 2018 Oxfam report called to action the world's leaders and governments to do something about the increasing inequality between the very rich and the very poor.

Here's a summary extract:

> 2017 saw the biggest increase in billionaires in history, one more every two days. Billionaires saw their wealth increase by $762bn in 12 months. This huge increase could have ended global extreme poverty seven times over. 82% of all wealth created in the last year went to the top 1%, while the bottom 50% saw no increase at all. Dangerous, poorly paid work for the many is supporting extreme wealth for the few. Women are doing the worst work, and almost all the super-rich are men.

Even post-2020, and the flow-on economic downturn the global pandemic caused, the richest 1% grabbed nearly two-thirds of all new wealth (worth $42 trillion), almost twice as much money as the bottom 99% of the world's population, according to the Oxfam report 'Survival of the Richest' (published in January 2023).

Of course, I'm not going to get all political and point fingers to the far-right conservatives or the social left, nor look for who or what's to blame for the current situation. None of what I have written so far is about one-sided or single-issue blame or specifically gender focused – yet. I'm speaking broadly, in general terms. From decades of personal observation … yes, and frustration.

Let us act on this NOW.

Frustration is a key driver to motivate disruptive action. In writing this section, I'm very aware of my frustrated tone, but I don't feel the need to apologise for it. Being real, raw and authentic is a strong value of mine. Besides, frustration is a valid emotion that fuels the drive to disrupt the status quo, and – like all emotions – it can be used resourcefully or unresourcefully. Why not use that in a resourceful way to instigate positive change?

Believe me, I've tried the gently-gently approach. It doesn't bring about change; just mild conciliation. You know: smiley faces and nodding heads, followed by a sigh of relief when I've gone, and then no follow-up action. Nothing but avoidance. I understand people get stuck in the comfort zone, but I'm not willing to give up. For me, being stuck is scarier than change.

This is why I don't shy away from a challenge easily. I do have a radar for what needs to change. I do think it's time to disrupt. I do feel a sense of urgency. On the flip side – I also sense a massive, tsunami-size wave of excitement for the possibilities ahead. That's what drives me forward; a strong gut sense or intuition that it's time to make a bigger difference. To be the game changer I was born to be.

Perhaps that's your purpose too?

Be a game changer. The world has enough followers.

IT'S TIME TO CHANGE THE GAME

Just as I choose to live by the beach, where I can feel the sunrise shining its new energy across the waves each day … right now, there IS a noticeable shift. A ripple of positive energy and enthusiasm. A renewed, excited feeling among many of us that the time for real change is *now*. That it's time to disrupt old thinking, old models, and yes, dare I say it: the old boys' clubs.

I believe it's time for women to rise together, to support each other, in a renewed feminist wave or movement; only this time, it's not about ditching aprons, burning bras, or who changes the kid's nappy. Surely we've moved well along from those debates.

What I love about this current equality movement (some call it the 'third wave') is that it's universally and unapologetically about promoting more women into lead roles. It's time for more diversity at the decision-making tables to drive change. It's time to change the leadership game.

Really? You say: *Hasn't it been 'that' time for a long time?* Yes – it has. Australian long-standing political leader Tanya Plibersek agreed when she said in her rousing 2018 International Women's Day speech:

Rock Your Stripes

'Back in 2007 — we said: "It's TIME". But in 2018 — we are saying: "TIME's UP"!'

I agree.

Time is up. It was up then — and we're still not there yet!

Wishing, shoulding and hoping hasn't worked. Targets with no affirmative or procedural action haven't made enough difference. Quotas have worked to some extent, but there's been a lot of resistance towards making that a rule or accepted procedure.

I understand the well-debated gender quota dilemma. No professional woman I know wants to win a role just because of some gender balance rule or numbers game. However, we need to be mindful to not use that as an excuse for not doing anything, or not implementing any changes in the way we currently recruit, because clearly it is not working in our favour.

When Gerry Harvey — a long-term member of the Financial Review Rich List and best known from founding the Australian Harvey Norman retail giant — commented in a televised interview that there aren't enough suitably educated women in Australia to reach the goal of gender equality at board tables (or even a 30% target), I almost choked on my dinner. He went on to say that many males in his circle are annoyed at having to appoint lesser experienced women than alternate male candidates, just to meet a target and so they 'look good' for shareholders. Oh, please! What utter crap. Women outshine men in university degree achievements, and in numbers of graduates with high-level degrees. Organisations across the globe with women at the helm or on their boards outperform companies that are run by men only. Let us not forget which countries handled the global pandemic crisis with the best possible results in decisiveness, compassion and courage; yes — they all had women leaders making those crucial decisions.

I believe the real story is that the rich and powerful old boys' club clearly DO view women as formidable opponents; *that's the issue*. They know female applicants are highly educated, innovative, adaptable, collaborative, compassionate, engaging communicators, and astute negotiators. These men are fearful. The competition has risen to greater heights. Men who used to outsmart other mediocre men for position and power are now – perhaps for the first time – having to compete with 100% of the suitable candidates – not just 50% (only the males). Astute women who are eager to demonstrate their capabilities. So, the 'women are not good enough' argument from the old boys' club is not valid or factual. It's driven by fear, based on the need for self-preservation.

Disruption of these limited, entrenched views is necessary.

'We cannot change what we are not aware of ...
and once we are aware, we cannot but help change.'

Sheryl Sandberg, former COO of Facebook

EQUALITY MATTERS

Just a moment ... while I put on my favourite T-shirt ...

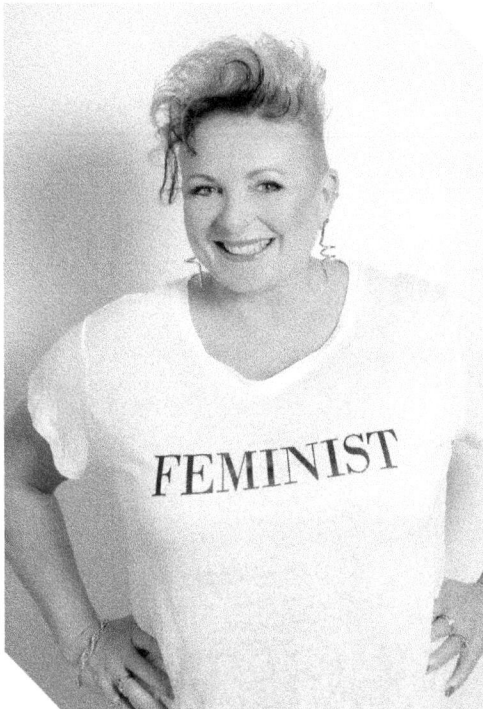

Rock Your Stripes

A random purchase from a quick department store stroll a few years back, I really love wearing this off-white, shabby-chic T-shirt.

As it's my casual weekend go-to comfy shirt, paired with funky casual pants, I've often worn it at the local shopping centre for Saturday-morning grocery shopping with my partner (his idea of a fun way to start a weekend – not mine). Of course, once out and about, I forget that the word FEMINIST is boldly displayed across my most prominent body area as I stroll up and down the supermarket aisles. BUT, believe me – I'm often reminded.

It's so funny – and rather entertaining – to watch the reactions of others. All smiles and thumbs-up from the ladies. Some older ladies then take a good hard look at my man, as if curious about what sort of man is proud to walk beside a 'feminist activist'? I feel like saying to them: 'He's one too – a feminist, an equal partner, a real man who is just as comfortable using pegs as power tools.' I'm going to get him a T-shirt that says: 'Yep, me too'.

By far the most noticeable reaction is that of senior males. You know – those pale, stale, conservative older gentlemen. From them I get anything from a frowning glare to a snarl and snub to a deliberate wide-berth trolley movement away from me. Mind you, I suspect they are already unhappy about having to do the grocery shopping. Of course, my response is to be overly friendly; lots of eye contact and engaging smiles. I really do find it amusing.

I understand that gender inequality suits some males; especially the older generation who are used to having a mother/carer/house-keeper as a wife … so, basically being looked after their entire life. Thank goodness that scenario is now becoming minority thinking. I often wonder: if they only knew how much happier their lives could have been with an equal partner. A happier partner, a partner who achieved her dreams and enjoyed a full and satisfying career. A financially independent partner who doesn't need an allowance. A partner who smiled a lot more because she didn't have to do 80% to 100% of the household tasks, or have a 'second job' (six or seven hours per day) as well as her 'real' job. A partner who wasn't too tired at the end of the day (usually 11 pm or later), and who subsequently suffered less from those bedroom headaches 😖.

It makes sense, doesn't it? We know teamwork and collaboration achieve greater results, happier workplaces and better retention in our organisations. Why should it be any different in our homes? Real equal partnerships mean equal sharing of household and child-raising responsibilities, resulting in equal career opportunities, equal financial gains, and a greater chance for equal happiness levels.

Sheryl Sandberg – former COO of Facebook, author, and founder of the Lean In global movement – spoke about the need for equality to start in the home in her 2010 TED Talk 'Why We Have Too Few Women Leaders'. The three powerful suggestions she gave to women were:

1. **Sit at the table, not on the sidelines** … so many women hesitate or hold back until invited.

2. **Make your partner a real partner** … equality starts in the home.

3. For the younger women (20s to 30s) about career choices: **don't leave before you leave** … don't check out from career opportunity or drop your career ambitions too early, before you have to, or at all.

While this may seem like an old view now, given Sandberg shared her strong message about these core issues over a decade ago, the sad thing is that the advice is still relevant. It still needs to be stated. In many countries, communities, inside our own homes, and within the women's circles I facilitate, these things are still the core underlining issues fuelling inequality.

It's no wonder we have fewer women sitting in the top lead roles if many women hold back due to already having too many balls to juggle. It's no wonder women initiate divorces more than men do, especially once children are independent. It's no wonder many of our younger women ditch their corporate career plans in their 20s and 30s to settle for more flexible options like a small home-based or online business, often earning a fraction of what they could be. It's no wonder – and a very sad fact – that in Australia our older women are fast becoming the most disadvantaged group, with the lowest superannuation retirement savings and increasing homelessness and financial destitution.

Until we have 50/50 partners, 50/50 household management and 50/50 child-raising and family-care duties, we will not achieve 50/50 opportunities in workplaces for women, especially in senior leadership positions.

Women can do anything ... but we can't do everything.

Nor were we meant to ... nor do we have to. Men can't do everything either ... nor will they.

Fairly balanced, mutually respectful relationships

Okay, so I don't mean 50/50 literally, with point-scoring lists and end-of-day hourly calculations. It's about firstly acknowledging and understanding the imbalances, then exploring and negotiating adjustments, and committing to more equitable arrangements. It's about mutual respect. It's about two-way love and support. It's about fairness.

For me, that all just makes sense. I learned early in life that fairly balanced, mutually respectful relationships are not a given, they are deliberately designed by the choices we make. And there are always choices. I've made some pretty bold choices and changes right from my late teens, and I'm still making them. But, I know many women who have never really sat down with their partners to have a serious discussion about these things.

Acceptance of *that's just the way it is* often leads to feeling stuck, which can quickly become resentment, and then the more debilitating, depressing 'victim thinking'. Have you given in or given up?

Women have a giving disorder ... from entrenched behaviour of giving in, which is often learned early in life.

It's time to disrupt that cycle ... cure the disorder ... and claim your worth.

GET OFF THE BARGAIN RACK AND RAISE YOUR VALUE

I joined forces with the Lean In global movement in 2013, as one of the first Australian-registered facilitators of Lean In Circles, and in 2019, as founder and Network Leader of Lean In Queensland. The purpose of forming peer circles (8 to 12 women in each) is to encourage and enable women to lean in to decision-making tables, to build their courage to challenge the status quo, and to step up into lead roles.

Prior to the global pandemic impact, there were over 80,000 registered Lean In Circles, spread across 170 countries. At the time, surveys showed 85% of participants credited their involvement in these circles as supporting significant positive changes in their lives, disruptive changes that they may not have dared to do without the shared learnings, coaching and support from their circle peers.

Likewise, women in our ElevateHER Australia network, which promotes and supports circle leaders nationally, come from a variety of life experiences, ages and stages, and a range of careers. Some are stronger for their past experiences, some are struggling with current experiences, and some are searching for the next experience. What I love is how supportive they become of each other, providing advice, genuine concern, and a shoulder to lean on or even stand on.

However, after almost every circle or network event, I'm amazed at the stories shared of unequal, unfair, blatantly sexist behaviour some of these women experience, particularly in workplaces. Yes, it IS still happening. Women doing the bulk of the hours; men taking the credit. Women expected to do 'office housework'. Women being undervalued in remuneration packages compared to male colleagues. And when they try to negotiate, they're made to feel 'lucky' to have the job with responses like: 'Do you want the job, or not?' Like – take what is offered or they'll find someone else who will.

Women need to negotiate better deals. We need to support each other to disrupt the belief that women will just keep giving, without negotiating a fairer outcome. We need to believe we deserve equal treatment, equal choices and equal opportunities.

Together, we can achieve so much more.

Not wanting to turn this section into an advert for any particular equality movement, I also acknowledge the many other women's groups and movements – both those well-established groups and the wave of new ones popping up to address gender inequality. Over the years I have joined and supported numerous other women's groups, movements and campaigns. I love that there is an exciting 'next wave' of disruptive feminism.

Why? Because we're not there yet. Movement towards greater equality is so slow that global studies conclude it could take 150 to 170 years to reach economic gender equality. That's totally unacceptable, especially when subsequent research data shows that organisations with women on their boards and in their executive leadership teams consistently outperform those with fewer or no women at the decision-making tables.

Seriously, that's just not good enough. My generation has clearly been dabbling around the edges for way too long. The reports don't lie. The stats are clear.

THE FACTS

Now, I'm not about to provide you with pages of all the stats on why the push for equality just makes sense. There is much research and many yearly updated reports available for public scrutiny that support the ongoing need to address inequality. Google them. Or check out links to the latest Australian ones from our ElevateHER Australia website.

But, just in case you are not into doing your own research, I've collated just a few that I use in my presentations. Perhaps you'd like to use these in your disruptive debates too ☺.

WHY NOT YOU?

So ... by now I've hopefully convinced you that the status quo is unacceptable and there is a chronic and urgent need to disrupt and change our approach, to support a more equal way to live, work and enjoy life.

DISRUPT ... the status quo

After the continuing downward slide in 2020–21,

Australia's overall *Global Gender Gap* ranking has steadily improved – up 24 places since 2021, up by 17 spots since the conservative LNP government was ousted (2022).

From 15th in 2005, down to 50th in 2021, improved to 26th by 2023

- Iceland is #1
- New Zealand #4
- Ireland #11
- United Kingdom #15

Australia's 2023 ranking break-down was:

- Economic participation and opportunity: #38
- Educational attainment: #1
- Political empowerment: #29

Global Gender Gap Report 2023
www.weforum.org

Australia's gender pay gap is

22.8%

which equates to ...

Women being paid, on average,

$26.6k less

than men a year

7/10

employers have a pay gap that favours men

in fact ...

Every industry has a pay gap that

favours men

Men are

twice as likely

to be in the top income bracket as women

Only **22.3%** of CEOs are women

Only

1 in 5

boards have gender balance

10

percentage points

or more in

female representation

on boards of Australian ASX-listed companies leads to a

4.9% increase

in company market value

3/5

employers offer paid parental leave,

92% of those offer it equally to men and women *but ...*
only 13% of all paid carers leave is taken by men.

WGEA – Australia's Gender Equality Scorecard report 2022-23
www.wgea.gov.au/publications/australias-gender-equality-scorecard

As an experienced leader and Change Champion, I find it annoying that many people continue to hold back from influencing or driving changes to stuff that's clearly not working. Not just the inequality issues, but lots of ineffective traditions, limited thinking and entrenched behaviours.

The reasons may be wide and varied, but mostly we make excuses as to why it's 'too hard' to change or 'won't work', from listening to the BS (aka: bullshit) voice in our own heads.

The problem with our inner voice is we often don't question its validity. Instead, we tend to quickly turn thoughts into stories, and when we run the same story in our head a few times, it soon becomes an entrenched belief. This is often called a 'limiting belief', because it's generally not the full story, just a quick take (or limited version) that helps us deal with and discard an 'issue' as quickly as possible.

Why do we do that? Well, the neuroscientist experts tell us we have about 2 million bits of information coming at us every second, but we can only process about 130 bits or approximately seven chunks of info at a time. This means that we are constantly deleting, distorting or generalising information so we can process the bits we consider relevant and leave out what we consider to be irrelevant. It's just how we make sense of our world.

So, in reality, the version you are running in your head may feel real, correct and the right approach for you, but it's good to remember that it's YOUR limited version, based on the sum of your experiences, your values, your judgements, your thoughts and ideas. Your map of the world. Your perception. It's perhaps quite different from my perception, or the perception of others. That's okay … if it's working for you.

Changing your thinking

But the questions are: is what you are leaving out, twisting to suit, or generalising about working for you? Are you brave enough to question your own thinking and beliefs? The stuff that may not be working as well for you as you thought it was?

Yes, you can change that. Because if you made up your reality as you see it today, you can just as easily create a new reality. Well, maybe not 'just as easily'. With entrenched habits, your brain may need some conscious reprogramming. Cool – brain disruption ☺.

Recent neuroscientist studies into habitual behaviour confirm that our brain's neural pathways become stronger and more solid the more times we transmit the same messages using those same comfortable pathways. So, our brains become lazy and subconsciously default to go in that same well-trodden direction. Like choosing the easy, low-hanging fruit, our brains constantly choose the easiest route. So, that's why changing our thinking and our habits is hard, however NOT impossible.

Disrupting entrenched habits and forging new neural pathways takes intentional effort.

In human behavioural science and coaching circles, the accepted punchline to the common joke:

How many psychologists (or coaches) does it take to change a light bulb?

Is:

None – the light bulb has to want to change.

Similarly, *you* have to *want* to change; to disrupt your status quo default thinking.

I encourage you to become more aware of the stories you run in your head. Not every thought that comes up is necessarily correct, logical or good for us. As the loudest voice is often the one in our own heads, learning to question that is a good place to start disrupting.

WHY CHOOSE TO BE ORDINARY?

Reflecting back on my early teens, I had needed to DISRUPT the small-p plans that others had for me, to ASPIRE towards my own dreams and meaningful goals, to REACH for broader, higher levels, and continually EVOLVE into who I was meant to be … to find my own purpose in life, be anything but 'ordinary', and make the biggest difference.

I'm so glad I had the courage to make destiny-changing decisions from those early years. True, a lot of water has flowed under many bridges since then, and yes, I've continued to shake up a few things along the way. I'm still courageously challenging the things that need to change … those entrenched practices that are clearly not producing great outcomes. Like that Gerry Harvey interview I mentioned a few pages back; immediately after it aired, I took to Facebook, tagged in some famous and powerful Australian feminist connections, named and shamed the ridiculously out-of-touch comments, and suggested women all over the nation boycott Harvey Norman stores. The posts went viral, and several women's online publications wrote articles on this same matter the next day. I love the social media super-highway effect that connects likeminded people and turns a small ripple into a tsunami-like movement.

That's what **stepping up, standing out and speaking up** about stuff that is just wrong is all about. I'm not famous or particularly influential on a broad scale, nor do I need to be in a C-suite or lead role to play a part in driving positive change. But, I do write articles and do media commentary, I do speak out and present at events, I do mentor and coach other women, and I do join with other ladies and proactive groups to collectively help influence change. A passionate 'do-er'.

My point is: leadership can come from anyone, based from anywhere.

Yes, it takes courage to put yourself out there in all your vulnerability.

As I mentioned in my Introduction, one of my favourite authors and renowned researcher of human behaviour Brené Brown wrote a book about how having the courage to be vulnerable can positively transform your life and increase your ability to confidently lead change. Entitled *Daring Greatly*, reading it fuelled a fundamental shift at a time in my life when I intuitively knew I needed to unshackle and play a bigger game.

I've lost count of how many times I've re-read parts of it, regularly picking it up as a great source of encouragement and strength. Vulnerability takes strength … it IS a strength, and you become stronger from using it.

I've spent the last decade passionately helping others to become disruptive, dynamic change leaders, building their courage, confidence, intentionality and resilience levels to cope with the pushback. And, believe me, there will be pushback. I have strong, broad shoulders for good reason – it takes strength and courage to stand up to those who try to knock you back down to suit their own agendas (more sharing on that later).

But it's worth it. You become stronger and more resilient for the knocks. After each experience and learning, you care less and less about what others think (those unimportant opinions based on fear), and become more and more focused on using your passion to make a bigger difference; ready to leave your mark. Your legacy.

What will you be remembered for?

A CHALLENGE FOR YOU

Is it time for you to disrupt things that are not working well in your life? Entrenched bad habits? Poor relationships? Toxic friends or workplaces? Maybe your own internal negative voice that holds you back? I challenge you to build your disruptive muscle.

It doesn't matter if you are 15, 19, 39, 59 or older. It's never too late to change stuff that is clearly not working for you anymore. Perhaps there's stuff that has never worked for you, and you've been accepting it for way too long. What are you waiting for? Change that now!

The time to disrupt inequality is NOW.

Rock Your Stripes

The time to play a bigger game is NOW.
Let's stand together as strong, determined, extraordinary women.
Together, we will make a big difference.

So ... I DARE YOU ... go a little nutso ... become a crazy disrupter.

I love this too much not to share the full version:

Here's to the crazy ones.
The misfits. The rebels.
The troublemakers.
The round pegs in the square holes.
The ones who see things differently.
They're not fond of rules,
and they have no respect for the status quo.
You can quote them, disagree with
them, glorify or vilify them.
About the only thing you
can't do is ignore them.
Because they change things.
They imagine. They invent.
They heal. They explore.
They create. They inspire.
They push the human race forward.
Maybe they have to be crazy ...
How else can you stare at an
empty canvas and see
a work of art?
Or sit in silence and hear a song
that's never been written?
Or gaze at a red planet and
see a laboratory on wheels?
And while some may see them as
the crazy ones, we see genius. Because
the people who are crazy enough
to think they can change the world,
are the ones who do.

Steve Jobs

Create your own personal DISRUPTION list ...

The STUFF YOU WILL NO LONGER ACCEPT

Disrupt

CHAPTER 2

ASPIRE ...

to your greatest version

There is no passion to be found playing

SMALL ...

in choosing to live a life that is less than the one you are capable of living.

Adaptation of Nelson Mandela's original version

UNLEASH YOUR ASPIRATIONS

Aspirations are important. Although synonyms for *aspiration* include the words *hope* and *wish*, I generally think of the word *aspire* as having more passionate and deliberate thought; like it carries more grit, ambition, determination, and expectation of result. More oomph than just a wish or a whim. More strategy than just hoping.

I'm referring to the stuff that gets us up, feet firmly planted on the floor and ready to stride out in the mornings (apart from the coffee). Aspirations that become the clear vision that drives us towards achieving our goals. It's what motivates and keeps us going. It's fuelled from our core, by an inner sense of purpose and passion.

> **'The two most important days in your life are: the day you were born, and the day you figured out why.'**
>
> Mark Twain

Success happens when a reoccurring dream or desire becomes a personal aspiration, and you turn that into an action plan, from which focused-fuelled persistence drives the daily efforts required to reach the goal. Underpinning all that is one crucial factor: a strong inner self-belief, tenacious and unwavering (more on how to build that in Part II).

Without aspirations, we simply go through robot-like, mindless motions or we allow the winds of life to just toss us around; like we have no plans, control or care factor. People who are like that have generally never built strong personal power, or they've let go of it at some point, discounted their self-worth, or lost faith in their ability to make wise choices.

Do you know people like that? No ambition, no drive, no enthusiasm about anything? Yes, I've met a few. Even lived with one for a while; now there's way too many energy-sucking years I'll never get back. These people are not happy, bright or bubbly to be around. Instead, they are often sad, depressed or anxious. Resigned to believing the story they run in their heads: that life is hopeless, they are hopeless (or at least – nothing special), that one bad outcome means all outcomes will be bad, and that nothing is ever going to change or improve. At their core is often a belief that they don't deserve to aspire for greater things. Sometimes, they are simply not aware there is any other way to be.

Recently I was coaching a young female manager who had learned behaviour from childhood to squash her emotions, to the point of being comfortably numb. Subsequently, she was struggling to identify her feelings in our sessions. She shared that her Mum had taught her a coping mechanism throughout her formative years; one of not getting too excited about anything. The principle being: if you don't get enthusiastic, don't set the bar very high, don't expect much, you won't get disappointed. No emotional investment equals nothing to lose. Like a coat of armour, she had chosen to protect herself from the potential hurt of disappointment or possible failure. Subsequently, her aim was just to survive each day, and anything else that manifested was a bonus, but not expected to last.

How sad to be that fearful of failure or disappointment, to choose such low expectations, dumb down your talents, stop believing in your potential, play small, and just accept whatever life dishes out. No personal aspiration; just acceptance of whatever crumbs are thrown your way.

Are you choosing to play a smaller game, to be beige and blend in, to keep your head down, your mouth shut and not rock anyone else's boat?

Have you lost your will to aspire to be your greatest version? Given up after one or two knocks?

Are you fearful that you might not have what it takes to succeed?

I know for some of you the answer to all three of these questions will be: 'Yes, probably'.

But there's good reason why you picked up this book, right? Don't be too hard on yourself. You are not alone. Women hold back and play small for all sorts of reasons, but it often starts with those potentially crippling fears I outlined in the Introduction.

SMASHING THOSE FEARS

You may recall in the previous chapter I mentioned that the language we listen to and use, and the stories we run with, are often a complex web of illogical, unfounded bullshit; well, fears can be the same. They are just stories you've embedded into your brain as a protection mechanism. Some fears are good for us – they keep us from harm. Some are definitely not – they hold us back from better outcomes.

So, let's look at the insidious ones that cause us to hold back, and unravel them a bit more. A good place to start clearing the way for your aspirations to surface and soar is by getting rid of the main blockages.

Over the years, I have found these fears to be the major constraints that either held me back or held back others who have shared their stories with me. To fully embrace your aspirations, to realise your full potential, you need to smash these unresourceful F words …

#1 FEAR: Fear of failure

Firstly, there IS NO SUCH THING AS FAILURE. I know, you've probably heard that cliché thrown around before. Seriously though, what is failure anyway? How major does crap have to get before we call it that fearful 'F' word? Does it kick in at – big disappointment? A let-down? Perhaps a family disaster or crisis? A relationship breakdown? Losing your job? Losing your house? Flunking an assessment? A poorly thought-out decision? Misplaced trust? Wrong career move? A major business flop? Life can be a series of all these experiences (and more).

Truth is, I have experienced ALL of the above (seriously, I had to stop myself writing a full page). But, that doesn't make ME a failure. It just means some things didn't work out. I'm richer and stronger for all of those experiences. Way more resilient than I would have been if I'd let the *fear of failure* hold me back from giving it a go. Just because shit happens doesn't mean it will always be that way, or even happen again. It doesn't stop me from trying again or leaping to the next goal. The important thing is to learn and grow from those lemons.

Like the old, well-used saying:

Turn your lemons into lemonade.

Every zigzag path or brick wall we run into provides us with a lesson and chance to grow wiser. So, instead of focusing on the problem, take on the feedback and new learnings. Don't try to disown or hide your screw-ups. They are what makes you a whole person; the person you are today. Embrace the richness that you've gained. Explore the alternative choices, then rise up, make some changes and take new chances. You will build more resilience and mastery, ready to launch into the next goal or chapter.

Owning our full story (warts and all) and loving ourselves throughout the journey is the bravest thing we can do ... and the best way to become our full-arse version 😊.

In my coaching work, be it with individuals or within client organisations, when I notice a strong indication of the *fear of failure*, it's often linked to this belief, which comes from a commonly thrown about line: *Failure is not an option.*

Really? When did that saying become a mainstream phrase?

If you're on the receiving end of that statement, it might have some intended shock impact to spur you to try harder so as NOT to fail. However, the pressure to be perfect all the time will eventually weigh you down with bucket loads of fear, anxiety and guilt. Some become too stressed to perform their best or too scared to attempt innovative ideas.

For others, that statement causes an immediate shut-down effect, like: *'Might as well give up now'*. The personal risk becomes too high. The environment doesn't feel safe. Trust is eroded. Innovation and creative ideas die within such risk-averse cultures. Good people walk out the door. Millennials run. Gen Z (born after 1995) won't even walk through the door to begin with; they won't consider working in an environment like that.

Here's the thing: if you're scared to fail, you'll be too scared to try. You won't do things at 100%. You'll be too busy checking that Plan B is in place to focus fully on Plan A. So, success of Plan A (your aspirational goal) becomes at risk of being limited from choosing a half-arsed, fearful approach.

Failure IS an acceptable option …

Failure provides opportunities to embrace new learning and growth; so, in many ways, those who fail fast and often are potentially wiser for it (as long as they learn from it and don't keep making the same mistakes).

Many of the world's most famously successful people, who we look up to in amazement at what they've achieved, experienced lots of failure on their path to success. They set aspirational goals, and had abilities and ideas that not everyone initially saw value in. They made mistakes along the way, but the one thing that got them through was their tenacious self-belief, aspiration, determination and drive.

People like:

Oprah

A multi-billionaire, who became globally famous for her successful TV endeavours, Oprah lives on a 65-acre Californian estate in a massive neo-Georgian mansion. She is an author, actor and motivational speaker. An African-American woman from a poor Mississippi family, Oprah has inspired so many women globally, and continues to give generously to charities, causes and individuals in need. Well, turns out she got fired from her first TV job as a presenter in Baltimore, after being told she didn't have what it takes. Along her journey she's had movie flops, television network flops, and openly talks about a life-long yo-yo struggle with her weight.

In a personal interview, Oprah (in her 60s) said: *'I have no angst, no regret, no fear.'* Her reflective view on failure:

> **'There is no such thing as failure. Failure is just life trying to move us in another direction.'**

JK Rowling

Before there were any globally renowned wizards or book publishing contracts, JK Rowling was a broke, depressed, divorced single mother on welfare, who decided to write a novel while studying. From child-hood, she had always wanted to be an author; that's all she aspired to be, but her parents told her that it was not a real career – not some-thing you could live off, but a nice hobby. So, she became a teacher, but persisted with writing on the side, in coffee shops and on trains. Her first book in the Harry Potter series was rejected by 12 publishing companies, before it was picked up by a little-known company. The rest is history, still in the making.

Now one of the richest women in the world, Rowling reflects on her early 'failures':

> **'It is impossible to live without failing at something, unless you live so cautiously that you might as well not have lived at all – in which case, you fail by default.'**

Richard Branson

Knighted by the British Government for his services to entrepreneur-ship, and said to be worth more than US$5 billion, Richard Branson owns so many companies he has trouble keeping track of them all. But his career has certainly had its share of zigzags. Here's just two:

- His first business venture – *Student* magazine – didn't make any money, so he pivoted into music, starting Virgin Records, which was eventually successful beyond his dreams.

- His launch of Virgin Atlantic Airways almost failed before it flew. Its only plane, a rented Boeing 747, was extensively damaged on an accreditation test flight when a flock of birds flew into an engine. He couldn't get the airline accredited without a working plane, and he couldn't get a loan to fix it without airline accreditation. So, he sold off and borrowed against other ventures to fix the plane and get Virgin Atlantic Airways off the ground.

Such is his aspirational strength, determination and unwavering self-belief, he knows he will always be okay; despite the ups and downs. At any one time he has hundreds of proposals and ventures on the go, and a significant percentage of those fail or at least need serious realignment. His advice:

'Do not be embarrassed by your failures, learn from them and start again.'

Jilinda Lee (me)

Okay, so I'm neither famous nor a billionaire. Fame and amassing a fortune are not featured among my aspirational goals, or at least, they are certainly not what drives me. My aspirations are all about making a significant difference; to drive positive change, to use my experiences and passion in raising leadership expectations, and to encourage more diversity at decision-making tables. Broadly simplified: I want to leave a positive mark on the world, as a Change Champion who refused to play small, and courageously challenged the unacceptable status quo of gender inequality.

Writing this book was an aspiration of mine for over five years, before I achieved that big audacious goal. After five decades of zigzagging through career (and relationship) opportunities, making some brave decisions (some good, some not), and continually seeking chances to keep evolving, I started saying the throwaway line: *'One day I'll write a book.'* That became more of an announcement – *'I'm writing a book'* – after attending a one-day 'how to write a book' workshop and subsequently scribbling down some journal notes, very occasionally. After a few years, it turned into an embarrassing topic as colleagues regularly asked me: *'How's the book coming along?'* Ooops – it had started to feel like an unachieved goal.

Of course, there were always valid reasons (read: excuses) why the book was not yet written. My partner changed job contracts, requiring shifts to different regional communities several times; subsequently, re-establishing our business in each new location was the stronger priority. As an extrovert, I like to be involved in the communities we live in, so it's easy for me to get caught up after hours with networking groups and establishing community development initiatives such as my women's Circles. Then there's all the social media distractions (read: addiction) that I use daily to stay connected with people we've met along the way.

Truthfully, excuses aside, in essence: I never really made my book writing a #1 priority goal.

Like JK Rowling, I was treating it as just a hobby, until frustration got the better of me (remember: frustration drives disruption of bad habits). I sought out wise guidance from a wonderful mentor – Andrew Griffiths, an internationally successful author, a dynamic speaker, master marketer, and an all-round genuine guy – who just happened to live nearby (at the time). Not only did he provide a process, structure and useful tips; he taught me that sharing my stories in the form of a book was absolutely core to achieving my bigger aspirational goals. More of the crucial missing link, rather than a loosely linked hobby. Writing this book then became my greatest goal. Priority #1.

So, with that revelation, I was off and running: an author retreat in Bali, book planned and scheduled, determined to launch by the end of 2017. Ooops again ... what happened to that plan? Life threw a few more curveballs (just to test out my resilience), and one big, unanticipated boulder that consumed both my partner and me for several months (that's a major story for another time).

However, through all those frustrating hurdles, I also became increasingly aware that there was something else holding me back. A self-sabotaging wall I had to climb over; a fear that kept coming up from my core. No, not the *fear of failure*. Like Richard Branson, I learned a long time ago to pivot from zig to zag when things don't work out. Straight paths are so overrated, believe me.

Here's the thing: every colourful learning experience (read: mistake) provided an opportunity to share my learnings with others. But in sharing all that looms another wall: what to share and how much to share? The more personal experience stories I wrote, the more I became aware of another major fear blockage …

What will others think? … How will they react?

The greatest prison people live in is the fear of what other people think.

#2 FEAR: Fear of what others will think

In those earlier days of writing, for me this fear was more of a deeper concern about the personal impact on others … how they might think, feel and react. You see, I'm very aware as I'm sharing my journey – which may at times include others (some I am close to, and some I was closer to) – that those people may not like my version of the story. The value I place on authenticity drives my need to be real and open about the lessons I took from each experience, but at the same time being conscious not to cause undue angst to anyone.

That's a fine balance for someone like me, having deliberately unlearned the art of eggshell walking or tiptoeing around whole truths since finding my loud and proud voice in my teens. Remember the elephants? I believe in flushing out the big, obvious impactors. Subtlety is not my forte … nor is it a personal aspiration. *Authentically me.*

Overcoming this particular fear has not been easy; but I assure you, it's been so worth it. I am acutely aware of the years of work I had already put in to smashing this *fear of what others will think*. Long before the concept of writing a book ever emerged, I spent much of my 20s and 30s consciously reprogramming my thoughts to eliminate this debilitating fear, which was so entrenched in my psyche from childhood.

> **'If you fuel your journey on the opinions of others, you are going to run out of gas.'**
>
> Dr Steve Maraboli

My mother was consumed all her life with this fear: *'What will people think?', 'What will God think?', 'What will church people say about our family?'* She lived her entire life with so many rules and restrictions based on outdated and irrelevant expectations (in my opinion) that she was ruled by what others (and her God) expected. For her, others' opinions and her fear-based belief that she was being judged by God on a daily basis outweighed the more realistic, fluid opinions that her family has. Sad, really; but it was not my role to try to change her thinking. She chose that narrow pathway, as was her right. I respect that, but I never subscribed to it. I've seen what it does.

The strictly religious, almost cult-like immersion I experienced throughout my childhood, reinforced decades later with my much broader observations of the 'life coaching' industry, provided me with a strong radar for spotting manipulative behaviour designed to prey on the fearful and needy for the purpose of keeping them that way. I have no respect for those who do that. Their motives are generally driven by a need for power, profit and control. I cannot condone any action that depletes another's inner power and makes them feel so fearful and undeserving of aspiring for something better. Likewise, I do not condone the use of NLP tactics used by some coaches to manipulate vulnerable clients into dependency on their services. Manipulative upselling; I witnessed that play out at a coaching institute I attended for a short time. It immediately triggered childhood memories of evangelistic preachers manipulating and breaking people's inner strength to entice unquestionable followership. I have a well-honed laser radar for spotting such unethical practices.

While I understand this example may be confronting to those with religious faith or a tad extreme for the many who don't subscribe to that, I firmly believe from experience that the *fear of what others will think* – often steeped in traditions and stereotypical beliefs – is one of the strongest, more hideous fears that holds many women back from their full potential.

Yes, it's true; we are each on our own journey, and we experience things from differing perspectives. The stories we take from each experience or chapter can also differ greatly, reflecting the impact that it had on us as individuals. I've had to keep reminding myself that is okay. People will have different opinions. There will always be variables.

What I know for sure, from years of working on smashing this fear, and I now share with others, is that **these FIVE THINGS** have allowed me to hold on to my aspirations and keep sharing my stories:

1. I can't change how other people feel and think … I have no control over that.

2. Not everyone will like or agree with my stories or learnings … but not everyone matters.

3. I am fully responsible for and only have control over what I feel and think, and how I respond.

4. I remain unwaveringly focused on my personal motivation for sharing my stories; to help others step up, stand out and speak up … so if I was to hold back, that would be inauthentic – playing small.

5. I regularly apply the fairness THINK test:

T – is it TRUE?

H – is it HELPFUL?

I – is it INSPIRING?

N – is it NECESSARY?

K – is it KIND?

Is it KIND? is the hardest one to answer for me, because that's subjective to how others feel and think; their personal sensitivity levels. And let's face it; I'm aware that sometimes what I write and speak about – and how I convey that – can be rather blunt. I'm a straight shooter and expressively use tone with intent. However, I have tried to ensure that even the most challenging stories I share are more focused on how I responded, the lessons I learned, and the key points I think you may find useful on your journey. After all, that is my intentional purpose for writing this book.

Value your own uniqueness and self-esteem over the superficial opinions of others.

Perfectionism is a curse

For women, probably the most common occurrence of this *fear of what others will think* comes from the conditioning we receive from our formative years of what's portrayed as the 'perfect woman'. Take our obsession with the perfectly shaped, pretty, softly spoken, model-like, nurturing, age-defying woman. Perpetuated from glossy advertising, mass media, fashion models, movie stars and a whole gamut of unrealistic external influences around beauty, size, style and gender stereotypes, women are trained to think that is the acceptable and expected standard. Like we are constantly comparing each other with the 'perfectly portrayed' models and latest fashions:

What will people think if I wear this same old thing again?

What if people notice I've put on five kilos?

What will they say if they see me without make up?

What if I don't look like my touched-up media profile photo in real life?

What will they think if I cut my long hair off to a short style with attitude? Or let it go grey? Or get a nose piercing? Or a tattoo?

Again, I could write a full page of these, but that's unhelpful. I'm sure there are plenty already in your head, or you know of many others who are consumed by this fear for these reasons.

Smash this fear. Firstly, it is none of your business what others think (they own that shit). Really, most people are too absorbed in their own fears and issues to be spending any time thinking about you at all. I love Eleanor Roosevelt's saying:

> **'You wouldn't worry so much about what others think of you if you knew how seldom they do.'**
>
> Eleanor Roosevelt

Here's the thing: be your own person – other people's opinions really don't matter. It is an absolute waste of time and energy to be consumed by such an unrealistic level of competing perfection. This fear has no logic or reason, other than to keep the consumerism model alive by making us **feel like we don't belong** to the 'in crowd' or that we are in some way **inferior or inadequate** if we don't buy the latest stuff, or look like the cover models, or become like that perfect supermum.

Interestingly, those bolded phrases are also major fears; they are all connected and act like multipliers or bricks in the wall. Keep reading … keep smashing these inhibitors of your aspirational goals.

#3 FEAR: Fear of rejection (or not belonging)

Having shared my rather different start in life (elephant #3 in the Introduction), and always knowing I was given up for adoption as a baby (no surprise revelations later in life), you might think I'll have a lot to say about this *fear of rejection (or not belonging)*.

Actually, I haven't. On reflection, this is one of the hardest fears for me to articulate, because I smashed this one out of the ballpark at a very young age. Oh, I certainly knew what it felt like to not quite belong or not fit in, but rather than allowing that to hold me back from my aspirations, I decided very early in life to simply accept the situation and not need it. Really, it was more than just acceptance;

I wholeheartedly seized the opportunity that situation provided for me, to justifiably embrace individualism and aspire to be deliberately different (more on that later).

In those formative years, I don't recall ever feeling rejected. We (my adopted sister and I) were raised in a loving family, had all our basic needs catered for, and were totally accepted as part of the wider family. That is not to say that I don't know what rejection is. Those lessons came much later in life for me.

As a change agent (read: disrupter), and not afraid to put new ideas forward, I've certainly had my share of rejected proposals and pushbacks, especially from those risk-averse public-sector policy makers. By the time I left my regional leadership role in State Government (after 10-plus years), I had built a reputation as someone who didn't accept rejection; more to the point – didn't accept *'no'* or *'you can't do that'* in the first instance. I became known for finding another way around it – creatively. Ironically, I received statewide recognition for several of the left-field 'pilot programs' I led that were initially rejected.

If I had to describe myself using only one word, it would be: 'DOESN'T FOLLOW DIRECTIONS'.

So, while rejection of an idea or proposal is annoying, it generally hasn't held me back. I just do it differently, or do it with different people, or do it anyway (quietly), or move on to the next idea. That grit and determination comes from a strong focus on my own beliefs, values and purpose, a willingness to stand up alone and be vulnerable, with an inner knowing that I will be able to cope with whatever life throws my way.

And that is how you **smash the fear** *of rejection or not belonging.* Build a strong personal power around your own beliefs and passion, so that your strongest sense of true belonging is first and foremost to yourself. Know this one important thing:

You are a complete, whole person in your own right.

You don't need others to complete you or prop you up. I'm not suggesting you become a loner or recluse and stop connecting with others. I love people and being part of community groups, but I choose to do that – selectively. I don't do that to feel like I am accepted. I'm not needing validation. I spend time with those who complement who I am and who connect with the fundamental principles of my aspirational goals. Because I want to, not because I need to. Yes, there's a difference.

So, I can honestly say: I have very little active fear around rejection. Pushback (and I do get that – a lot) from any individual, community, group or client doesn't cause me to crumble or feel hurt. Just perhaps a little disappointed. It means I choose carefully who I spend my time with, where, and doing what. I set the boundaries, and I think that's the key. I'm in control of what I accept and what I reject. Living life on my terms. My choices.

Here's the thing: surround yourself with those who allow you to be YOU; those who accept you for who you are and what you bring to the relationship. And, if the 'fit' doesn't feel right, be willing to bravely stand alone in the wilderness, with that inner knowing you will be okay.

If this is a big blockage for you to overcome, and you'd like to dive a little deeper into understanding how to smash this fear, grab a copy of Brené Brown's book *Braving the Wilderness*. Like all her books, her advice is rich in research and real stories to back up her theories; this one is about the *'quest for true belonging'*.

> **'True belonging doesn't require us to change who we are. It requires us to BE who we are.'**
>
> Brené Brown

#4 FEAR: Fear of not being good enough

Well, here is my biggy – the major one. This was one big fear (or BS internal voice) I had to contend with for much of my formative years, right up until I left the town I grew up in – Toowoomba (in my mid-20s).

As we drove away (me, husband and two toddlers), I remember feeling like a massive burden had just rolled off my shoulders. For the first time in my life, I felt free. Free of the impossible burden to measure up to others' limiting expectations; to be someone I knew was NOT who I wanted to be. From that moment, I knew I would never return. My husband thought we were moving to a new regional community (10 hours north-west) for a three-year 'country service' teaching position, then returning to 'our home town'. But I knew I'd never go back to live there. I also knew this was just the start of a new story. Finally – 'my story'. A whole book of exciting new chapters waiting to be written.

You see, I grew up in a family where the expectation was that you would surrender your life to the church, constantly being compared with other 'good Christian girls', even to the point where spinster women doing overseas missionary work were hailed as the pinnacle to aspire to. I learned to hate such 'narrow road' comparisons and the restrictive impact that has on one's individualised thinking.

Having the courage to move away and distance myself from all that was the first time I recall experiencing the joy of what I now refer to as *'turning the page and starting a new chapter'*. Rather than subscribing to those external forces, I built immense internal strength. During those following years, I was able to work out WHO I WAS, and became more and more trusting of my own intuition, listening to my own inner voice of reasoning.

I've turned a lot of pages and started several new chapters since then, courageously and confidently, each time with similar feelings of burden-clearing elation.

Rock Your Stripes

The ones who say 'you can't' or 'you won't' are the same ones who know 'you can' and are scared that 'you will'.

You are good enough. You were always good enough.

Just like the *fear of rejection*, this feeling of *not being good enough* is steeped in comparison and competition. Not good enough compared to who? Why do you need to be the same as? Or do the same as? Or have the same aspirations as?

To this day, I detest the concept behind beauty competitions, fashion on the fields race-day competitions, or going to gala events where the whole focus is on outdoing each other's glamorous dresses. All of those things send a message that you have been judged compared to others. Deemed as 'not good enough', unless you win of course – but then that's subjective to others' views too. Oh, the pressure! But what does it really give you?

Who needs that shit? How shallow is a competition that is judged only on looks? How does that evaluate you as a whole person, a complete individual in your own right?

Smash through that. Watch out for those people and repetitive things that potentially embed the *'never will be good enough'* fear message into your psyche.

> **'There are some people who will never see you as being good enough. That is their short-coming, not yours. Be merciful enough to yourself to cut them out of your life.'**
>
> Dr Steve Maraboli

Just a footnote to that quote: if you can't cut them out of your life, at least choose to spend less time with them, and walk away from any belittling behaviour. Just shake it off.

For many years now, I have felt no need to compete with others. Even when I'm being assessed in work interviews or at proposal pitches, I'm more comfortable being my 'out there', different, unique self and showcasing my strengths than focusing on how that compares with others. That's an interview or tender panel task, not mine. I'll either be a good fit for what they want, or not. Their call. Regardless of the outcomes (typically some wins, some losses), my value is not depleted by this process or judgements from others.

In fact, I always seek feedback, so I can gain an accurate understanding (not assumptions) and take on a learning from each such experience. You see, most times I know that I was and am good enough to do the role or project, so when unsuccessful, I'm not afraid to probe for deeper answers to help me grow and continually evolve.

My only competition is with the person staring back at me in the mirror each morning. The person doing sunrise meditation, yoga stretches, and setting intentions at the beach each day. I am my own competition. Every day, I strive to be better than I was yesterday. That's it. Not better than you. Not better than my colleagues. Rocking my own full-arse version, my way.

Here's the thing: *individuality* is the key to smashing this fear (more on that in Part II).

#5 FEAR: Fear of the unknown (uncertainty and change)

Aspirational goals are difficult for some people to focus on, especially those who need to engage all senses before believing it CAN and WILL happen. Feel it, see it, hear it, touch it, logic it, prove it; some need to see the results before committing. Their fear blockage is based on a need for certainty and a sense of security, before they will make that leap. For many, change feels too risky when there are no certain results.

Really? When was the last time you were certain about anything? To smash this fear, you need to be very clear on this one big truth. Repeat after me, and repeat again:

There is no such thing as CERTAINTY.

Never was. Never will be. Certainty is an illusion. You can plan all you like, set off in a particular direction, and even mark out your life like a personal plan of milestones and projected outcomes, but along the way there will be variables, unexpected hiccups, even crises. Nothing is a certainty; except perhaps that things will change.

Change will happen. Some level of change is a given. It's just that knowing when, what, how and why around the change is uncertain until it occurs. That's life. A journey of unexpected (or semi-anticipated) changes, and potentially lots of different chapters and outcomes.

It's far better then to prepare yourself with the willingness to accept, the strength to rise up from the knocks, the flexibility to respond, and the ability to adapt to other choices and opportunities. Resilience + agility. Build those mindset muscles. When you embrace the possibilities and excitement that change can bring, instead of being worried or fearful of it, you will **totally smash this fear**.

Don't make change too complicated
... just decide to change and do it.

BECOME A GAME CHANGER

If I had to pick just one thing I have high-level expertise in from personal experience, it would be the topic of change. Change has been a part of my life from day one, and I'm thankful for that each and every day. From an early acceptance of change, to seeking change, to exploring new opportunities, to designing changes, making changes, driving changes, leading changes; it's no wonder I'm known as a Change Champion. Change has provided so much opportunity in my life that I actively search for 'the next big thing'.

Now, before you judge me as 'flippant' (like I care anyway), or having some sort of long-term commitment phobia, I want to be clear about the type of changes I'm talking about.

You may have heard of the *'next shiny thing syndrome'*. It's a label that's used to describe a personality trait of someone who wants the constant stimulation of new stuff, is easily distracted (by shiny things), perhaps has an insatiable desire to buy the latest fashion or latest gizmos and gadgets, or someone who appears to lack what my Mum referred to as 'stickability'. Millennials are often labelled with having this 'affliction', because they've grown up in a fast-paced, throwaway world. Well, guess what. It's not a Millennial disease. It's a behaviour type; it's not gender or generation specific.

As an accredited behavioural science analyst, I know I have some of those tendencies in my nature. Distraction is something I work to reduce every day with mindfulness meditation and simple things like switching off all those beeping gizmo alerts! The anticipation and excitement of 'what's next' is something I crave, because I get bored with 'same-same' very quickly. Once I've achieved that thing, to continue doing the same thing over and over again is like marking time. Not progressing or growing. Stagnant. Stuck.

All behaviour traits can be used resourcefully or unresourcefully. It's a choice. So, I deliberately use my *'next shiny thing'* inclinations towards planning aspirational goals that provide continual personal and professional development, not constant shoe shopping or new hairstyles. Actually, those who knew me many years ago would recognise that change of focus as significant. I used to be known for my exotic shoe collection and seasonal hairstyle changes. Those quick-fix shiny things do not feature as much in my life now.

Over the years, with each new chapter (and move), the need for material possessions or owning lots of stuff has diminished. I love a good declutter. It takes another load off my shoulders, providing another sense of freedom and openness to embrace the next change.

I now focus my attention on the life-changing big stuff. Changes that provide opportunity to reach for those big, aspirational goals. Changes that align with my values – one of my top ones being continual learning and growth. Changes that challenge the status quo and challenge me to step up as an influencer of change, or leader of positive outcomes. These changes may be incremental or one big leap, but none of that is something to fear. It's something to embrace – wholeheartedly. Actually … I'm more fearful of being stuck than of making or embracing changes.

Here's the thing: make this your mantra that helps smash this fear and drive your aspirations:

> *Be more fearful of being stuck*
> *than of embracing change.*

Turning the page ...

So ... now that we've dealt with those blocking fears – or at least you are more aware of them and will question their hold over you – it's time to feel the freedom to aspire to YOUR goals. Yes, *YOURS*. Not necessarily the same ones as what others think you should do. Not needing to align with others' views on what *'success'* or *'achieving greatness'* means. Remember: that's *their* map of the world. It's important to get clear on YOUR own aspirations.

> *Aspire to become YOUR greatest version.*

Turning our aspirations into actions and then leaping towards those big changes requires us to be able to visualise the possibilities. It is harder to build a strong inner belief and smash those doubting fears if you can't see a way forward or sense some degree of realistic success.

That brings to mind the saying you've probably seen touted around quite a bit in recent years:

> *We cannot BE what we cannot see.*

Actually, I don't believe that statement to be entirely true, because with all new ideas or entrepreneurial projects, someone has to go first. Someone has to lead the change.

However, it IS more difficult to aspire towards something that we either haven't seen or haven't viewed as working well, or when we have to break through major barriers to get there. That's a much harder task. It requires an inner willingness to lead fundamental change and the courage to be vulnerable. Sometimes, you have to be the disrupter – to be brave enough to be 'the first' to make those changes. Perhaps this even means being the catalyst for pushing through fundamental change.

I believe this is one of the reasons we have a longstanding gender imbalance at leadership levels. It is difficult to get there. It shouldn't be, but it is, for a whole range of reasons. The flow-on effect is that the lack of female role models currently in leadership positions creates a degree of uneasiness for those women having to be 'the first female CEO for this council' or 'the first female chair of the board' or 'the only female sitting at the decision-making table'. Sad that these are still newsworthy headlines; it is still seen as a reportable, unusual or groundbreaking milestone.

Pushing through change can be uncomfortable, but is so necessary to reach our aspirational goal of more women in leadership roles.

GIRLS CAN ASPIRE TO DO ANYTHING

From the moment we are born, we have the capability to aspire. We aspire to get around so we start crawling, then we aspire to be upright so we learn to walk, then aspire to be understood so we learn to speak. Girls and boys alike. No differences.

At school, we start with aspirations and excitement to learn new things. Interestingly, studies show that at early primary school levels this capacity for aspiration is the same for both girls and boys. BUT … something happens during those formative years, and by the time girls reach about 10 to 12 years old, many have already started to hold back. To play second fiddle. Not wanting to be perceived as pushy or bossy. Not wanting to be loud or take over. Not expected to be as fast, or as strong, or as clever, or as ambitious as the boys.

What's with that?

It's societal gender conditioning. The subtle (and not so subtle) influences children observe from the adults around them. Sure, there is widespread espousing of equal opportunities, but in reality the observable behaviours and opportunities speak for themselves. We take the strongest message from what we see, not necessarily from spoken words. Actions always speak loudest.

Rock Your Stripes

Why do some girls stop reaching for their highest potential? Because they cannot visualise what it's like or how they need to be when they can't see it from those women who walk the path before them. Their mothers, aunties and family friends. Women in their community.

By the time they reach double figures, most little girls (and boys) have noticed how their Mum spends most of her time, and which parent's career or job status is more important. Yes, I'm generalising, and it's great to see some positive changes to that. But, sadly – we're not there yet in abolishing this often unintended conditioning. Observation of parent behaviour moulds young minds.

Think about it. Did your brothers play with toy trucks and cars, while you had Barbie dolls, tea sets and miniature replica cooking appliances? Were there pink butterflies and fairies hanging from your bedroom ceiling, while airplanes and spaceships hung from your brother's ceiling? Did the boys play football while you and your girl-friends learned ballet? Did you have to help Mum with inside tasks, while your brothers were mostly outside with Dad? Sometimes it's subtler than that, but sadly, it's still there.

In 2018, Target came under social media fire for selling children's pink and blue toy dress-up kits. Yes, they were the only colour choices, so straightaway most would think: pink kit for girls, blue kit for boys. Right? Well, just to make certain you could tell the difference, the pink kit was labelled 'My First Beauty Studio' and the blue kit was labelled 'My First Medical Centre'. Okay, so the kits did not say boy or girl on them, and children (or parents) were free to choose either colour for their child (as was Target's response). But, the subtle inference is there. Just another little hint of potential gender bias. We need to call that out. We need to ensure that we are not still caught up in gender-specific toy purchases for our children and grandchildren.

Does the special little girl in your life play with trucks and spaceships? Or the little boy have a miniature kitchen set with pots, pans and Play-Doh? My grandchildren do. My daughter made sure of that. Even when my five-year-old granddaughter started asking for Barbie dolls (after receiving her first one as a birthday gift), we (the family) mindfully selected 'diverse' Barbies – one dark-skinned, dark-haired skater girl, and one plus-size, short-haired female doctor (yes – there are much broader choices now than the original unnaturally shaped, glam Barbie versions).

Even if your upbringing was more balanced with widespread choices, the world in general has not been actively de-gendering to match; from the basic family household chores, to grocery shopping, to child-caring responsibilities, to flexible working hours options, right up to C-suite positions. Gender bias still kills many women's aspirations.

In fairness, it also reduces men's aspirations of wanting to spend more time at home and be more involved in their children's lives. I have coached many men, particularly in executive roles, who would love the option of more flexible hours, without it being a career-limiting move for them too. Point is: gender equality is good for both men and women, and in role-modelling a more equal world for the next generation.

> 'A better, more equal world would be one
> where half our institutions are run by women
> and half our homes are run by men.'
>
> Sheryl Sandberg

Organisational recruitment bias and lack of diversity programs across industries is one issue, but there is another concerning pattern. Young women coming out of university know that at some point in the next 10 years they will potentially have to drop out of the workforce to care for children, working part time or flexible hours around that. Young men don't think about that as they leave university or apply for promotion after promotion.

Sheryl Sandberg, former COO of Facebook and author of the book *Lean In*, tells a story about one of her staff – a young woman in her 20s with great promise. There was a management role on offer and Sheryl, who saw her potential, encouraged her to apply. To Sheryl's astonishment, the young woman declined, stating that she would be having a family soon and planned to either leave or work part time. After Sheryl congratulated her, the young lady revealed that she wasn't pregnant yet. In fact, she didn't even have a boyfriend. She just had accepted her destiny that sometime soon she'd meet her man, marry, and have children. So, she believed that it was a waste of time, money and effort for the company to train her up into a management role. Thankfully, Sheryl set her straight.

Here's the thing: too many women start to lean out of their careers, or give up on their aspirations, way too early. They hold back from those promotions, like they have already accepted that their career progression is less important than their male partner's (or male colleagues') aspirations.

Smash that thinking. You have the right to aspire to be your greatest version. To make choices that suit your aspirations.

SAY NO TO KITCHEN BITCHIN'

You were NOT born to cook, clean, and be the main carer of children. I knew that 30-plus years ago, and honestly, I've never been a house-wife. Both my husbands were house-trained before I married them. You could say it was a very clear prerequisite. Frankly, if they wanted to eat, they needed to know their way around a kitchen and the local supermarket.

I feel so strongly about this that these two random lines regularly feature in my International Women's Day talks:

> ### Woman are born with a womb, not a broom.

… and …

> ### The only reason I have a kitchen is it comes with the house.

My adult awakening came at age 19. I had completed my hair-dressing apprenticeship with a well-regarded chain of salons, was appointed as Salon Manager for a busy new salon with five staff, became an accredited Trainer, and was rewarded with a company car. My career was going well, but I'd come to a personal crossroad. I realised my aspirations for my career were not a good match with those of my long-term boyfriend. So, to the shock of many friends and family who had us written off as the next couple to be engaged, I broke off the relationship.

You see, after three years, I realised that if I was not the #1 priority (or at least equal priority) in his life by now, I never would be. I came somewhere further down the list, after his sportscar, motorbike, mates, and his own entrepreneurial business plans. I was just the token girl-friend. Destined to be his home-office assistant and 'go-for' girl.

However, by far the biggest concern was his gender-taming agenda for my life, clearly demonstrated with the extravagant gifts of a Rena Ware saucepan set, Noritake dinner set, and stainless-steel cutlery set with my name engraved on each piece. Kitchen bitch, perhaps? Like, if I had the best tools, maybe I'd be more interested in learning how to use them and become a house-wifey type? I was only 19! I swear, if the next gift was a vacuum cleaner, I'm pretty sure I would have seriously harmed him with it.

All that aside, there was another growing desire in me at that time: to leave the restrictive, conservative town I'd grown up in. I'd outgrown it. I wanted to explore other things, to spread my wings, to check out other choices. I aspired for something better, or at least – different. To be in charge of my own journey, which clearly did not include any in-depth exploration of a kitchen.

BE THE CHANGE YOU WANT TO SEE

Truly aspirational goals are not 'pie in the sky' thought bubbles. You need to spend quality reflection time on what YOU aspire to achieve. What does aspiring to YOUR greatest version mean to you? What does achievement look like for YOU? What do YOU value? What are YOU passionate about? Because YOUR aspirations need to come from YOUR core.

Not long ago, the Australian Prime Minister of the time, Malcolm Turnbull, responded to a question relating to the future plight of typical middle-income earners under his government's proposed tax package – the example given was aged-care workers. The PM's rhetoric provided yet another gob-smacking moment for me. His view was that workers in those lower paid roles should be more aspirational in their career choices. Really? How insulting for the wonderful people who aspire to be 'the best aged-care support workers'. That IS a valid aspirational goal.

My point is: not everyone aspires to earn large sums of money, or own three properties, or be the CEO of a Fortune 500 company. Aspirations belong to the individual, based on their personal values, passion, motives, priorities, and what gives them personal satisfaction.

As a Change Champion, I love that Millennials are actively disrupting the old, traditional, hierarchical, ladder-climbing, class-structured society. They are openly questioning the aspirations of past generations. Good on them. I have been doing that for quite a while, too.

Let's look at one of those yesteryear aspirations, still being touted by the old brigade – the 'great Australian dream' or expected aspiration to own your own home: get a mortgage you can't jump over that ties you up financially for 30-plus years, just so you may eventually own your home (even though it's increasingly likely that the mortgage will never be fully repaid). Not only has this become an unrealistic pipe dream, it is NOT what many 20-somethings want; at least not the ones I speak with. Not even in their top 10 bucket list.

Millennials are waking up to the fact that old thinking, old models, old ways won't work for them. They and the next generation will have a life full of career opportunities, changes, experiences and adventure that could take them anywhere in the world. From watching their parents' and grandparents' generations, they know that working on an assembly line, or with one company for their entire career, or living and working in the same suburb or city for life, is no longer feasible. Nor is it a very personally fulfilling career or lifestyle. Agility is the new sought-after currency, to enable aspirational goals to be reached. Those goals may not include owning a house; instead, it may be to see and experience as much of the world as possible. That's okay.

I recently saw this clever Millennial aspiration list that was reposted on social media (author unknown), and loved it:

1. Get married ~~before turning 30.~~
   when you're really ready.

2. Retire with ~~$5 million.~~
   loads of memories.

3. Become an ~~entrepreneur.~~
   influencer.

4. Fall in love with ~~someone beautiful.~~
   inner beauty.

5. Make my parents proud of ~~how much I earn.~~
   how happy I am.

6. Make ~~many~~ friends.
   real

7. Find happiness in the ~~luxury items.~~
   ordinary things.

8. Find someone whom you ~~can live with.~~
   can't live without.

I think it says it all, really. Aspirations are personal, not a one-size-fits-all.

YOUR JOURNEY … YOUR ASPIRATIONS … YOUR LIFE

It took me a couple of decades to understand the importance of having my own aspirational goals, and where aspirations come from: deep within ME. It took me a few years longer to really believe that I deserved a richer, more colourful life; that what I aspired to be was totally up to me. To realise that I was not a product of my circumstances or upbringing – I was a protégé of my own unique journey. A journey I could design, change, redesign, and fill with as much excitement and opportunity as I chose to leap towards.

Rock Your Stripes

All this reflective writing has got me thinking: I wonder what my aspirational list would look like now, or what I would tell my younger self, or indeed my younger female mentees today? So, I decided to create a similar list; a thought-provoking version for today's aspirational women. Perhaps you'd like to add your ideal outcomes too … or create your own amended aspirational list. I've left room for you to add some of your own ideas.

1. Get into a career I ~~can fall back into doing part time hours later.~~
can learn, grow and keep achieving in
can build transferable skills in that will take me anywhere
am passionate about and empowers my aspirations

_____

_____

2. Fall in love with ~~a good, hard-working man who will provide for me.~~
someone who shares my values and supports my aspirations
someone who loves all of me, not just the pretty bits
life's opportunities … and my dog ☻

_____

_____

3. Get married ~~before turning 25.~~
whenever I want to, if I want to …
when I've found a real partner I want to share my life with
or not … it's a choice

_____

_____

4. Have children ~~before turning 30.~~
whenever I want to, if I want to …
only when I'm ready and have a shared parenting plan in place
or not … it's a choice

_____

_____

5. Get a mortgage to buy a home ~~before turning 40.~~

        if I want to, if it's feasible

        only when I'm ready and able to commit

        or not ... renting is a valid, flexible choice

_____

_____

6. Make my parents proud of ~~how great a Mother and Wife I am.~~

        how I'm achieving my dreams and aspirations

        how I'm raising my children as independent equals

        how happy I am

        or don't – it doesn't matter what they think

_____

_____

7. Find happiness in ~~the luxury items and material possessions.~~

        the ordinary things and daily surroundings

        a life without clutter or unnecessary complications

        an adventurous life full of aspirational goals

_____

_____

8. Retire with ~~$5 million.~~

        the satisfaction of kicking those aspirational goals

        knowing I've made a difference and left my mark

        heaps of adventures and loads of memories

        or don't retire – keep being adventurous and writing lots of stories

_____

_____

9. Make ~~many~~ friends.

        real

_____

10. Find a partner you ~~can live with.~~

        connect with and complements you.

_____

Create your own personal BRAG list ...

Those BIG RADICAL ASPIRATIONAL GOALS

Aspire

CHAPTER 3

REACH ...

for your goals

REACH ... for
your goals

Only as **HIGH**
as I reach
can I **GROW** ...

Only as **FAR**
as I seek
can I **GO** >>>

THE RESILIENCE RIDE

Reach high. Simple to say, but not always easy to do, right? There's no easy way to reach your aspirational goals. There is no express lane. No straight and narrow road that guarantees a smooth glide to the finish line of your desired successes. Unless you are extremely lucky and have a tail wind helping to push you along all the way, you will have to do it like most successful people: dig deeply, push forward, jump the hurdles, rise up from the knocks, ride the zigzags, and keep reaching higher.

The big question is:

Do you WANT it badly enough?

First and foremost, the foundational step is to passionately, unquestionably, and with cemented resolve that comes from deep within your inner core, believe these two things:

1. YOU CAN DO IT: Believe in your purpose and your linked aspirational goals, with unwavering self-belief.

2. YOU DESERVE IT: Believe that you deserve to live your life to the fullest extent – you deserve to achieve your aspirational goals.

YES, YOU CAN … take personal responsibility for your own journey of learning and growth. Back yourself first, and don't give up on your dreams and personal goals.

YES, YOU ARE … deserving of something better. Refuse to settle for an ordinary, preordained life. Shake things up, hold on to your aspirations, embrace the possibilities and opportunities, and choose to live an extraordinary life. To be disruptive – a rule breaker. To be aspirational – a thought leader. To be a game-changing woman – a leader of groundbreaking decisions.

My intention in writing this section and sharing more of my personal journey is not to say 'do it my way'. I certainly don't have all the answers. I'm no guru. My life has not been perfect, and at any point I could have made other decisions to reach the same, different or even better outcomes. But, I don't waste time there. It's not helpful to look back and dwell on the *'woulda–coulda–shoulda'* scenarios. The most important thing is to keep reaching and enjoy your journey.

> ### Don't keep looking back over your shoulder. You're not going that way.

One big thing I know from personal experience is that every goal I have achieved, every outcome I am proud of, I have had to stretch and reach for and keep pushing forward. I share some of those stories here to encourage you to bravely step up, as I have chosen to on many occasions; to be bold, be brilliant, become your best, biggest, full-arse version. Your version. Rocking every one of those well-earned stripes.

DIG DEEPLY

From all the heart-wrenching excavations over my adult decades, what I know for sure is that there will be times when you have to dig deeply. So, so deep. Deep enough to find that rich internal fortitude you need to help you climb back up to the surface. Deep enough to take responsibility, and do what needs to be done; sometimes even taking the lead in times of crisis.

> ### Pull on those big girl panties and just deal with it.

My Dad's big, generous heart of gold stopped beating suddenly in his mid-60s; a massive heart attack took him instantly while he was sitting at the breakfast table one morning. No second chances. He'd just retired, built their dream home on acreage, and they'd been planning their first of many adventure trips; this one to Tasmania.

I was mid-20s, working part time while coping with two toddlers under three years, mostly as a single parent while my husband was living and studying in Brisbane (two hours away) during the week. He was in the middle of sitting for final exams. I was certainly already wearing big panties, but the elastic was about to be stretched further when my Mum rang me.

Dig deep, Jilinda.

In the hours that followed, my Mum went numb – understandably; trying to process the reality that she'd just suddenly lost her one and only love, and the most important person in her life. The reason she got up each day. The reason she had done most things for the past 40-plus years. My sister, who lived close by, was out of town that day, so when she found out on her return that evening (pre-mobile phones), she spiralled through the emotional states of denial and then immobilising grief. Also understandable. We all handle crises in our own ways. *Dig deeper, Jilinda. You can do this.*

So, I pulled my big panties up high enough to support my heavy heart, and just got on with it. I made the phone calls to rellies and friends, helped Mum plan the funeral, and literally walked her through the worst days of her life, holding her up all the way. Like a detached, robotic project manager, I did what needed to be done. My time for grieving would wait. *More deep digging to come, Jilinda. You can do this.*

I don't know why, but life seems to throw such challenges our way just when we are making exciting plans to reach higher; when we're about to move towards aspirational goals. Perhaps the universe is testing our resolve? Like – *how badly do you want that thing?*

You see, when my Dad died suddenly, leaving my Mum to fend for herself on a seven-acre semi-rural block 30 minutes out of town (more his retirement dream than hers), it was just one month before we were to leave Toowoomba, to live in a remote location 10 hours' drive away. You may recall I shared that story in the previous aspirational section. I'd been excitingly planning this escape to start a new chapter for several years. I was so ready to reach for new, evolving goals. To go where I could become the 'real' me (whatever that was – I wasn't yet sure). Testing, testing? How strong are my aspirational goals? *Dig deeper again, Jilinda. You can do this. You deserve this. Your Dad knew that.*

Life's challenges are there for a reason; there's a lesson in every one of them. Despite all the 'shoulding' messages that were screaming at me (some internal, some from external sources), the strongest, deepest message I chose to take from my Dad's sudden death was this: life is short. Life is unpredictable and uncertain. Do what you want to do NOW. TODAY. Because tomorrow is not a given. *Rise up, push forward, reach higher, Jilinda.* Mum was an independent, strong, and very capable woman. *She can do this. You can do this. Follow your dreams.*

It's hard to believe that lesson occurred 30 years ago. So many incidents of having to dig deeper and keep pushing forward have occurred since then. Unfair, crappy stuff like rising back up from incapacitating injuries, surviving on inadequate funds, lost assets, ended relationships, job redundancies, malicious personal attacks, and flopped initiatives. Eeeek! So many tough lessons. So many stripe-earning moments.

Rather than allowing those slap-downs to kill off my aspirations, I know that I became stronger each and every time I have had to dig deep and rise back up – more courageous and confident to personally choose the challenges that require me to dig deep, so I can reach higher.

My inner strength is such now that I know I'll be okay, no matter what happens. I'm not afraid of the future, and to be frank, I don't spend much time worrying about all the possible scenarios. I have learned that trying to predict certain outcomes is wasted energy.

REMEMBER:
There is no such thing as certainty.

When you have clear values and beliefs that drive your purpose and passion, that define your aspirations, and strengthen your inner resolve to reach for your goals, I believe the right opportunities will come along. New doors will appear. But, you have to step out from behind the door. You have to be ready and willing to reach out, grasp the handle, and yank open those doors when they appear.

Here's the thing: to keep pushing forward and reaching up towards your aspirational goals, with high-beam focus and unwavering determination, you have to want it badly enough. Sometimes it takes pure guts. Sometimes it takes quiet patience. Always it takes a deep inner strength. *Dig deep … you'll find it.*

NO magic potions.

NO fairy dust.

NO-one to do it for you …

Just me, I will push you,

**show you how to put one determined
foot in front of the other.**

That's what I will do.

I AM INSIDE YOU …

I'm called your inner strength.

Dig deep down and you will find me.

You CAN do this …

I'VE GOT YOUR BACK.

PUSH FORWARD

Six months after we left Toowoomba (for good), and I felt those wonderful first waves of freedom, I also realised that some major life-changing decisions I'd made in my early 20s were not right for me. I don't refer to them as mistakes, and certainly not as failures. I just reflected and acknowledged to my inner self at that point in time that I had made those decisions for the benefit of others. All about pleasing others and conforming to norms. To fit in with the values of those closest to me at the time. I'd come to realise the outcomes were not a good fit for me or the aspirations I initially had planned for my 20s.

In essence: I had done what was expected of a 'good girl' of that era; a young women at 21 years (gets married), and what normally follows two or three years later (has children). Perhaps I did it to prove to others I was 'good enough'? To follow along with traditional expectations? Well, on the surface anyway. My inner, unconventional voice certainly did a lot of screaming at me in those days. But, I didn't trust it enough yet to listen and act on it. *Push forward, Jilinda.*

Twenty-one seems such a young age to get married now, but most of my church friends and many of my workmates were already married. My bestie, who had been a bridesmaid three times already, was so pleased when I told her: *'I'm not having any bridesmaids'*. You see, I did try to disrupt some traditions by refusing to have bridesmaids, or wear a veil (why cover up a great hairstyle!), or have a train of fabric dragging behind me in the dirt (makes no sense!). I wore a champagne cream, ankle-length designer dress, decorated with deep pink- and peach-coloured open roses across the shoulders, topped off with a pearl headband that dipped down low on my forehead. Anything but the usual lacy white fru-fru bridal attire. Defiant; but only to a point.

You see, by that age I had embraced my individuality but not yet trusted my independent mind enough to design my life on my terms. That strength kicked in a few years later.

As my Dad was walking me down the aisle, I remember clearly my inner voice was yelling at me: 'What are you doing, Jilinda? What about all your dreams to travel and see the world in your 20s?'

So, fast forward a few years: there I was at 27, with the realisation that I'd married way too young, to someone much older than me, who I had little in common with (apart from Miss 3 and Mister 1), and to top it all off, I was crap at the mumsy stuff. Somehow, the naturally nurturing maternal instincts just never really clicked in for me. Or maybe, I just never accepted the concept that being a mother had to change anything; certainly not change who I am.

I'd literally spent the prior two years in robotic survival mode, project managing the entire household affairs, scheduling child-raising routines to clockwork timetables, so that I could still fit in part-time work and my sanity time of three gym sessions per week (yay – free child minding ☻). Then, when my husband came home from college on weekends, I spent many of them writing HIS university assignments (not bad for someone who left school at 15).

Now, with his first teaching job and me stuck in basic public housing with two toddlers in a small rural community, I knew I needed a life that was more than playgroup and patty cakes. It was time to create the next chapter. *Dig deep, Jilinda. Push forward.*

Rock Your Stripes

'People who get on in this world are those who
get up and look for the circumstances they want,
and, if they can't find them, make them.'

George Bernard Shaw

One of the great things about small communities is the willingness of others to help and the opportunities there are to make a positive difference. They say it takes a village to raise children; well it certainly did for mine. Within weeks I had found a wonderful, older daycare mumsy mum whose last two (of six) kids were in high school, so she had time to look after my two. Within months, I designed and organised the re-furb of an empty shop, and opened my first hairdressing business. Initially planned to run just three days a week, within three months that changed to six days a week, and within six months, I'd employed my first apprentice.

Thank goodness the daycare mum was amenable to increased hours and adored our kids. In fact, she was their primary carer right up until both went to school. A substitute granny-mum. After that, their Dad worked the same hours and had the same school holidays, so – problem solved. *Riding the zigzags.*

The response to my new business was amazing. People travelled from anywhere within a three-hour radius to have a stylish haircut and colour from a 'city-trained' stylist. It became usual to be solidly booked a month in advance. After three years, and by then having to squeeze three staff into a tiny space, and with clients having to wait on a bench seat outside, we built a much larger salon. *Push forward, Jilinda. You can do this.*

Our initial three-year 'country service' teaching plan ended up with me being fully immersed into this wonderful regional community for seven years. We stayed for greater reasons than just my successful business; it was a period of immense personal and professional development growth for me. I was like a sponge; sucking up every opportunity. I created an independent life that made the most of the situation;

filling my diary with anything that fuelled a new learning or growth, and driving positive change wherever I could.

So, from a young, disillusioned Mum to small business owner/manager, to starting the community's first business network (with several other progressive business people), to being one of the first two women elected to the board of what was historically the rural town gentlemen's club (ending the 'old boys' club brigade'), to running numerous community events; this was when I first realised my influential leadership capability.

This was my leadership training ground. The chapter of my life when I grew massive inner strength and a deep personal conviction to be a leader of change. A Change Champion. A disrupter of ordinary. A challenger of the 'play it small' thinkers. A real purpose.

Seriously, at one point I considered staying put and putting my hand up for a local councillor position. Many clients were encouraging me.

Those wonderful, wise women who became my unofficial mentors at that time were strong, resilient country women who were not only supportive of my change initiatives in their community, they willingly shared their rural knowledge, invited me into their circles, and provided valuable advice. I grew to love this rural community and its potential. But, I knew I would outgrow it.

What I also grew was a realisation that life's opportunities come in chapters, each with its own set of limitations and end dates. I could foresee that at some point I would need to make major personal-life changes to enable me to reach bigger aspirational goals. I knew those changes would need to take place elsewhere. The next chapter was already in the making.

By the time we moved from this small rural community to larger coastal civilisation (with Miss 10's high school plans a priority), I was ready for a new career. Over the years I never stopped learning, travelling to attend yearly industry expos and completing many business courses. Now, it was time to reach higher. I was keen to get a university degree. So, I pushed open those heavy doors and was accepted into post-graduate studies at age 35, as an external student. And what's more, just to smash that old fear of *'not being good enough'* right out of my head, I got a high distinction for my first assignment. *Keep reaching higher, Jilinda.*

Here's the thing: life is a series of chapters, all of them full of choices to explore, chances to take, and changes you can make. You are not born to excel at everything. You are not born to be mothers, born to be successful business owners, or born to be leaders. You are born as an awesome human being with the potential to choose to do the things that excite and energise you. The stuff you are passionate about. *Push forward. Find what that is. Rock the socks off it.*

> **'You are born into genius ... but have you resigned yourself to mediocrity?'**
>
> Robin Sharma

JUMP THE HURDLES

It is really concerning to me just how many women don't reach up or push on towards their aspirational goals. I've coached many women over the years who are holding back from making those big changes, like starting a new business, or growing their current business, or committing to studies, or – particularly – taking on a leadership role.

Apart from smashing those core fears I've outlined previously, their reasons generally match recent findings from a local business women's network survey identifying the top four hurdles to women progressing their career:

1. confidence
2. time
3. competence (education and experience)
4. money.

These survey results are not surprising. Many women put their own professional development needs last when it comes to family budget and time allocated to focus on their own aspirations. I do get that sometimes it just seems all too hard when dealing with competing priorities. But …

Is it time to question what you are prioritising?

As I shared earlier, I've been a facilitator of women's Circles since 2014, starting them up in the various regions we moved to. The Circles were held on a week night, once a month, after hours. While I do this as a community development service (read: I give my time), I charge a small membership fee to cover for folders, printouts and venue incidentals, so that I'm not out of pocket. Each time I offer a new Circle and call for expressions of interest, there are always several ladies who are initially really keen, until they have to commit by paying the small upfront membership fee. Like it's a huge stumbling block. Like they can't possibly stretch their (family) budget to spend anything on their own personal and professional development.

Honestly? In reality, I'm talking about less than the cost of their takeaway coffee purchases per week. I know these same women would think nothing of regular lunch outings with friends, or buying a new dress, shoes, handbag and hat to attend local races – spending 10 times that amount for one afternoon of fashionista competitiveness. Priorities people? Which investment provides longer-term benefits?

The sad reality is that this type of inaction (or 'on hold' status) often leads to women lacking competence by not having the required levels to competitively apply for higher roles; especially when there are gaps in their résumés. Then, the flow-on effect is: the more knockbacks, the more confidence levels take a dive. What I've observed is the longer you hold back and put your own needs last, the harder it is to rise up and push forward. *Rise up … explore your options. Invest in your personal growth. You deserve it.*

When you decide to take those next steps, to reach and keep pushing forward, to keep learning, your inner confidence will grow, and your external courage will show that with every new action you take.

> **'If you are not willing to learn, no-one can help you ...**
> **If you are determined to learn, no-one can stop you.'**
>
> Zig Ziglar

From my own experiences, I know that continual growth of competence levels has massively benefited me in reaching aspirational goals. Knowledge IS power. Education is important; formal and informal. Credibility and capability matter when it comes to applying for that next level, or a new career leap, or simply standing out from the rest (more on that to come).

Frankly, in these days of so much information provided freely by the devices we surround ourselves with, ignorance is a choice. A poor one. The reality is, growing your knowledge has never been easier. There are no excuses, with so much online and flexible learning, much of it at low or no cost. Lack of funds doesn't have to hold anyone back.

Is it time to check the BS money stories you are telling yourself?

Honestly, I completed ALL my studies while on a shoestring budget. No-one funded my formal studies but me; something I'm very proud of. During most of that chapter, I remember budgeting to live on $150 per week; that's groceries, fuel, and limited social outings. Luckily, I could do my own hair! I also discovered that my skin responded better to $30 products than $100 supermodel-endorsed cosmetics. That a brisk esplanade walk and swim in the public lagoon kept me in better shape than a gym membership I struggled to use. Besides, the fresh outdoor air was better for mind clearing and stress release.

It's true, university studies in Australia these days are a major financial and personal commitment. By not continuing on to university straight from high school, I missed the boat on the Gough-Whitlam-driven, no-uni-fees era. When I started my degree in my mid-30s, I funded the course enrolment costs as a part-time employee on low hairdressing wages. Then, for two semesters, I was recovering from shoulder surgery and unemployed. Later, despite being employed in State Government leadership roles while completing my Masters in Management degree, the decision-makers above me refused to recognise my study as *essential or highly desirable*, thereby not entitling me to any course fee assistance. So, consequently, I could only ever afford to do one subject per semester, and my degree took 10 years to complete (after work hours), including several deferment breaks to allow financial breathing space along the way.

Back then, gaining such a degree wasn't highly valued in the public sector (especially for women), and was certainly not considered to be essential by those serial seat-warming executives above me; none of those guys had tertiary degrees. They had worked their way up through the ranks of the public sector since joining as 17-year-old recruits straight out of high school, in the days when women were employed as 'tea ladies' (yes – delivering cups of tea and warm hand towels to their desks!), or 'typists' (an administration pool of women who typed up all the outgoing letters, reports and minutes). With job-for-life attitudes, these blokes had reached their career destination – the comfortable 'director's chair brigade' – and were happy to sit there watching their superannuation accounts grow. *Rise above, Jilinda. Don't be like them.*

Interestingly, I have coached some public-sector guys like that; those who need help with accepting change and learning new ways to think and act. Many live in fear of having to re-apply for 'restructured roles' or apply for another job elsewhere in the twilight years of their working life. Many are very fearful of the high-achieving women they now have to compete with for jobs that were previously handballed to them by other blokes (read: mates).

The thing is: these days I believe education levels DO matter, both for competency and currency reasons. The world is changing rapidly, so it is increasingly important to not get left behind.

> '**A mind that is stretched by new experiences
> can never go back to its old dimensions.**'
>
> Oliver Wendell Holmes

There were so many great learnings I took from those education-focused, financially skint years; the most enduring one being – I don't need all that extra stuff. Minimalist living is far less complicated. Finding joy in the simple things and experiences trumps the clutter and weight of material possessions. Hands down. The only exception (read: obsession) for me these days is my ever-growing library. Kindle copies just don't have the same appeal to me as printed books I can dog-ear, highlight, sticky-note and scribble over.

Push forward. Have a clear focus on what really matters.

TIME IS ON YOUR SIDE

Now, let's take a look at another big blockage; the TIME issue that holds many women back from progressing their career. I think of the TIME dilemma in two ways:

- finding enough time
- not the right time.

Let's have a look at each of these.

Finding enough time

Really? Is it time to do an honest hour-by-hour audit on exactly what you are choosing to spend your time on? Perhaps you are not prioritising the right things, or not delegating enough, or not asking for help, or are just too distracted?

We each have the same 24 hours per day and the ability to choose what we spend our time on; but many women suffer from a common female affliction – a giving disorder. Giving of our time, our energy, even our best years, for the benefit of others in our family.

Take stock of how much time you are giving away. If you are choosing to do that and it's working for you, or it's part of a staged, short-term plan, that may be okay (for a short while). As long as it's genuinely a choice YOU are making, and not a chain around your neck holding you back.

Australian author Kate Christie's book *Me Time* provides a step-by-step guide with practical exercises to help women find '30 guilt-free hours a month'. Frankly, I think that equation of one hour a day or half a day per week is a very small goal, but I realise it's a starting base for some. These 'take back' hours are often found in the simple things we think of as just 'normal expectations'. That might be cooking the evening meals, washing, ironing, folding clothes; a long list of all the little things that add up to 'no time left for you'. If you've never done an in-depth time audit, Kate's book is the bomb; especially for working mums coping with numerous house-management tasks.

'I don't have time' is the adult version of 'the dog ate my homework.'

When I was a business owner with two toddlers, there were some 'normally expected' women's chores I rejected from very early on. One was ironing. I hated it with a passion. My husband (of that chapter) loved it. It was his excuse to spend countless hours watching weekend sport on TV, while ironing (slowly but with knife-pleat perfection). Honestly, he was so proud of his precision ironing skills that when my Mum visited and did some ironing, he waited until she went to bed, then took his work clothes back downstairs and re-ironed them. So, there were no arguments about who did the ironing in our house. *Winning.*

Years later, when I left that marriage, I never bought an iron. I simply decided that I would never buy anything that needed ironing; and

I never have. I love my wardrobe of comfortable, stretchy, wash–hang–wear clothes. No linen or silk items allowed, unless they have the fashionable crinkle or crushed look. So great for travel too; just roll up into a suitcase, roll out and wear. Choices, ladies: we all have them.

Speaking of better choices – these days, there IS an iron in the cupboard. It came with my wonderfully house-trained partner; about the only household item we didn't have two of when we merged. After following my best-practice lead in laundering T-shirts and jeans (precision peg placing and purposeful hanger choices), he only uses it to iron business shirts for in-person meetings. By the way, if those 1970s stretchy men's body shirts ever come back into vogue, he'll be ditching the iron too.

(Note to the entrepreneurs: *someone needs to invent stylish men's business shirts that don't need ironing.* My partner will order them in an instant. Seriously, there's a real market opportunity.)

Similarly, as I mentioned earlier, kitchening has never been my thing. While we eat healthy, fresh food (not takeaway), it is generally something that takes less than 10 minutes prep. Frankly, I've lost interest after that time. As a busy couple, each working on our own projects, we've established a simple food routine that works for both our timetables and our health needs, incorporating one or two small meals of meat/veggies/salad, and one or two protein fruit smoothies a day. Just love my smoothies; two minutes prep, three minutes drinking, and back into the important stuff. My kind of re-fuelling. No Master Chef aspirations in our house. Really, I just can't be arsed. Quite sure I could make a list of 500 things I'd rather be doing than cooking. We both agree on that one. *Winning again.*

One last thing about time wasters: social media is not only a distraction, it is an addictive decimator of time and energy. I know. I have suffered from the addiction. It takes continual discipline and serious deadlines (like this book writing launch date) to make me realise how much time can be wasted in that space. If you use it for business and providing inspirational messages to your followers (aka: your tribe) like I do, schedule a time to do your posts, then switch it off. That's what I've had to do. Like all addictions, it takes constant effort to mitigate the relapses. *Push on, Jilinda.*

REMEMBER: you can do anything ... but not EVERYTHING.

Right timing

This is a slightly different aspect of a 'timing' issue or blockage. It is a reality I have painstakingly grown to accept over the years. Things often take longer to happen than my ideal timing (like this book!), and people take longer to get on board with change or new ideas than what I expect. Or sometimes – it's just the wrong timing.

You see, I'm naturally impatient. It's a well-honed, reactive emotion (read: frustration) to the sometimes-unrealistic expectations I have; fuelled by my naturally optimistic personality. Change Champions like me tend to think up solutions, then want to do it NOW, without needing to work out all the details or waste time doing an in-depth risk analysis. I just want to see results quickly. A risk-taker. Not afraid to jump in head first and work it out along the way.

Subsequently, there have been many career moments, particularly as a manager, when I've been way ahead of the pack. Then, after looking behind me to find where everyone else is at, I've had to stop, re-engage, inspire, encourage, support, and wait for them to catch up. There's even been several occasions when stuff I was trying to make happen, that never got enough traction at the time, finally occurred like two years after I'd moved on to the next role. Frustrating, right?

So, I often have to dig deep to find enough patience. The best way I've found to stay motivated on the important goals is to keep visualising the desired outcome, and then plan out the next move, so that step is ready to roll out when the timing IS right. Sometimes, I've had to just trust that the lagging bits will eventually catch up. All in good time. Often, my patience bucket runs dry, and I lose interest and move on. Nice idea, wrong timing. Acceptance is often better than ongoing annoyance.

Now, I do think there's a time and place for those calming, reassuringly Zen-inspired sayings like:

'The universe will provide' ... or ... 'Everything happens when it's meant to.'

But ... that woo-woo guidance is not where I place my trust. I learned from leaping into independent adulting at an earlier age than most that you don't become your full-arse version by sitting back and waiting for the right opportunities to just fall from the universe into your lap at the right time. Like it's somehow preordained from some higher power above. I stopped believing a long time ago in the notion that a higher being (such as 'the lord') will provide me with a purpose, plan and schedule; that all will be miraculously revealed and unfold when the time is right. What I've discovered is that the universe (or whatever higher power you speak to) needs you to manifest your dreams and goals, work towards them, and regularly hold up a sign, because the right timing often needs some 'hello' alarm bell reminders.

That said, since writing the original version of this book (2018), and experiencing unexpected pandemic pauses and impacts, like many others I took the opportunity to rest, reflect, reassess life choices, rejig my mindset, and add some new self-care, soul-fuelling rituals. Through daily morning beach sunrise meditation and journalling, I have developed a deeper respect and understanding of the need for personal spiritual connection (that is totally separate from religious teachings). I've learned to accept the natural ebb and flow of life, to be grateful for each day, to be open to new opportunities and direction changes (without needing to push or control all that), and to trust the process or journey more deeply. Trust that there is a bigger reason why things don't always turn out in line with my ideal plan, and trust in my own ability and agility levels to leap forward when the timing is right.

One pertinent example is the timing of publishing and promoting the original version of this book. Launched mid-2019, book tour in August and September that year, speaking engagements in the fourth quarter ... then BOOM! – my left knee meniscus suddenly tore in

January 2020, which meant hobbling around on crutches for two months, physio, rethinking travel …then BOOM BAM! – COVID hit Australian shores and the whole country closed borders and shut up shop.

As the pandemic dragged on and women were significantly impacted by increased care duties with everyone home (feeding the masses, schooling the children, juggling work at kitchen tables, career aspirations on hold); the core message of my book – to *unleash your full-arse version* and *step into the arena* to *courageously lead change* quickly became – wrong timing. Many women in Australia couldn't step outside their own doors, let alone into a public arena. At least, if they dared to, they would have been safely alone – no audience or crowds.

A huge lesson in why right timing matters, and in patience and belief in the core message. I trusted that the right time would emerge, and the impact would be greater than initially planned. *Divine timing, Jilinda.*

Let's smash a few more myths that plodders, naysayers, or those who try to hold you back tend to use:

Patience is NOT a virtue if it is used as an excuse to do nothing while waiting for the perfect conditions ... (which never happens, because there's no such thing as perfect).

By all means be patiently and methodically persistent in reaching for your goals, but not just patiently waiting for the stars to line up. Without persistent effort, you won't get there.

And another … despite what my mother told me, I've also discovered that:

GREAT
~~Good~~ things happen to
those who wait.
DON'T

105

I learned that one the hard way. Whenever I have not trusted my gut instinct and opted instead to wait a little longer to see if it works out – yep; *wrong again. Oh, the wasted years.* All the many times I could have done that thing yesterday or last year or 10 years ago! (*Yes, like writing this book!*) I go with my gut instincts a lot more these days. I've learned to trust my intuition. Somehow, that deep inner voice seems to know what's best, before my head tries to over-complicate it with other random 'what if' thoughts and worst-case scenarios.

My point is this: you have to curiously keep exploring opportunities that pop up, to see if they match well with your goals, then courageously take small steps towards them and keep pushing forward until the timing is right for that big, bold leap. Love those giant, exciting leaps.

Here's the thing: pushing forward is not a one-time effort. To become your full version and reach your greatest potential, you are going to need to *keep* jumping hurdles and pushing on. Become really mindful and focused on your priorities and take personal responsibility for the choices you make every day. Call out those BS excuses. Tell your negative voice to sit down and shut up. Stop waiting. Stop holding back. *Just do it.*

> **'You have to sit by the side of a river for a V E R Y long time before a roast duck will fly into your mouth.'**
>
> Guy Kawasaki

RISE UP FROM THE KNOCKS

Jumping back to my mid-30s; apart from wanting to take my career to a higher level, I knew I had to leave the hairdressing industry after 20 years for another good reason. For several years, I was having shoulder massages at least fortnightly, just to keep going. What I didn't know was just how bad the damage was. You see, I'm vertically challenged – a shorty – so my arms had been constantly held above shoulder level for decades. I ended up needing surgery to repair my supraspinatus tendon which had worn to thin threads, and was fully torn through on one side.

Recovering from that surgery was one of my darkest, deepest down times. Not because my hairdressing career was over; I was already over that and several semesters into my degree studies. I was knocked down by the inability to do anything for months. I'm an active person. An extrovert. Highly independent. My patience was tested to its absolute limits. I remember teaching my 15-year-old daughter to change the gears in my manual car, so I could drive with one arm, just to get out of the house. I also became quite proficient at typing one-handed to complete my uni assignments.

But by far, the biggest blow was to my personal next chapter plans. The big, radical change. I was ready for a giant leap. I'd been planning it for years. Nine months of surgery recovery and not earning put a major hole in my progression towards that. Another testing of my resolve? *Dig deep, Jilinda. Push on. It's just another hurdle. Rise up.*

What I've learned from unanticipated knocks like this, and the end results, is sometimes there's a better plan in the making, at a slightly different time than I had envisioned. There's that need for patience again, and trusting the universe's timing. I've learned to trust that when you rise up from the rubble, you don't always see a clear path; sometimes you have to wait just a little bit longer for the dust to clear. But, know that it will clear, and be ready to fly when it does. *Focus on the end goal. Trust the process, Jilinda.*

So, after my shoulder surgery, the work rehabilitation program temporarily placed me with a State Government department that aligned with my self-directed studies. Travelling into the city from a coastal hinterland hub by train each day was my first taste of the corporate worker grind. I absolutely loved it. Twelve hours out of the house each day! I was immediately able to use some of my new human resource management degree learnings in the industrial relations arena. Again, I was like a sponge. So excited to be learning and building new capabilities. A massive career leap. It turned out to be the start of what would be a 10-year, fast-paced career climb through the public sector to senior regional management.

Eighteen months after commencing this new career, I was offered my first permanent position, a two-level promotion to District Manager in the North Queensland region. They needed a change leader with HR expertise and performance management focus. They wanted to bring in fresh thinking and a new approach; something that was rare within the public sector at the time. I ticked all their boxes, and the career opportunity and relocation aspect ticked mine. Finally, a chance to invoke my big, radical change. To be free. Divorced. Financially independent. Single. To travel. Explore. This was not just another new chapter, it was like finishing part one of my life story and commencing a whole new part two. *Turning to a blank page. Designing a new life. Rise up. Be brave, Jilinda.*

So, with just two suitcases of clothes and two boxes of household essentials, I drove a one-way hire car and headed north. Once again, I felt the burden of what had been a struggle in silence for so many years just roll off my shoulders. I remember playing my favourite CDs and singing all the way. No tears. My time to rise up had come … as I knew it would. *Reach higher. It's your time to shine, Jilinda.*

No chapter, situation or relationship is a waste of time. If it didn't bring you what you want, it taught you what you don't want.

Here's the thing: often the greatest lessons and the most powerful personal growth happens when you are knocked down and forced to sit in the rubble, just long enough for it to cement those life-changing plans into place. Long enough to gather inner strength to rise up and be ready to take another shot at life.

RIDE THE ZIGZAGS

As this book is not intended to be a chronological autobiography, I'll jump forward a few years, skipping along an exciting zigzag path of many choices, chances and changes. (You can check out more about my zigzag journey in the next chapter – EVOLVE.)

What I've become really skilled in is to simply ZIG when I hit a ZAG, and I've grown certainty in these two things:

■ I know there will always be choices.

■ I trust I will always be okay.

That said, I'm not expecting the universe to provide these things; it's up to me to explore choices, jump on opportunities, and make things happen. To design my zigzag journey.

Along the way I've also accepted that life is not going to be an easy ride. It hasn't been so far, and I know I'm richer for all life has thrown at me. The reality is: game-changing disrupters will always experience some level of pushback. But, some ZAGs are really crap to go through and ZIGing back from those takes a little longer, and a bucket load of resilience.

When my partner – Mr G – and I met, neither of us was particularly looking for a life-long commitment. We had both come out of marriages we'd responsibly spent too long in, both had young adult children off doing their own things (yeah!), and for several years since, had both been enjoying the flexibility of independent lives and busy careers. Unencumbered. Ours was firstly a meeting of likeminded executive leaders at a board table, then a discovery of well-matched values, drivers, and jointly held aspirations to make a bigger difference. Like a pair of matching socks, it was comfortable right from the start. A pair of Change Champions; we were sometimes referred to as a 'dynamic duo' (or perhaps by some – 'double trouble'). Since becoming partners, we've zigzagged our way around several regional locations, moving each time for career opportunities that match our expertise and desire to lead positive change.

In 2017, just two years after we had made commitments to settle and do meaningful work in a remote regional community for a three-to-six year chapter – a place where we were already making positive differences – we were slapped down with a vexatious assault on our highest held value: our integrity. We were falsely accused by a threatened species (read: CEO in self-preservation mode) – he and a couple of his power-hungry mates concocted a plan to deliberately discredit us and drive us out of town. Apparently, we asked too many questions they were uncomfortable answering, and we'd pushed for too many innovative changes that impacted on their comfort zone kingdom. That ZAG blow was a biggy to rise up from. *Dig deep, dynamic duo.*

With unexpected, unfounded allegations, which triggered absolutely unnecessary investigations, the incident caused us to dig deeper than perhaps we've ever had to before; especially as a couple. The personal assault was against both of us, as we were both driving positive changes in this small community. It smashed through our planned personal goals, ruined our proactive community development goals and career aspirations at the time, and totally rocked our world.

Without a doubt, it was the biggest reminder I'd felt for some time that there is no such thing as certainty. Not even a three-year contract certainty. One thing we have absolutely no control over is other people's maliciously motivated behaviour. But, we do have control and choices over how we respond.

Sometimes, the easiest and best thing to do is to walk away and move on. After all, we've done that before; we're experienced zigzaggers. Adept at turning the page and just pushing forward to start the next new chapter. However, when it comes to an assault on our integrity and reputation as role models of ethical leadership practices, we needed to rise up and fight to clear our names, and distance ourselves from such corrupt, wrongful behaviours. Yes, even diving into the whole murky litigation process. If nothing is done to change this sort of atrocious predatory behaviour, nothing will change. *Time to drag out those big girl panties again.*

We both firmly believe that the behaviour you walk past is the behaviour you condone. As leaders and mentors to other leaders, we could not do that. Wrong is always wrong, even if others have gotten away with it before. *Dig in. Keep holding our heads high.*

Now, on the flip side, because we choose not to rumble below the positive line for long, one thing we know is there was valuable learning from this big ZAG incident. A lesson I feel compelled to share so that many others learn from it as well.

'Integrity is choosing courage over comfort. Choosing what is right over what is fun, fast or easy. Choosing to practice our values rather than simply professing them.'

Brené Brown

Contrary to what you may think, our own reflective lesson is NOT to *never do that again*. We are proud of what we achieved and what we did for that community. It actually fuelled our desire to *turn the dial up*; step up sooner, stand out from the rest, speak up earlier, and reach up higher. We became even more determined to raise the bar on leadership expectations – both in quality and quantity.

In the rumble months following, we refreshed our consulting company brand name to Vital LEADERS, and strengthened our mission on developing dynamic leaders: authentic, genuine, ethical, emotionally intelligent and engaging. We've certainly had firsthand experience of what happens when that's missing. *Now that's how you turn a nasty ZAG into a positively energised ZIG.*

Rising up is easier to do when you reach out with greater-good intentions, focusing on the solution rather than the problem.

While the outcome of the formal investigation into this insidious personal attack totally cleared both of us of any wrongdoing (as we knew it would), thereby confirming that the allegations were unfounded and of malicious intent, subsequent consequences for the offenders was personally disappointing. But bringing this to the attention of relevant authorities added to the broader investigation of a number of local government councils for a range of similar and quite serious charges, our case being just one of those. I often share this 'shit-storm' story in keynotes and workshops to emphasise the importance of ensuring leaders have the right character, competence, values and motives, consistent with the organisation or community they lead. Of course, when people are popularly elected into lead roles without the desired leadership attributes and ethics, that adds a whole other complication to the matter of removing the 'problem' (THINK: ex-President Trump ... or closer to home – ex-PM Morrison).

> 'There is NO GREATER THREAT to the critics, cynics and fearmongers than those of us who are WILLING TO FALL because we have learned how to RISE.'
>
> Brené Brown

Here's the thing: when you dare to disrupt the status quo, when you aspire for greater outcomes, when you are brave enough to reach up and drive much-needed change, you have to be prepared to take the knocks and ride the zigzags, knowing you can always rise up again and push on. Knowing that every time you do, your resilience muscle strengthens. Knowing that every experience is a lesson to share. Life is a journey, not a destination.

Ride it out. Keep reaching. Rock your well-earned stripes.

KEEP REACHING HIGHER

Remember those BRAGs? Those BIG RADICAL ASPIRATIONAL GOALS you wrote out at the end of the previous chapter? Well, now it's time to reach up and grab hold of the railings, and climb those steps to make them happen. You need to manage your life and career like you're the CEO.

No more excuses. I've heard them all. Yes, sometimes I still hear my own internal negative voice whisper them, before I quickly tell it to sit down and shut up with something like:

> 'Really? Where on earth did those BS words come from? As if ... '

Be mindful that those limiting stories you are listening to are likely to have come from other people's flippant remarks, or risk-averse advisors, or maybe even unresourceful beliefs you still hold on to from childhood. Lots of people have influenced you along your journey, and mostly with good intentions; but it's wise to question any thought that pops up and tries to hold you back. You don't have to subscribe to those issues. They probably just belong to someone else you bumped heads with along the way.

I remember a phone chat with my elderly Mum a few years ago, excitedly telling her about the projects I was working on and a few of my BRAGs that were gaining momentum: like my book writing, published articles, joining a speakers' bureau, and becoming a national ambassador for the Institute of Managers and Leaders' (IML) Chartered Manager professional designation. I think I overwhelmed her with all this news, as her response was:

'You be careful not to get too big for your boots.'

Frankly, I was gobsmacked that her immediate response was to instil some fear that I shouldn't be reaching for such high goals. There's that ugly, deflating word – 'shouldn't'. That fear of daring to be anything but ordinary, average, or blending into the shadows. Did she think I wasn't good enough? Didn't I deserve to have some recognition for all the years of hard work? How is it a bad thing to stand out from the rest?

I asked her in a rather strong tone: 'Why on earth would you say such a thing? What intended message am I supposed to take from that?' After a little silence, she simply added: 'I don't know. I guess it's just something my Dad used to say to me.' No doubt to keep her from dreaming of having a life other than being a dutiful wife (read: house servant).

So there you have it, folks. That's a perfect example of exactly how easily those limiting beliefs and fears are formed from flippant statements that have no positive use and don't serve us well. While I had no intention of taking that remark seriously, I think the reason I reacted so intensely was that it brought up old memories. Childhood recollections. It wasn't the first time I had heard that line. I'd spent years since building up my personal inner strength, independence and resolve to never let anyone or anything hold me back. Besides, the saying makes no sense:

If you outgrow your boots, you don't slice a piece off your foot ... you just go get bigger boots.

My point is: don't allow others who failed to reach their own goals talk you out of reaching your greatest potential. Just walk away, rise above and reach higher.

> 'If people are doubting how far you'll go ...
> go so far you can't hear them anymore.'
>
> Michele Ruiz

In 2018, I achieved what is touted to be *'the gold standard for managers and leaders'*; I became a Chartered Manager. A professional designation offered by IML in Australia and New Zealand, it is globally recognised through a strategic alliance with the Chartered Management Institute in the UK. I jumped on the chance to have my leadership competence levels, the work that I do, and the outcomes I'd achieved more broadly recognised. To reach a little higher and continue to raise the bar, as a role model for others, particularly women.

Some colleagues and people I spoke to about this asked me why I bothered. Why I felt I needed another credential. After all, I already have a few and I am known for continually researching and updating my knowledge in my areas of passion, and sharing that in my blogs and programs.

When you reach for higher goals, there will always be those who question your intentions, and some who make assumptions from what they may perceive as an unhealthy *'look at me'* desire for recognition. You know: no-one wants to be like the serial trophy collectors; the ones who self-nominate for every award that's going. The ones who keep adding more letters after their name. Perhaps even those who write a book about their achievements … right?

Now, in my home country – Australia – this reaction is like a national sport (read: affliction) that seems to be ingrained in the DNA of dinky-die Aussies. Perhaps it stems from our roots back to the British penal colony era; discarded from the United Kingdom class-ruled society and dumped on the other side of the world. That old feeling of *not being good enough* raising its head? Whatever the reason, this resentful attitude towards successful people is sadly still very prevalent. It's called *'the tall poppy syndrome'*. The aim of the game is to cut down any poppy (or person) that stands up taller than the others. They must question and speculate about the 'tall poppy's' motives. Try to discredit their achievements. Dismiss the effort as nothing more than what anyone else could do.

The irony is that, yes, lots of people COULD have achieved the same successful things I have and probably much more. I'm not special. BUT, the fact is: they didn't. They chose not to. They couldn't be bothered putting in the work. They'll generally have myriad excuses. The thing I find frustrating about this sport is that the side-liners holding the secateurs assume shit; they don't ask or bother to find out the person's real intent. So, I reflected on that and decided to write a blog to explain my purpose and intent, which IML shared broadly through various media promotions.

Overleaf is an extract from that blog … just in case you are starting to see a very long-stemmed, bright red poppy on my head and are searching for your secateurs. My point in sharing this is that, as a leader of change, I know how important it is for others to understand WHY; especially those I am wanting to inspire and influence. People want to follow leaders who are doing things for the right reasons; for the greater good, not just their own good. Intentions matter.

Ironically, the timing of gaining my Chartered Manager status could not have been more beautiful and meaningful. Beautiful – because I was able to combine my final assessment with the CMI UK assessor with a family trip to meet my first grand-bubba, who lives in London. Meaningful – because it was just a few months after rising up from that shocking big ZAG experience. *Reach higher. Integrity matters.*

WHY I BECAME A CHARTERED MANAGER (14 MAY 2018 – EXTRACT)

Why did I bother? After all, I already have a Masters in Management (MMgt), and numerous other accreditations in coaching and human behaviour assessments. Well, while that's great underpinning theory, we all know that it's hands-on experience, proven results, and continual learning to stay current that matters most.

Just like other professions, standards of practice vary. For example, there are bookkeepers, qualified accountants, and there are Chartered Certified Accountants. As a leadership coach, it concerns me that in the coaching industry, there are numerous life coaches, wellness coaches, transformational coaches – a whole raft of labels anyone can use. From attending a weekend coaching course, to completing a full Diploma in Coaching, credibility varies greatly.

On 16 January this year (2018), I officially achieved the internationally recognised, designated status of Chartered Manager – CMgr …

The process required me to submit a comprehensive assessment outlining how I manage change and lead others, including outcomes and learnings. I also had to demonstrate how I stay current, including outlining my professional development plan for the next 12 months.

Honestly, the process was more challenging than I initially thought it would be – but that's a good thing. It required considerable introspective reflection on why I do what I do, and particularly, what I learn from each experience.

What being recognised as a Chartered Manager means to me is these three core things:

- **Credibility** – international recognition of my expertise as a currently practising company manager, leader of change, trainer and mentor of aspiring leaders.

- **Currency** – acknowledged value of what I currently do, how I resolve issues by challenging the status quo and driving change, how I meet client expectations by using the latest practices, and recognition of positive outcomes achieved.

- **Commitment to continual growth** – acknowledgement of my insatiable thirst for continual professional development (CPD), and commitment to research and learning, for which I will be held accountable each year.

Embedded into the leadership development programs I deliver is a trust formula for leaders, which is fundamentally about building credibility.

Character + Competence + Consistency = TRUST

The Chartered Manager process gave me the opportunity to provide evidence of my ethical, honest and intentional character, my competence levels and achievements, and my consistent approach to continually learn and grow. Being awarded the Chartered Manager designation and proudly upholding those standards means I stand out from the mediocre, and stand proud as an intentional leader – as a trusted role model and mentor.

Yes, it means more than just another paper certificate.

Yes, I'm proud of being globally recognised for my achievements.

But above all that, I'm honoured to share my journey and what I've learned so that others can aspire, reach and grow.

Intentional Leaders develop and mentor other leaders … and my intention is to keep doing that.

Leadership credibility matters.

The message I want you to take from sharing this achievement is that no matter what small-minded people think, say or do, the gold is in how you choose to respond. You can always rise up, reach higher, rise well above their level, and be the better person.

Oh … and just in case you are wondering: no, I didn't need to go and buy a new larger size pair of boots, or a bigger hat.

Here's the thing: whatever you decide your BRAG goals are, deliberately and unapologetically focus on them. Look for opportunities to keep learning and growing your credibility in that area. Keep reaching for higher standards, new approaches. Stretch up higher than you (or others) thought possible. Don't be afraid to stand out from the average. Do it intentionally – to make a bigger difference. To leave your positive mark in this world.

Rock your stripes – proudly.

THERE IS AN INNER
BEAUTY ABOUT
A WOMAN
*WHO BELIEVES
IN HERSELF ...
WHO KNOWS SHE IS
CAPABLE OF ANYTHING
SHE PUTS HER MIND TO.*

THERE IS
BEAUTY IN THE
STRENGTH AND
DETERMINATION OF
A WOMAN
*WHO FOLLOWS HER
OWN PATH,*

WHO ISN'T THROWN
OFF BY THE OBSTACLES
ALONG THE WAY ...

THERE IS BEAUTY
ABOUT A WOMAN
WHOSE CONFIDENCE
COMES FROM
EXPERIENCES,
WHO KNOWS SHE
CAN FALL,
PICK HERSELF BACK UP,
AND MOVE ON.

Create your own personal GROWTH opportunities ...

When do you need to:

Dig deeply ...

Push forward ...

Jump hurdles ...

Rise from the knocks ...

Ride the zigzags ...

Reach higher ...

Reach

CHAPTER 4

EVOLVE ...
keep learning and growing

EVOLVE...
KEEP GROWING.

CHANGE
is
inevitable.

EVOLUTION,
while optional, is
VITAL.

CHANGE IS NOT AS SCARY AS *NOT* CHANGING

'Everything changes. Everything on this earth is in a continuous state of evolving, refining, improving, adapting, enhancing ... changing. You were not put on this earth to remain stagnant.'

Dr Steve Maraboli

If there's one big, overarching challenge I am intentionally wanting you to take on board as you read through this book, it is this: BE OPEN TO CHANGE. Embrace change. Explore choices. Initiate changes in your life. Drive change. Lead and influence others to change.

Why? Three things I know for sure from personal experience:

1. Your current circumstances will not improve unless YOU decide to actively implement changes; to make different choices, take chances and do stuff differently. It's okay to change your mind. It's okay to choose different things. It's okay for things to run their course and finish. Take personal responsibility to make the changes that are right for you – *now*.

2. You will not grow and improve, and will risk becoming insignificant or even irrelevant to society, if you refuse to embrace, learn about, and adapt to changes happening around you. Stay curious, ask questions, and – as much as practicable – keep up with the world. Keep evolving with it. This has become increasingly, vitally important.

3. When opportunities knock, first ask yourself: '*Will it potentially take me closer to my goals?*', and, '*Will it most likely hold me back?*' If it's a yes and a no – take that leap of faith and work out the details along the way. Every experience, while not always successful, provides key lessons and opportunities to grow, enabling you to evolve into your greatest, full-arse version ☺.

Harsh words? A little 'preachy' perhaps? Maybe 'scary shit' for some, or maybe a much needed wake-up call? But it IS the reality check we all need reminding of, especially in the fast-paced world we live in. Never before has it been so crucial to continually learn and grow. To evolve and keep evolving. I urge you – don't get left behind.

So ... the first questions to challenge yourself with are:

■ **How OPEN are YOU to continually learning new things?**
Are you putting that out there? Do others know that?

■ **How READY are YOU to embrace changes quickly?**
Are the right people, the decision-makers, aware of that?

■ **How WILLING are YOU to help influence and drive positive revolutions?**
Are the proactive movers and shakers aware of that?

■ **Are you currently EVOLVING or are you avoiding the inevitable?**
Only you can change or improve on that. It's YOUR choice.

If you're not changing and evolving with the times, there's a pretty good chance that you're stagnant, dying, already dead, or just a rock in someone's shoe.

Right O. Message received – loud and clear, you say. We all know CHANGE is the new NORMAL.

Given I've shared quite a few personal stories about embracing change already, I hope that you've arrived on this page with an increased curiosity to explore the changes you could make, and at the very least, an acceptance of the notion that change is inevitable. Okay with that? It's a given.

Ouch

CHANGING THE GAME

Throughout this book and across media, I mention that I've built a reputation as a *Change Champion*. What's a *Change Champion*? Simply put: I advocate for changes to the status quo, initiate change projects, embrace and drive change in my own life and business, and help others to make positive changes. To me, change is exciting, stimulating and full of opportunities and lessons.

Oh my goodness – yes, some of those lessons have been freakin' massive, and some were scary! But I know this for sure: I truly am so much wiser in thought, richer in spirit, and more centred to my core values for ALL of those experiences. The good, bad and downright ugly ones.

What's particularly special about this current chapter in my life is how in sync my partner and I are – a pair of *Change Champions*. Our passion for driving change, and making a positive difference in helping people and communities develop and grow, is what brought Mr G and I together over a decade ago. We were both enlisted onto a State Government led regional 'rapid response committee' during the fallout of the Global Financial Crisis (2008). It was a meeting of solution brokers, creative minds, a collaboration of purpose, and, as it turned out for us – a melding of strong personal values with matching drivers.

Ironically, we had both arrived at that point in life from similar zigzagging journeys. I clearly remember our first dates – we talked all night, sharing our experiences and learnings. So many 'me too' moments. Mind you, he would probably say: *'She still talks all night'* … but that's more a reflection of our differing needs when it comes to 'wind down' evening time. I'm a detailed over-sharer and storyteller, he's a dot-point strategist with limited 'need-to-know' capacity.

Rather than finding change 'scary', we view it as a positive opportunity to fix things that are not working, or change things that are no longer relevant; like the stuff that has simply run its course. Both of us are well-experienced in driving life-altering changes; not for the thrill of change, but for the purpose of personal growth and making a bigger difference for the greater good of our society – our core drivers. 'Stuck' is not an option we choose to accept.

Sure, I may have had a jump-start on others, having experienced change from day one (arriving in this world alone, adopted at two weeks old), but it was during my formative years (7 to 14) that I recognised the stark differences between being held back by traditional, old-fashioned beliefs and reaching to embrace new ideals with greater choices. The more I stepped outside that small, suffocating box, took a chance and made changes, the more I evolved into the REAL me. The person I was meant to be (more on that in Part II).

Of course, it was such an exciting time for young women to be growing up in the '70s – an era of pushing the boundaries, individual expressionism, and free love. The invigorated feminism wave was flowing strong, and let's not forget the evolution of music into rock concerts; so head-bangingly defiant of mainstream music. Intoxicating rhythm and free-form dance movements. Years of classic piano lessons were wasted on me. I just wanted to bash out the chords to songs I heard on the radio, my only access to the latest releases until I started work and my own music collection.

Luckily, my music training unleashed a natural ability to quickly identify major keys and chord changes in songs by ear (just listening and tinkering on the keyboard), so I had no need to wait until the music manuscripts came out. Winner – as buying most of the stuff I liked would not have been allowed. I clearly remember my old music teacher's feedback from a classical exam piece I had to play for her:

'Jilinda, that was really nicely played ... it's just a shame it's not what was written there.'

Oops; caught out. I was playing what I thought it should sound like; more upbeat and lively, no doubt.

While I constantly belted out and sang Helen Reddy songs – *I Am Woman, Hear Me Roar* and *I Don't Know How To Love Him* – and had fleeting daydreams of being the next Suzi Quatro, none of that was going to happen in the home environment I grew up in. Nice girls don't look like, sound like, or act like that. Although I do recall one

127

early win: I talked my Mum into taking me to a proper hairdressing salon for a shaggy-dog, Suzie Quatro–inspired haircut. I would have been 9 or 10 years of age at the time. Don't think I've ever worn piggy or pony tails again. *The evolution had begun.*

What about the '70s fashion, though? How awesome were all those bright colours (orange, green, purple, hot pink) splashed into psychedelic-patterned culottes; the first wave of ripped jeans and short, frayed denim shorts; itsy-bitsy string bikinis and topless sunbathing. Yes, I grew up in the Queensland sunshine and 'got wrecked' on Great Keppel Island with hundreds of other adventurous young adults (a popular holiday destination for 18 to 30s at the time). Tropical islands are still my favourite holiday destinations. The beach is my re-energising space.

Throughout this era, it was clear that the 1950s good-girl, housewifey, floral-frock, pastel-cardigan and gender-biased submission rules were under considerable pressure. Without doubt, the 1970s was a thrilling time of disruptive influence and significant change, fuelling my desire for 'what else'.

Subsequently, it's fair to say that much of my sheltered childhood was a noticeable mismatch with what was going on in the broader world. I excitedly dreamed, craved, and planned for the day I could immerse into all that the 'real' world had to offer, without the religious-based restrictions. Life would have been very different for me had I not had the courage to step out, explore choices, take chances and make changes from my mid-teens. And, I'm still doing that. Continually exploring and evolving. Still excited about the possibilities of 'what's next'. Every day brings new choices.

From all the revolutionary 'change' experiences I had through my early adult years, I took on what is perhaps the greatest learning and personal ACCEPTANCE. It is the thing that has continued to bolster my resilience and fuelled my courage to go on and make more changes. It is this:

Nothing stays the same ... and I'm okay with that.

Nothing. Nor would we want it to. Life would be boring if we plodded along doing the same stuff, day in–day out, for 80-plus years. Individuals need to grow and evolve, or they die. I know some people who have died on the inside first. Benjamin Franklin knew that when he famously stated:

> **'Some people die at 25 ... and aren't buried until 75.'**
>
> Benjamin Franklin

You have already evolved

Right now ... take a moment to think about how much you HAVE evolved.

You are not the same person you were last year, last week, yesterday, or even an hour ago. You can't un-learn, un-see, un-hear, or un-feel things. Everything you take on board (consider and form a belief about), process (explore further), and make a decision about (take action) shapes who you are becoming. Yes, 'becoming' – because you and I are not 'there' yet.

The world keeps evolving around us, and these days with increased mobility and worldwide media, there's no getting away from that. Unless, of course, you choose to live a reclusive life up in some remote mountains where there is no wifi or connection with the real world. Nice for a getaway retreat perhaps, but not sustainable long term. At least, not for me. I'd go nutso after 24 hours.

My point is: change is constantly in our faces. Our brains keep taking it all in and processing it. And that's a really good thing. It is how we evolve personally and continually adapt to an evolving world. *Exciting.* Think about this for a moment:

- Do you drive the same car you did 30 years ago ... or even 10 years ago?

- Do you buy the same food, cook the same way or eat the same things you did 20 years ago?

- Do you look the same and wear the same clothes you did 20, 10 or even 5 years ago?

I know I don't – except for a few zebra-print favourite pieces, and several pairs of rather stylish corporate heels that as an 'exec escapee' I now refer to as my 'stage heels'. Seriously though, if you saw photos of me in the '80s you'd be saying, 'thank goodness fashions change'. Believe me – the last thing my top-heavy body shape ever needed was padded shoulders and fru-fru taffeta gowns with enormous puffy sleeves. More lessons learned along the way – one being that a sense of style that evolves into your personal brand definitely trumps fashion fads.

No sense resisting or hiding

Need I mention the advancement of mobile connectivity and global reach? If you are not on board with that you're already well behind the rest of the world, and dare I say, choosing to live in a small, protective bubble. Yes, I know plenty of Baby Boomers who have resisted changes, particularly in the technology space. I get that it's hard to keep up. Tech devices and the way we communicate have changed rapidly over the past 10 to 15 years, especially in the social media space.

New technology scares me too; mostly because I'm a techno peasant who takes a little while to work it out on my own. My neuroscience colleagues would likely conclude that it's an area of my brain that I've not built strong neural pathways to (read: I avoid going there), so it takes more effort to light that part up. It's not a well-trodden path for me. But inevitably, I get frustrated enough and my 'need to know' kicks in, so I push myself to learn the crucial stuff from other experts. Change Champions are not fearless; we use our inner courage to push through the fears and do it anyway. *Pushing forward is often uncomfortable.*

However, I'm amazed at how many of my colleagues still 'don't do' social media, like – at all. No LinkedIn profile, no Facebook presence, no Messenger. No online interaction with the broader world other than work emails and conversations with their closed circle of family and friends. When I've questioned some of them about the reasons for this resistance or refusal to embrace wider connectivity through social media, it often comes down to deeply held fears:

- **Fear of the unknown:** *'don't know how'* (technical skill) or *'don't know why anyone is interested in anything I'm doing'* (lack of understanding of the benefits of connection) or *'don't trust big data security'* (unknown impacts).

- **Fear of what others think:** *'I'm a private person ... I don't want people seeing what I'm doing and commenting on it,'* or, *'What if they think I'm "up-myself"'* (read: egotistical, narcissistic, a self-promoter).

But what if ...

Something that's fascinated me for years is the number of people who immediately respond to proposed change with the worst-case scenarios of what might happen. I call it 'catastrophising'. For them, literally E V E R Y T H I N G new has possible catastrophic results:

> **'What if this happens ... and then it turns into this ... and then even worse stuff down the track' ... blah, blah, blah ... as they tell themselves 'it's just all too risky.' It's all too hard.**

If this sounds like you, please get help for these crippling fears that are holding you back from evolving into all you could be. This brick-walling, self-protective attitude will reduce your ability to accept and adapt to the inevitable changes that get thrown your way. Your resilience levels will be in a vulnerable state; but, it doesn't have to be that way. You can choose to change that now. Build your agility muscle.

Here's the thing: most of us DO embrace lots of changes, as the world keeps developing, improving, and implementing new ways to do stuff; but how often do you initiate change?

Step out of your comfort zone and push yourself to learn some of that new, exciting stuff. Build your capacity for change. You are not your full-arse version yet ... it's an evolutionary journey.

Rock Your Stripes

All the magic happens outside your comfort zone.

LEARN FROM THE EXPERTS

One of the increasingly difficult things about writing a book these days is how quickly specific examples and data included in it can date. During the months it took me to finalise the first edition content, I lost count of how many edits and changes I made to ensure my words and quoted data were as current as possible. That's what happens to prolific readers and avid researchers like me (and I must admit – those of us who still struggle with distraction and perfectionist tendencies). Not only do my original ideas keep evolving; the experts and thought leaders keep publishing amazing new work. Some of it is similar and links well to the stuff I'm sharing with you. You see – everything keeps evolving.

You ain't seen nothin' yet

Mindful that I don't have all the answers, nor am I professing to be the guru of all things evolutionary, I've included a couple of brief summaries and extracts in this section from two such experts in their field. Why? Because the pace of change is about to take off like a rocket. If you think that there have been lots of changes in the last 15 years, get ready for a rapid increase in the speed of change, particularly around advancements in technology and artificial intelligence (AI), and the impact that will have on career choices. *That's not just my thoughts …*

Chris Riddell – Global Futurist, Media Commentator and Inspirational Speaker – challenges people around the world to unlock new ways of thinking about the digital economy. Google him. Back in 2018, in a video streamed to organisations around the world, his core message was:

'The next three years will shape and define the next 100 in a way that we've never before seen in history ... at home, work and in our global interactions. Speed is the new disruptor in our world. Your ability to reinvent and keep adapting to global market conditions will define your relevance ahead; both in your individual career options, and your business or organisation you work with. The future is not an extension of the past, it's the reinvention of everything we see today.'

NOTE: this prediction was made two years before the world was thrown into a global pandemic, which necessitated instant adjustments and subsequent widespread reset on how, where and when we do our work.

Flexible, agile, virtual, remotely connected, global-reaching workforces; this has become the new way to work. Woo-hoo! That's exciting, and a potential solution to many pain points, both for individual workers and urban infrastructure pressures. The idea of working from anywhere in the world; well, that's my kind of lifestyle. I mean – who needs a suburban house and all that commuting? Not me. Travel to interesting places – yes, please. Daily, same-old traffic trudging – no thanks. Clocking on to rigid hours in CBD office towers – never again!

Frankly though, it's nuts that it took a global pandemic to significantly disrupt such rigid practices and move towards greater flexibility. Women and men I coach would prefer more flexible work options to assist with shared juggling of family responsibilities and improving life balance versus equal opportunities for career continuity. The take-up of technology-driven, flexible work practices in Australia has been way too slow, and it's disappointing to see some organisations slip back from enforced hybrid and flexible work arrangements to the management ease of rigid same-for-all, in-office hours.

We have all the technology and ability to perform work from any-where in the world, to access stuff at any time, and to engage through all sorts of media platforms; globally spread organisations have been operating that way for years. BUT for many Australian organisations the willingness to explore or use these options more broadly is still not there. Of course, those of you within corporate entities know that entrenched work structures and patterns come from decisions made (or not made) at the top levels; the executive tables. I truly believe that's where we need the biggest changes; evolution of the thought processes at decision-making tables. And dare I say – more diversity? Of course I dare. *Dare to SHOUT it!*

I truly believe that when we have more women in leadership, and particularly in representative or policy-changing positions, there will be stronger focus and push for action on increasing flexibility in work-places (for both men and women), and increasing government support for sharing family responsibilities, including greater childcare options.

We need to DISRUPT old, structured (yes, predominately male-advantageous) thinking. Companies must rethink their rigid work structures, because the world of work is changing more rapidly than ever before. Adaptability and flexibility are core to attracting and retaining good staff – especially women – and for future sustainability. Diversity at the leadership tables will be the key to organisational suc-cess (and political party relevance).

The career-hopping era

That said: let's bring the focus back on YOU; back on the decisions you CAN make. What about your individual career progression and success? How can you take charge of your career evolution?

The days are long gone of working for life in the one job, or for the one company, or even in the one industry sector. If you are still plod-ding away at the same old job or even the same industry you were in last decade, stand up, look out the window, survey the horizon, check out the new opportunities, explore your options, enlist the help of a career coach, and take charge of your career. Why? Because there's no such thing as job security or certainty. That entitlement era has passed.

If you were not convinced of that prior to 2020 (the pandemic flow-on effect), there is no disputing that now. *Get out of stuck mode.*

We are in the job-hopping era, and the next generation coming through know that. They are far more agile and adaptable. They have no interest in standing still or wasting precious time. They have no intention of making their mark with mindless widget tweaking on an assembly line, or monotonous admin, or just meet and greet receptionist tasks. But, that's not a bad thing. *Exciting change is coming.*

Many of those jobs will not exist soon due to the increasing automation of repetitive tasks. Think about how much you currently do online: all sorts of appointments, travel bookings, fashion and furniture shopping, weekly groceries, prescription orders, banking; we add to this automated list every week. Most occupations have already changed or are set to change. Therefore, agility is exactly the skill needed to survive and succeed in today's world of work.

So, what does that mean for you? Unless you are working for a great company that is progressively evolving, innovative, and in an industry that will continue to provide essential hands-on services into the future, AND they are providing career progression opportunities for you, keep your eyes open and your exploration mind on high alert. Actually, I say – *do that anyway.* It makes sense to stay open to an increasingly diverse range of new industries and opportunities, and ready to leap towards more sustainable options.

Career Change Champion

Michelle Gibbings, a fellow Australian change and career expert, in her 2018 book *Career Leap: How to reinvent and liberate your career,* offered some really practical advice and useful exercises for taking control of your career. Here's a little taste:

> 'The upside of all this change is the new opportunities it brings ... to embrace a role that you love, that inspires you, that makes you want to get up for work every day. Perhaps it's a role that ...

> *provides you with a chance to do truly meaningful work that makes a difference on either a local or global scale. If you sit back and wait, these opportunities will pass you by and go to someone else, so it's up to you to do something about it.'*

In addition to both being champions for change, Michelle and I have something else in common. We're both mature-age career leapers, sometimes taking rather large leaps into very different industry sectors and across different geographical zones. You may recall I mentioned in the intro, I'm up to 11 different locations, three different career paths (fourth one in the making), various organisations, numerous roles and projects (but who's counting?). It's not a scoreboard or a competition.

Why is that even significant, you ask? Well, for both of us it was not the normally expected practice of the day, and therefore was seen by many 'play-it-safers' at the time as risky, or maybe even disloyal.

What has driven me (and others) to take those leaps is a need to continually learn, grow and challenge the status quo. Sometimes things had run their course; I'd achieved what I set out to do, and it was time for the next chapter. Sometimes interests and needs changed, or it ended up being the wrong role, the wrong organisation, and/or the wrong time. Those latter scenarios and subsequent decisions to move on were generally motivated by weak or toxic bosses, widely known as the number one reason good people leave organisations. Often it is best to take a zig step (or maybe a running leap) to another opportunity.

Good employees leave bad bosses AND the companies that allow bad bosses to survive.

Sure, there have been times when I have slammed that door shut and bolted it closed on the way out, so as never to go there again. Other times, I've left it open a little, in case a better opportunity arises in that space later. But, throughout all that, having a broad range of career experiences has helped me achieve far greater things than I initially set out to do (as a 15 year old entering the hairdressing industry).

When referring to today's Millennials and Gen Y'ers, I often hear senior people in organisations complain that they are 'disloyal'. But, loyalty – like respect and trust – is earned and is not a given. While those relationship bonding ingredients form part of a formula of successful character traits, respecting others' rights to choices far outweighs the type of yesteryear or institutionalised loyalty that commands unquestioning allegiance.

Frankly, I think loyalty is an overrated trait and overused word; often misused as a judgement (for example, a threat of character assassination) with the intent to keep others in line, under control or playing small, for the benefit of those in control. Or it's a throwaway line used to deflect the blame away from the real reasons a person decides to move on. It's just not an acceptable accusation when it's motivated by expectations of submission or suppressing another person's dreams and desires.

As a leadership coach, I help aspiring leaders understand that their core responsibility is to encourage and enable others to grow and evolve into their greatest version – to be leaders in their own right, not hold them back as subordinates. It's not about power over others. An employment contract is not a right to own someone's career progression; the individual owns that.

Richard Branson nails it:

> **'Train people well enough so they can leave.
> Treat them well enough so they don't want to.'**
>
> Richard Branson

Here's the thing: take charge of your career. Be the CEO driving the evolution of it, and not at the mercy of some other CEO or supervisor. Make sure you stay current. Keep evolving. Embrace every chapter.

CHAPTERS OF A CHANGE CHAMPION

Exploring choices ... taking chances
... embracing changes.

Here's a graphical capture of my journey; the quick-trip career time-line version. I'm not sharing because it's better or more interesting than other people's journey, or in any way spectacular; I'm sharing to encourage you to create your own version. Reflect on how far you've come, how much you've evolved ... and how much longer and richer your timeline could become. I know mine is still evolving ...

Born in Brisbane Adopted at two weeks, raised in Toowoomba	1962	1975	**First feminist stance – age 13** Objected to cooking and sewing school subject 'education' options
First job – Career #1 – age 15 Hairdressing apprenticeship – Toowoomba	1977	1981	**First lead role – age 19** Salon Manager of five staff – Toowoomba
Train the Trainer – accreditation Apprentice trainer for chain of salons	1982	1989	**Moved to Barcaldine – Western QLD** For husband's career, with two toddlers
First business ownership – Barcaldine QLD Hairdressing salon and children's clothing	1990	1993	**Business expansion – new bigger salon** Hair and beauty, retail and jewellery
First community leadership roles Barcaldine Business Council – founding executive Barcaldine Club – first female on board	1993	1996	**HFQ Industry Rep. for QLD** Industry advisor for national training package
Certificate III in Training – accreditation Sold business to pursue next career chapter	1997	1997	**Moved to Sunshine Coast Hinterland – QLD** For husband's career, children's education, and next chapter planning
Started uni studies – USQ Business management – part-time study, part-time work	2000	2001	**Shoulder surgery – work-related injury** End of hairdressing career – YAY! Over it. Ready for next career.
Commenced public sector – Career #2 Dept of Employment, Training and IR, IR Advisor, then first promotion – Training Officer	2002	2004	**Moved to Emerald – Central QLD** Second promotion – Senior Development Officer

Moved to Townsville – North QLD Third promotion – District Manager	2004	2005	**Leadership development course** Public sector statewide succession planning Introduction to leadership principles
Won two statewide DETE Leadership Awards Ideas & Innovation and Collaboration & Partnering	2006	2008	**Moved to Rockhampton – Central QLD** Fourth promotion – Regional Manager – DETE Extensive regional travel and leading change
Won a statewide DETE Leadership Award Partnering – joint project with stakeholders	2008	2010	**Graduated – Masters in Management – USQ** HRM Major, Leadership Specialisation Completed externally, entirely in own time and self-financed
Left public sector leadership roles Political impact – mismatch to my core values and driving forces	2012	2013	**Started new business – Workforce Vitality** 'Creating Employers of Choice' consultancy – workplace culture focus
First keynote presentation – Rockhampton QLD Workplace trainers' conference – SRDS	2013	2013	**Coaching and behavioural science accreditations** ICF/ABNLP – Coaching, ISEI –EQ Profiling, DISC and Motivators – Facilitation
Launched Lean In Circle #1 – Yeppoon QLD Facilitator for Lean In global movement	2014	2014	**Moved to Barham – NSW/VIC border** For partner's career opportunities
Launched Lean In Circle #2 – Swan Hill VIC Successful grant to initiate BPW Women in Leadership program	2015	2015	**Moved to Cooktown – Far North QLD** Greater career opportunities for us both (or so we were led to believe … ☹)
Launched Lean In Circle #3 – Cooktown Elected to Chamber of Commerce Committee Keynote presenter at local events (e.g. CWA, Business Conference, IWD)	2016	2017	**Professional development – writer/speaker** Author Academy – course and mentoring Speaker Academy – course and mentoring Book writing schedule – launch goal Dec. 2017 (Oops …)
Launched Lean In Circle #4 – Cooktown (#2) Lead and coordinate IWD celebrations Elected President – Chamber of Commerce	2017	2017	**Moved to Cairns Northern Beaches – FNQ** To make a bigger difference – to disrupt unethical practices and lead change

Refreshed our leadership company brand Launched Vital LEADERS Keynote presenter at National IML Conference	2017	2017	**Established ElevateHER – Regional Chapter** Registered business partner of Lean In Inc.
Launched Lean In Circles #5 and #6 – Cairns Revised book writing schedule – EOY goal 2018	2018	2018	**Awarded Chartered Manager status – CMGR** IML – gold standard in leadership excellence National Ambassador – IML CMGR designation
ElevateHER partnerships – WLA, AGEC, ALGWA Joined #100daysforchange – Women and Leadership, Australia's gender equality campaign, Australia Gender Equality Council and Australian Local Government Women's Association – QLD committee	2018	2019	**Launched Lean In Circle #7 – Cairns** **Book Launch** – *Rock Your Stripes*
Launched Lean In Queensland network Established ElevateHER Australia – NFP company, providing online support for Circle Leaders nationally	2020	2021	**Created and facilitated** 'Women Leading in Local Government' state-wide program for 90 councillors Elected Director of Australian Gender Equality Council – national board
Delivered Team Dynamics programs, workshops, online Masterclasses Turned 60! Increased interest in ageism research	2022	2023	**Paused** our Vital LEADERS contract work to focus on creating my next chapter Balance of self-care, inner spirituality, research, writing, speaking, coaching others Launched *Jilinda Lee* brand

TO BE CONTINUED ...

Two key things about this personal career timeline I've shared with you:

- I've deliberately left out marriages (two), births (two) and deaths (both parents) … to protect others' privacy; but I want to acknowledge that every chapter, every experience is valued (not just career-related ones), and I continue to grow and evolve through each one. The entire journey has made me who I am today, and I am grateful for each experience.

- I've not added additional spaces (past this latest version) because I don't want to pre-empt just how long and zigzaggy the rest of my timeline will be. I assure you, I will keep optimistically cha-chaing my way through my next chapters to an unknown finish line … and I plan to share more on that journey in my next books.

Taking a step backwards or sideways after taking a step forwards is not a disaster, it's more like a cha-cha.

If you'd like to reflect on your personal and/or career evolution, try making up a similar table, listing all the career changes and zigzags you've made. Be sure to focus on what you achieved in each. This exercise is a great way to also check if your CV and LinkedIn profile adequately outline your experience. *Your personal profile matters.*

BE A GAME CHANGER

By now, if you've worked your way through the previous sections before landing here, it's probably clear that I'm on a mission to enable more women to step up into lead roles, to stand out from the ordinary, and to speak up for equal rights and representation at decision-making tables. I trust that some of you are already feeling more inspired and inclined to do that. Ready to get out there. *Rock those stripes* ☺.

There is no question that the world needs more women to rise up into lead roles. Now, more than ever before …. YES, yes. Okay, *I know*.

I've said all that 'boys' club behaving badly' inequality stuff in previous pages. But right now, my excitement levels are soaring and I want to share that with you.

Why?

As I wrote this book, women across the world (and thankfully, in Australia too) were rising up to say: enough! Time's UP. Overflowing frustration with the unacceptable status quo is evolving into a new 'pink wave' revolution, with more women speaking out and standing up to lead change. *YAY!*

Some have called it 'the third wave of feminism', with reference to the previous two notable significant push periods for equality – the early 1900s (women winning voting rights), and the 1970s (birth control, abortion rights, higher education choices, and more). Now, it feels like the right time to build on what our brave forbearers fought for. The journey to reach gender equality since the 1970s has been painfully slow. It's time for pushing, driving and actioning real change; to finish the job.

Who would have predicted a few years ago that in 2019 Ethiopia would lead the way in empowering women into their country's top leadership roles? In an unprecedented push for gender parity, in 2018 Prime Minister Abiy reshuffled his cabinet to have women in at least half the ministerial posts, and then installed a well-known women's equality advocate as head of their country's justice system, intentionally to drive much-needed culture change.

Following closely from that, the 2018 US mid-term elections saw record numbers of women voted into the House of Representatives, and in 2021, Kamala Harris became the first female Vice President and highest-ranking female official in US history. This was widely believed to be a deliberate pushback against the Trump administration's denigration of women's rights and backwards policy-making that had widened the gender equality gap even further in America. Overall, there are record numbers of women putting their hand up to get involved, record numbers of women nominated, and records smashed all over the country, including the most number of women and youth casting their votes. Their voices mattered.

Woo-hoo, I say. About bloody time. *Rising up.*

In Australia, my island home affectionately known as 'the land down under', we also needed to ensure we jumped on this global evolutionary movement and not become known as 'the land of the downtrodden'. Australians showed they had run out of patience with the conservative patriarchal status quo at the 2022 election; voting in a new progressive government, led by Prime Minister Anthony Albanese, whose first cabinet was Australia's most diverse ever. Not only did women make up approximately 43% of cabinet ministerial positions, they were from diverse race, ethnic, and religious backgrounds. A cabinet that was far more representative of the country it serves. 'We are one, and we are many, and from all the lands on earth we come', is our unofficial national anthem so beautifully acknowledging our rich and diverse culture.

Ladies, it's our time to lead the way forward. The ripples of change are gathering momentum. Let's ride that pink wave together and turn it into a multi-coloured tsunami.

LEADERSHIP IS NOT ABOUT POSITION

But, what if you don't want to be 'the leader'? What if you're tired of pushing upwards into the same solid concrete, corporate ceiling? We all know it's not made of glass; anyone can smash glass. Sometimes it feels more like a solid reinforced cement block barricade of entrenched behaviour; perhaps you have the bruises to show for bumping against it. I know I have some. What if all that responsibility and pressure to be leading from the front is just not your thing, right?

Don't flip past these pages. Don't drop the book.

You don't have to be in a lead role to be a game changer.

Leadership tip: Leadership is NOT about position; it is a mindset, an attitude, a set of principles and observable behaviours. You can lead and influence change from any chair, any situation, any location. And you can certainly lead changes in your own life.

I fully understand that not everyone wants to be the CEO, or sit in the C-suite tower, or be the next prime minister. Not everyone wants to be manager of a company or lead other people. That's okay. Growing your inner confidence and courage and self-leadership skills will help you evolve and reach your aspirational goals, no matter what they are. Remember: it's your journey. Keep evolving. Keep reading. *Skim over the next few pages if you must, but don't skip the next part.*

That said; I want to address the reasons I often hear women (and men) provide for not wanting to go for those leadership promotions or representative roles, like:

> **I don't want to be like that. I don't want to live, eat and breathe work, and work 12-hour days. I don't need that stress. I don't want to live for work. I want to work to have a life. I can't put my family through that; I don't want to put that kind of pressure (or media scrutiny) on them.**

My response to that is:

> **What if you didn't do it like that? What if you did it differently? Organised the work in a better way? More flexible? More hybrid role-modelling? More people and relationships focused? More inclusive and collaborative? Organised your life to support that? More balanced? What if your family were supportive — even encouraging? What if you and your partner equally shared the home life responsibilities?**

And specifically – to the women – I generally add:

What if you did it the 'womenwise' way, instead of thinking you have to be a 'manette'?

Because in many of the organisations I've experienced and observed, the rigid hours, traditional, one location, yesteryear approach is NOT working, nor is it sustainable. It's time we change that. Being a leader doesn't have to mean you have no life balance or other interests. Frankly, I regularly question the self-leadership and self-management competence levels of CEOs who think starting their office work day at 5 am and finishing at 11 pm is 'normal practice', or expected. Same goes for sending an email at 3 am and expecting a response before 9 am that morning. I know some who wear 16-hour work days like a badge of honour, not realising it's quite the opposite. It actually screams lack of leadership competence, and such people are often overwhelmed and not coping, or soon will be. This is certainly NOT leadership role-model behaviour.

My point is: be smarter than that. Explore how you could do it differently, with more flexibility. Negotiate a better deal. Call out unfair practices. Collaborate. Delegate. Enable others. *Speak up.*

As I mentioned earlier, I acknowledge the current reality, even post-pandemic, is that inflexibility is still a core problem. We all know that needs to be urgently addressed if we are serious about greater diversity at the leadership table. Research shows that it's one of the biggest barriers for achieving greater gender equality – inflexibility both in the workplace and the home, especially around accessible and affordable childcare. Again, this has been talked about so much, but there are so few actions that are addressing this issue.

While initially writing this section, I discovered disturbing results of a National Prevalence Survey reported by Australian Human Rights Commission's (AHRC) 2018 stats on the types of discrimination related to maternity leave. One third (32%) of the women reviewed had experienced discrimination in the workplace when they requested or took parental leave. Of those, more than 29% lost their jobs while on maternity leave, mostly due to business restructures or contracts not being renewed.

While I appreciate that employers have the right to restructure for efficiency gain, it is a little hard to believe that all those companies suddenly decided to restructure their workforce. Convenient excuse, perhaps? The thing is – at present, that type of action is technically legal under our Australian business and employment laws, and HR advisors know that. So, while it may continue until firmer laws are put in place to regulate misuse of a 'restructure' (a slow process), that doesn't make it right. These are not 'employers of choice' with ethical leadership practices. *Speak up. Share your stories.*

> **Leadership tip:** Ethical decision-making is understanding the difference between knowing what you have a right to do, and choosing what is the right thing to do. Ethics without empathy is empty. Soulless leadership. Actually, that's not leadership at all, because real leadership is about encouraging and enabling others.

Furthermore, from this same AHRC report, almost half (46%) of the women participating in this review reported discrimination in relation to their performance assessment and career advancement opportunities. Appalling; but sadly, none of this is new. It's been going on for a long time, and if we keep accepting that as 'just the way it is', women will continue to be disadvantaged in reaching their career progression goals. It's TIME to change that.

How? By changing how we've been playing the game. The yester-year society-driven rules ingrained in past generations are no longer relevant. Women are NOT the ones who have to change to fit in to these unacceptable and often ineffective practices.

This is NOT a women's issue ... it is a human-being equity and fairness issue.

One major concern is the longer-term outcome of this ongoing situation. There are increasing numbers of well-educated, qualified, capable women leaving professional careers or giving up on reaching for leadership positions in their chosen fields of expertise. It's alarming, but hardly surprising. Many women are sick of waiting for these barriers to be addressed. You can only keep hitting your head against that cement ceiling for so long. *TIME'S UP!*

The Workplace Gender Equality Agency provides yearly stats on women's workforce participation, which show that the number of women in full-time work since initial 2013 reporting either slipped backwards (2020) or has stagnated at 20% to 21% for the last decade. While overall employment engagement figures may have risen slightly, this is predominately in part-time or casual work, or in small home-based businesses. In fact, women-owned microbusinesses have increased in recent years from 31% to 35%, with microbusinesses now making up 89% of all businesses in Australia (2022 stats). While that may seem positive, it's worth noting that many of those women-led microbusinesses are under-resourced, resulting in lower profitability and lower incomes than in the professions they resigned from. And, many of these women left career positions with potential leadership pipeline opportunities. *Alarm bells.*

Women in the coaching circles I've facilitated have often shared that they left full-time progressive careers for greater flexibility (due to the inflexibility of their partner's job), for family care reasons, the ability to take control of their future, and to have meaningful work where they feel valued and their skills are recognised (away from toxic, gender-biased workplaces). In other words: they decided to become the CEO of their own career. Good for them.

Of course, those entrepreneurial women who start up their own businesses (often at home) expect their new venture to generate a decent income in time, rather than just be an expensive hobby. But many are willing to earn significantly less, especially at the start, accepting 'that's just how it is'. A trade-off.

The concerning result for many Australian women is that they will continue to be financially disadvantaged, ending up with far less retirement savings and superannuation than their male professional colleagues and their male partners. Right now, women over age 55 are the fastest growing poverty group (at risk of homelessness) in

Rock Your Stripes

Australia. This is due to years of being unemployed (read: unpaid home managers), or underemployed (part-time work), or employed in lower paid industries (for example, childcare, teaching, nursing, social work), or small business owners (unpaid, underpaid or periodic pay), or in lower paid roles within corporate sectors (non-executive roles).

Apart from the potential financial trade-off, some of the women I coach who have left their chosen careers become concerned about losing the currency of their professional skills in case they want to return to that sector in later years. With the rate of change now, even one year away on maternity or carers leave can significantly reduce professional currency. Some find the loss of intellectual interaction with likeminded colleagues also reduces their professional confidence levels.

On the flip side – some flourish, and never look back. It turns out to be one of the best decisions they've made. They push on, rise up from the knocks, zigzag a few times, learn new skills, and make a successful life out of their circumstances. *Leader of their own journey. Power to them.*

So, while it's true that women have other choices, and some (like me) may decide to take a chance leaping into something else, the key point in sharing these rather scary reality-check stats is this: these career trade-off options (successful or otherwise) will NOT fix the gender equality issue, specifically the male dominance of boardrooms, C-suites, and key governance positions.

Okay, so we already know this is a problem. Many of us are frustrated with how seemingly difficult it is to address this unfairness with sustainable, positive solutions. While I am encouraging you to keep stepping up, standing out, speaking up, and bravely disrupting the status quo, aspiring for more, reaching higher, and keep evolving – I also know in my gut those actions (alone) won't be enough to fix the broader, systemic gender inequality issue.

Here's why: YOU are NOT the problem. I know many of you are already capable, confident, courageous, strong-minded women. It is not your capabilities that hold you back or force you to settle for less. It is the system. The crap, unfair system – designed by men for the benefit of men. It's just wrong ... and it needs a collective push to change that.

Women don't need FIXING ... it's the system (built by and for men) that needs FIXING.

That is why I am passionate (read: obsessed) about and actively involved in helping to drive positive systemic change that enables more women to take on lead roles. Genuine recruitment. Meritoriously – of course, that goes without saying, surely. There's something seriously wrong with our recruitment systems when more than half our university degree graduates are women, and yet significantly less than half are offered appropriate level positions compared to male graduates. That outcome can't be based on merit or unbiased recruitment practices, so it's a bit rich for men to put up the 'based on merits only' argument, don't you think? It just doesn't stack up.

Let's be frank. Men have had the benefit of a tailwind for centuries. From the footy club deals, matesy mentality and talent spotters, to succession planning, formal and informal mentoring, and shoulder-tap promotions; it's like flying along in a smooth slip stream in a fast jet with priority landing. *Nice, easy-as ride.*

Women rarely have the same smooth-ride experience. They generally have to battle a blustery head wind that seems to get stronger along the way, as their family responsibilities grow. Pushing through the thick fog, navigating around turbulence, and often forced into a holding pattern; just circling and hovering until there is a clear opportunity to land. When it's finally 'their turn' (commonly at 40-plus years) and they've earned enough stripes, the new battle then is often gaps in skill currency, relevance of prior (particularly recent) achievements, and ageism. *So unfair.*

So, yes ... it's time to change all that, with real gender equality targets, mentors and sponsors, and the support of male champions of change – those who will open the doors and push you towards opportunities. *Seek out and surf the pink wave evolution.*

While I could share more on this topic from my own experiences and observations, writing about the equality issue and the current global rise of the feminist movement is not the core theme of this book. Sure, inequality is one key blockage that holds women back, but it's not the only one. Remember, it's just one of my three elephants in the room that I shared at the start of this book. *Dare to keep evolving.*

That said, if you'd like to delve deeper into current research and be more proactive in this space, I commend to you well-known Australian feminist researcher and author Catherine Fox's book *Stop Fixing Women*. Her work is impeccably researched, very factual, convincing, and she focuses on real solutions. Her overarching message in the book is that *'building fairer workplaces is everybody's business'*. What I personally love about it is the intentional encouragement of men to be part of the solution. *Evolutionary.*

Here's the thing: collectively, I firmly believe we can influence positive changes to the equality issue with proactive strategies. Actions, not just words or nodding agreement. I urge you to get involved or at least get behind the growing wave of game-changing activism to stamp out entrenched unfair practices, traditional gender-biased beliefs, and all those unnecessary workplace systems that potentially hold you back from evolving into your full-arse version. *It's time to change the game.*

If not YOU, then WHO?
If not NOW, then WHEN?

EVOLVE AT ANY AGE OR STAGE

> **'You are an endless project …**
> **changing, evolving, surprising.'**
>
> James Patterson

You are:

- never too old

- never too young

- not too feminine or too masculine

- not too out there or different

- not too ordinary or average

- not too dumb or under-educated

- not over-educated (Really? Surely there's no such thing …).

However … you do have to be ready, willing and able to jump on opportunities with grit and gusto.

Now, in my sixth decade of learning, growing and significant evolving, I live with a level of realistic optimism and expectation there will be more chapters of change yet to come in my journey. Exciting ones. Challenging ones. Soul-wrenching ones. Uplifting ones. Surprising ones. Each of them providing bucket loads of learning and rich wisdom, potentially to continue sharing with others. Not being one to leave all that to hopeful wishing, I'm working towards the next chapter, every day.

Like when writing this – my first published book. I was pretty sure it would not be my last one, as I had to park so many thoughts and ideas for 'the next one' (hint: focused more on influencing impactful changes).

While I know 'bucket lists' are the trendy thing to do, I don't have one. You know – that list of 'must do before you die' things to achieve and cross off in the race towards the finish line. That's way too prescriptive (read: inflexible) for me. I'd rather keep scanning the horizon for opportunities than tick off a wish list written at a particular point in time. Life changes quickly, as do our circumstances and priorities. Besides, who needs the added pressure of staring at a list of unmet (and often unrealistic) expectations? That's a recipe for disappointment and regret. It's more important for me to live each day to the full, and to stay agile; ready to shift gears, jump into action and adapt to new challenges.

SELF-CARE IS ABSOLUTELY CRUCIAL

Of course, to remain capable of doing that, I've learned a few things along the way about agility and resilience. Self-care is absolutely crucial; physical and mental wellbeing. These things have been important priorities of mine for decades: having a fit, strong body; a healthy, enquiring mind; and a centred, fulfilled soul.

More specifically, I've learned that I need to:

- start the day well and intentionally (sunrise beach stroll, meditation, journalling and set daily goals)

- keep moving my body every few hours (not sit to write at the computer all day and night)

- keep exercising my muscle groups (walk, swim and stretch daily, and regular gym workouts)

- eat nutritionally healthy food (smaller portion sizes these days)

- get good sleep (seven to eight hours each night).

As knowledge and continual learning are strong values of mine, I also read something new every day. It's not unusual for me to have three or four books on the go at any one time, and to scan-read internet articles and latest reports while relaxing at night. Yes, I have a busy mind; always full of creative thoughts. So, to ensure I give my brain a regular declutter, I regularly take a beach path stroll at dusk, and night pool swim with just the blue underwater lights on. That works for me. It's my way of staying agile and ready to respond to whatever life throws my way.

Again, I'm not perfect, and sometimes that healthy balance is disrupted. Rigid routines are not my forte, so I mix it up a bit, depending on work and social commitments; but that's what agility is all about. Being able to stay flexible; yes – in mind and body. Being able to rise up from the knocks and rejuvenate your soul with the things that strengthen your resilience.

So, I guess you could say: I'm still evolving into my full-arse version, although I'm quite sure there are some people with whom I've knocked heads along the way who may think my current version is way more than enough. Enough – perhaps … but never too much! I intend to keep leaping into more career opportunities and adding a few more colourful stripes to rock out.

Just as this book has continued to evolve (and grow in word count), I'm aware of how much I evolved from writing it. So many 'ah-haa' moments as I dug deep to reflect on why I believe what I do, what experiences embedded and strengthened those beliefs along the way, what important points to include, and why I feel the need to share that with you. I am grateful for this opportunity; and particularly thankful for my partner's support, my understanding friends, and my clients' patience, as I took considerable time off to complete this work.

During the process, I became increasingly aware of the time it took me to write this. It was a very long and somewhat slowly evolving piece of work. Many times, I felt stuck; a feeling that rings alarm bells for me. Stuck within never-ending book chapters. Stuck at home in my office – still writing. Stuck between balancing the need to finish this and the competing need to keep working in my leadership consultancy business. For a natural extrovert like me, the deliberately reduced client workload and lack of daily socialising tends to deplete my energy levels.

Yet again, the journey provided another valuable set of learnings, confirming all the things I have written about in this chapter: the need for grit, gusto, agility, resilience, flexibility – fuelled by a self-care routine that refreshes your resolve to keep going. Keep growing. Keep evolving.

One thing I know for sure; my next life chapter – the next zig leap – is already in the making. There is more evolving yet to come. More to do to become my fully full-arsed version. *I'm up for the challenge.*

Are you ready?

Here's the thing: dig deep and find the inner will and courage to keep evolving ... challenge yourself, change stuff, learn new stuff, grow some more, and keep your body, mind and soul healthy and agile, ready to jump on opportunities and keep evolving. It's never too soon or too late. NOW is the right time. *Rock those stripes.*

Dear past ... thank you for your lessons.
Dear future ... I am ready.

Reflect on your own EVOLUTIONARY journey ...

Create your ZIGZAG ACHIEVEMENT MAP

Evolve

It takes a lot of
COURAGE...

to release the
familiar and
seemingly secure,
to embrace the **NEW**.

But ... there is no
real security in
what is no longer
meaningful.

There is more
security in the
adventurous and
exciting ...

for in **MOVEMENT**
there is **LIFE** ...

and in
CHANGE
there is
POWER.

Alan Cohen

PART II

F.A.V.E. 5 FORMULA

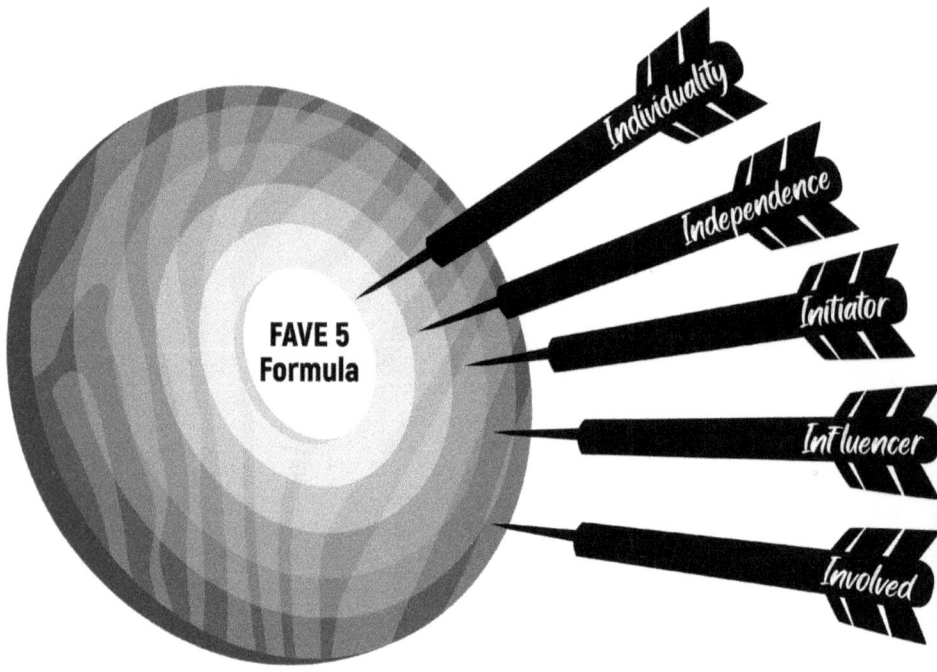

FAVE 5
Formula

Individuality

Independence

Initiator

InFluencer

Involved

CHAPTER 5

GET READY

to change the game ...

I CAN ...
I WILL ...
I AM ...
ready to:
STEP UP
bravely.
STAND OUT
boldly.
SPEAK UP
brilliantly.

STEP ONE – PERMISSION TO SHINE ...

Give yourself a promotion ... to CEO of your own life's choices, your own career, and Chief Planner of how you will make your unique mark in our world.

Perhaps you are already doing that? If so, please reach out, scoop up other ladies and help them turn their dreams into a reality. Share your journey with others. Your voice and your stories are possibly more powerful than you realise. Please be a proactive, positive influencer. Share this book with others. We need more women supporting each other and raising each other up.

For those of you who are wanting to step up into being CEO of your own life, and perhaps have been playing a smaller, more submissive game for way too long: I've written this 'how to' section to help you make changes – NOW. Please don't hold back any longer. You probably already know WHAT you need to change, or tweak a little, but maybe you're not so sure HOW or where to start.

Part I of this book is intentionally a call to action; an outline of WHY changes are both necessary and exciting, and why we need more courageous, game-changing women leading the way. Through the shared stories and research about stuff that's not serving women well – things like traditions, systems, entrenched expectations and behaviours of others – you may now be more aware of those, but as an individual you don't own that stuff. Much of it requires others to make changes, so in the meantime, we all still need to navigate our way around that. We can negotiate, influence, initiate or be involved in the changes, but making significant changes to societally entrenched expectations requires a collective willingness and ongoing collaborative effort from all of us. *Sisterhood.*

The reality is: fundamental change takes courage and extensive commitment; the willingness to bravely step forward, speak up, and join in with the game-changing disrupter groups. I'll get to that in the final chapter.

Firstly, let's focus on what YOU CAN DO – RIGHT NOW. Easy steps you can take to build your inner confidence and courage, so you can take that leap and drive the changes you want to lead and implement – as CEO of your own journey.

Regardless of where you are in your life journey or in your career, there will be times when you need to put those big girl panties on, bravely step up to the task, boldly stand in your power, and make big-shift personal changes; perhaps even radical realignments.

Some you will instigate by choice, in line with your current needs or your next-chapter interests and desires. Some will be forced by circumstances, perhaps initially uncomfortable, but dig deeper; remember you will always have choices in how you respond to shifts that happen 'to you' and around you.

> 'You MUST take personal responsibility. You cannot change the circumstances, the seasons or the wind ... but you can change yourself. That IS something you have charge of.'
>
> Jim Rohn

STEP INTO THE ARENA – LET'S DO THIS

In Part II, I'm sharing what I've personally discovered are the FIVE core igniters and strengtheners of my inner personal power. For decades now, these five fabulous 'I' competencies (yes, these are learnable skills) have continued to fuel my confidence and courage, which has enabled me to keep daring to disrupt, aspiring to greater things, reaching for new goals, and importantly – keep evolving. They have become my 'must haves' in life.

I now cheekily refer to them as my **FAVE (Full-Arse Version Essentials) 5 Formula**, which is:

- INDIVIDUALITY ... *discovered from childhood*
- INDEPENDENCE ... *embraced from teenager*
- INITIATOR ... *forced by circumstances*
- INFLUENCER ... *ignited by passion*
- INVOLVED ... *enriched by opportunities.*

Of course, this is not intended to be a complete set of 'must do' instructions. I'm not into numbered, prescriptive lists, as I believe in continually exploring the 'what else'. So, the FAVE 5 is not an 'only' or 'all-encompassing' formula; it's just MY top five core igniters of inner power that have served me well – so far.

With the somewhat volatile combination of Change Champion and female brain, it's highly likely I may add more at a later date, or I may find one or two less important than others as I go through various chapters in my life. So might you; that's totally okay. *Evolution rocks.*

I came up with these five 'I' behaviour choice titles while taking my first self-imposed writer's retreat on Great Keppel Island in 2015. It was at a significant point of unrest; just after making a life-changing zigzag, just after exploring various 'next step' career options, and just before taking another leap into a new, challenging chapter in a very different location.

I deliberately chose the seclusion of a basically appointed island beach bungalow, which had endured a battering cyclone the month before. The irony of that was not lost on me. It somehow felt in sync with where I was at. I knew there would be very few people about to disturb my focus, and I was pleased to support this small island resort (which holds a special place in my heart from my teenage 'get wrecked' days) at a time when they could really use my patronage.

I also knew that I needed some head-clearing time, to get clearer on my purpose and my message. Two strong writing themes kept coming up for me … my two passions:

- **LEADERSHIP** – leading change, the need for more authentic, genuine, ethical leadership (especially in the public sector), and helping others develop leadership thinking and behaviours to lead greater-good outcomes.

- **ELEVATING WOMEN** – inspiring, encouraging, enabling, empowering, elevating women to be all they can be; to play the game at 100%; to step up, stand out and speak up as equals in their home, workplace and society in general.

I'd been talking about writing a book since I voluntarily left the Queensland public sector in late 2012, after the notorious LNP politically motivated mass staff cuts and program decimation. Although, in hindsight, the book I had in my head at that time would have been a very different book to this one; likely peppered with a much angrier WTF tone at the poor leadership I had witnessed, and subsequently walked away from. *Evolution on the run.*

By late 2014, after going to a workshop on 'how to write your book in 48 hours', I decided to stop talking about it and just do it. The main thing I got from that workshop was I needed to get clearer on:

■ My 'WHY' – the narrow and deep purpose for writing a book (or several books … which one first?) …

■ WHO am I writing it for …

■ WHAT content would be most useful to that specific audience, and …

■ that 48 hours was never going to be enough time for me to get a lifetime of thoughts and experiences out of my head and into some sense of order.

Busy, enquiring minds like mine are like that. Always thinking, always joining the dots, with the neural pathways in our brains criss-crossing and working overtime. Always searching for more information, and often over-analysing much of it, just trying to make sense of its relevance in an ever-changing world. Constantly turning thought bubbles into creative ideas and potential opportunities.

By the time my toes touched the sandy shores of Great Keppel Island in early 2015, I knew there was something else that was really annoying me. Something I needed to flush out; the most common blockage for first-time would-be authors. What I had to address was the negative, doubting voice in my head that insidiously whispered to me:

'Why would YOU write a book?' … 'Why would anyone want to read about YOUR

stories and experiences?' ... 'What makes YOU so special?' ... 'What if no-one buys it, and it's just throwing money away?'

So, I dug a whole lot deeper while sitting at the shaded picnic table outside my beach bungalow, headed south of my over-active head space, and sat with my heart space for a while.

There's a saying that your heart already knows what your head is trying to figure out, and I've found that to be so true. The voices in our heads are often the loudest, most annoying, negative ones, constantly questioning the logic of stuff. It's necessary to sometimes tell them to sit down and shut up, so you can consult your core feelings – your heart and gut instincts.

What I know now from many years of this head versus heart tug of war is that I have to go to a quiet, peaceful place (generally involving sand, sea, sunshine and swaying palm trees) to hear what my heart is saying.

It is the heart that holds your inner feelings, that fuels your values and self-belief, ignites the passion, and drives your motivation and actions. It is the heart that holds the personal stories that mean the most to you. The ones that you learned the most from, and you have turned those learnings into core beliefs. That's what makes me unique. And that's what makes you unique too.

Those are the real stories that need to be shared, that will provide the most value for others to learn from. Not to compare or compete with other professional writers or researchers, but to simply contribute your unique experiences ... for the greater good of our society.

'It is the ultimate luxury to combine passion and contribution. It's also a very clear path to happiness.'

Sheryl Sandberg

Here's the thing: it took me three decades to follow my heart and trust my gut instincts, four decades to unshackle and become who I am meant to be, and to bravely rock those uniquely independent stripes, and five decades before I started actively sharing that with others; writing blogs and articles, facilitating workshops, presenting keynote talks, and mentoring – all for the purpose of helping others. Oh ... and it took the last three years of over-thinking and over-analysing to write this book, while continually practising, honing and truthing my FAVE 5 Formula. Writing books feels like a natural evolution into the next chapter of my life: that wonderful stage where I embrace opportunities to contribute and give back.

If I can, you can too

I trust you will find this FAVE 5 Formula uplifting and useful as you evolve into your full-arse version. *Rocking all your stripes.*

RULES ARE SIMPLY GUIDELINES

About the FAVE 5 Formula ...

There are no rules with these types of suggested 'HOW TO' formulas. I've never been one to abide by rules that restrict creative expression or exploration of other options.

From my many and varied questioning excavations to make sense of the world, I have discovered that way too many rules are made by those who like being in charge and want to stay that way, often deliberately restricting the ability of others to rise. Too many rules are just not necessary and make no sense at all when you take a closer look with the logical brain engaged, rumble with how it feels, and trust your gut instincts. Too many rules often make Jack happy and Jill a dull girl.

Rock Your Stripes

Have a think about the rules (read: entrenched guidelines) you are living your life by ... especially the ones that may be restricting you from being all you can be. Ask yourself:

- Where did that rule come from?

- When did I start believing that I had no other choice but to abide by that rule?

- Who made the rule anyway? (Maybe it was you? ... so just unmake it!)

Many rules, like beliefs, are formed from experiences (yours or others you've observed) and the stories you decided to take from them. A good point to remember here is: a story is made up, and while sometimes it seemed like the right thing at the time, if it's no longer working for you – change it.

My point is: you are in charge of the stories you create, the rules you make, the rules you break, and the rules you choose to abide by.

As CEO of your life, it's your responsibility to make sure your rules are working for you ... not against you.

So, go ahead: dig a little deeper into those restrictive rules and start using my absolute favourite questioning word: **REALLY?** (Said with head cocked to one side, slight questioning frown, one eyebrow raised, and lots of WTF tone 😉.) Like:

- **Really?** *Do I really believe that? ... Or is it what others expect me to believe?*

- **Really?** *Do I really want to keep accepting that? ... Or is it time to change that?*

- **Really?** *Is it that I CAN'T do that thing? ... Or is it really that I've decided I WON'T do it? (Won't is a choice you are making. Is it the right one?)*

One more thing: *A reminder from the start of the book: NO SHOULDING OR WISHING allowed … just:*

I can *(or I can't)* …

I will *(or I won't)* …

I AM already, or I AM becoming my full-arse version.

Get ready to rock those stripes.

There will be
OBSTACLES.

There will be
DOUBTERS.

There will be
MISTAKES.

But with hard
work ...

THERE ARE
NO LIMITS.

CHAPTER 6

BE AN
INDIVIDUAL

FAVE 5
Formula

Individuality

Colour me FUCHSIA ... or ... rock your own colours!

ZEBRAS ARE INDIVIDUALLY UNIQUE ...

Just like human fingerprints,
each animal's striped pattern is
their own unique design.
The mother zebra stays
close to her newborn,
often circling until
baby zeb learns to
recognise her individual stripes,
like imprinting a bar
code on its mind.
Zebra stripes symbolise balance,
a blending of opposites,
a variable mix of yin
and yang energies,
neither black nor white,
right or wrong,
or better than others ...
they know how to blend
within the herd
without losing their individuality,
**recognising and embracing
their differences ...**

INDIVIDUALITY ROCKS!

> 'There is no one in this world, more YOUer than YOU.'
>
> Dr Seuss

STEP OUT – GO DEEP, BE YOU, AND EMBRACE YOUR UNIQUENESS

From the moment of conceptualising the key lessons I wanted to share in the 'how to' part of this book, *individuality* was always going to be my top priority and the number one core strength to build and grow from. I say 'core' because that's exactly where it comes from. Internally yours. Uniquely yours.

Discovering the power of individuality was one of the first igniters of my personal power journey, embracing it from childhood. Throughout my life, it has provided my survival source and resilience force. I truly believe it to be a fundamental component for building both inner courage and outward confidence.

MY SEVEN-YEAR-OLD AWAKENING ...

One of my earliest memories of individuality being triggered in me was at the age of seven. Grade three. I remember clearly the teacher's name, the classroom and even where I was sitting. It was summer, fans were whirring above, and I was wearing sandals with my school uniform. Slightly less clear (and unimportant) are the details surrounding a playground spat I'd had earlier with my button-pushing, bullying older sister (also adopted), but I do recall my reaction to that. An awakening light-bulb moment as I walked away and up the stairs towards the classroom, with the gripping self-preservation revelation: *'She's not really my sister ... I don't have to like her ... I don't have to BE like her ... or take any notice of what she does or thinks.'* I am me. *Uniquely me. TFFT!*

Now, I don't share that to be nasty. Neither of us are better than the other, just very different people. But from that trigger point onwards, I don't recall ever trying to compete with her, or copy her, or try to follow her path – I just never felt the need to. I had no interest in competing or conforming to her wishes; no need to play the winner/ loser games. It was my first taste (that I recall) of standing in my own individual power. *Fist-pump moment.*

So, that revelation kick-started a much broader exploration into this strength of individual uniqueness, what it would be like to be my own person. Not like my parents, and all the hordes of cousins (most of them much older); they were NOT LIKE ME either. Somehow, I instinctively understood that each was on their own journey, and each of them had their own motives and their own idiosyncrasies. *Fascinating people-watching.*

Take, for example, my triplet cousins whose weddings we attended while I was a small child. They each looked totally different; the tall, lanky guy became a religious minister, the shorter, intelligent guy was a successful businessman, and then there was the big, burly, beer-swigging truckie with a heart of gold. Same birthday, same parents, completely different individuals, but all successful achievers in their own way. Just quietly, I secretly preferred the big, friendly, always loud and laughing, life-of-the-party truckie cousin (RIP 2017 – may he be rocking his bold stripes in the next life). *Full-arse version early influence?*

Rock Your Stripes

Becoming more and more fascinated with people-watching, I developed a deep curiosity in understanding what drives each person to do what they do. As I mentioned earlier, people in our close circles thought I was a shy kid, but I was quietly observing from the periphery during those formative years. Kind of like a hovering helicopter view of the surroundings, deciding where I wanted to land, if I wanted to land, or perhaps where I could fly off to explore other options. Always one eye on the horizon; it was the early days of my 'what's next' appetite for change.

Back to the grade three classroom; it was around this time that I was sitting in front of a large sketch pad, opened onto a blank page. I can't remember what we were supposed to be drawing (probably something about family activities), but I have a vivid recollection of what came up for me as I stared at the blank page in deep consideration for quite some time:

I am like this blank canvas. I can create whatever I want ... whatever I imagine.

I don't have to conform to the norm, or copy what others are drawing. I can create my own story.

I can splash as much colour onto this page as I want to ... be as colourful as I like.

I am me. Uniquely me.

There was no sadness in this moment; rather I recall a sense of wonder and excitement. It was like someone took the lid off the box I'd been crouching in. A *freakin' WOW* moment.

From that point on ... I knew I could:

- *Design my own picture* ... from my imagination and vision of what my life could be.

- *Plan my own game of life* ... make my own choices.

- *Embrace my uniqueness* ... and not feel I 'should' be like anyone else.

After all, I'd even been given a rather different first name, one my mother apparently made up. An original. My sister hated that; there were at least five girls with the same name as her in her primary school grade. It's only been in recent decades, since internet connectivity, that I've noticed a couple of other 'Jilindas' out there (mostly in the US, and mostly younger). So essentially, I grew up thinking I was one of a kind, and that was pretty cool. High school teachers tried to shorten my name to Jill, but I would immediately pick them up on it. I'm not a 'Jill' … I'm Jilinda. *Uniquely me.*

Of course, I know the whole adoption thing really made no difference to my individuality dexterity, other than it being the initial trigger of my personal power exploration process. I never felt like a 'nobody'; on the contrary – I felt 'special' and was determined to become a 'somebody'. Like rising up from that blank canvas, I was excited to boldly splash on as much colour as I could find and explore all I could be. A life of adventure, by design.

Sure, I probably embedded a strong desire for individuality earlier than others. Most of my friends were more inclined to conform to religious constraints, or family norms, or compete with their siblings for attention, or copy their friends. Normal, conservative, family-tradition stuff; but I always knew my circumstances were not normal, and I secretly loved that. *The power of individuality.*

As I mentioned in the earlier *disrupt* section, what I know from decades of experience and curious observation is that 'normal' is not where you will grow your personal power to fuel and sustain the desired outcome – to rock your full-arse version. Sitting in the mediocre, average, bland, beige, or same-sameness box won't give you the opportunities to shine your light. You have to leap up out of there to where the magic is. Anyone can choose to do that. Sit there subdued or leap up and shine; your choice.

READY TO SHINE?

Just before I share a few 'how to' tips with you, it's perhaps worth another reminder about those fearful BS voices that are bound to surface when you step outside your comfort zone. Those five core fears that stifle your ambitions, as outlined more extensively in the *aspire* section:

- Fear of FAILURE … *there is no such thing as failure.*

- Fear of WHAT OTHERS THINK … *you have no control over that, so don't waste energy on it.*

- Fear of REJECTION (or not belonging) … *you are a complete person on your own. Belong to YOU first.*

- Fear of NOT BEING GOOD ENOUGH … *you are enough. Strong enough. Capable enough. Brave enough.*

- Fear of THE UNKNOWN … *there is no such thing as certainty. Embrace the excitement of change.*

Flip back and revise them again if you need to, or simply be aware of them. They will just keep holding you back if you don't learn to question and smash those illogical, debilitating fears first.

Ask yourself: REALLY? Do I *really* believe that? Do I *really* care what others think? Especially those who are choosing to play a smaller game themselves – do I *really* want to conform to their ideals? Do I *really* think I'm not capable? Or not brave enough? *REALLY?* (All with lots of WTF tone ☺.)

Here's what I know for sure: there is a profound sense of power in being uniquely you. In understanding and embracing your inner core, knowing what's important to you and what's not, knowing your strengths and passionate drivers, and above all: believing that you deserve to shine as an individual. Wholeheartedly. Unapologetically. Courageously. *Rocking out all your stripes.*

BE BRAVE … do what the ordinary fear.

PREPARE TO GO DEEP AND NARROW

Are you ready to demolish more unresourceful thinking and behaviour patterns that may be holding you back? Because – *drum roll* – we have another smashing party to attend.

What, there's more?

Yes. To clear the way to building your individuality muscle, we need to drill through a few more restrictive layers. Not too far down from the surface is a set of commonly entrenched behaviours that seem to become ingrained in our psyche, especially in women. It's part gender conditioning (the perfect-woman syndrome), part media marketing (the perfect look), partly our education system (to conform and compete), and driven by most of the five fears I just mentioned, especially the fears of NOT BEING GOOD ENOUGH and REJECTION (not belonging with the in crowd).

It pains me to see so many women getting caught up (and dragged down) in one or more of these things, just to feel good about themselves and their achievements. The fact is, they are trying to gain fulfilment from external sources, rather than doing the deep work of self-discovery and valuing their own strengths and uniqueness.

THE FOUR CRAPPY 'C' CONSTRICTORS

So, here they are. Get ready for some serious smashing …

Drop the need to Compare, Compete, Copy or Conform to the norm

Way too much energy is wasted on that crap.

Smash these constrictors. If you want to build your individuality muscle and increase your confidence levels and courage to rock your own unique stripes, you must drop the need to:

■ Compare – *it leads to constant discontent*

■ Compete – *it leads to destructive behaviours like passive bullying*

■ Copy – *it is a clear indication of not being happy with oneself*

■ Conform – *it suffocates creativity, stunts growth and leads to half-arse results.*

Let's explore each of these a little more.

Smash the inclination to COMPARE …

Comparison leads to constant discontent. It stems from the fear of 'not being good enough' compared to others. It's a total time waster to be constantly checking out (read: social media stalking) what others are doing, especially your colleagues and competitors in business or in the workplace. That's like having one eye on the ball and one looking sideways; one hand doing and the other hand distracted.

I've personally seen this constant comparing and measuring success with others lead to unhealthy competing for supremacy, which then fuels destructive behaviours like passive-bullying traits of undermining others, side-lining or ostracising perceived threats (both in workplaces and social groups), and aggressive self-preservation tactics. None of that ends well.

My point here is: it's far better to spend all that time and energy focusing on your own goals and rocking your own space. *Rise above the need to compare.*

> **'Comparison is the thief of joy.'**
>
> Theodore Roosevelt

Smash the need to COMPETE …

I briefly mentioned earlier that I detest the concept behind beauty competitions and any kind of parade that encourages women to compete on external presentation alone. Things like: race-day fashion competitions, best-dressed awards, online or magazine competitions for 'prettiest face' or 'best bikini babe', and in recent years, the TV shows of beautiful, model-like women competing for the one male bachelor (anything but a 'reality show', I think).

What concerns me the most is the appalling message these types of competitions give to our young women about desirable goals to aspire to. Much of our media-driven society is portraying the 'successful pathway' for a woman as a pretty face with a hot body in a sexy gown designed to snaffle a good-looking man, like the fairy-tale princess who needs rescuing and her every whim provided for, ever after. Please! Surely this is not a valid life ambition for most women anymore – if it ever was. Certainly not a sustainable one.

This unnecessary pressure to constantly compare and compete with others comes from such a shallow base, and it leaves the discarded people to process the message that they have been judged as 'not good enough'. *Really?* No-one needs that shit.

Now, I'm NOT stating, *'Don't make an effort to present as your best'*. In fact, I provide tips on how to do that later. I like getting dressed up in my-style clothes, funky shoes and out-there hair, as much (if not more) than most women do. I love how it makes me feel: confident, bold, and beautiful. But, it's MY individual style and forms part of my personal brand. I'm not comparing or competing with others. I've simply learned to rock my own style and not waste precious thought space making judgements about who's got the nicest dress, or who's the fittest, youngest-looking 50-plus lady at networking events. Seriously, who cares? How is that even important? *Rock your own space.*

While we're on the topic of competing, I feel compelled to mention the competition dilemma I know women struggle with: achievement recognition awards. To be honest, it's something I'm not all that comfortable with myself. Sure, I've won a few awards, and had the odd achievement recognised and showcased in media articles and industry promotions, but each time nominated or proposed by others. I've never really put myself out there to gain an award or collect trophies. I'm not saying that's right or wrong, it's just my journey to date.

However, I do acknowledge the role that many achievement recognition awards play in inspiring others. For my support and involvement (mostly on judging panels these days), the purpose of the awards has to fit well with my values and passions, and the intent of the nominees has to be about showcasing positive outcomes that inspire others, and not just shining a 'look at me' light on themselves. *Intentionality matters.*

My point here is: focus on creating your own individual style, intentionally aligned with your personal brand, developed in congruence with your inner values and purpose. Style that comes from your core (more on that soon).

Rock Your Stripes

Smash the desire to COPY ...

I have to share: copy cats frustrate the hell out of me. With my strong individualism values, it's really annoying when people pick up and run with someone else's stuff that took hours of creating. Frankly, I view copying as a cheap act, not dissimilar to theft of one's personal property or a breach of rights to one's intellectual property. There is nothing individualistic about copying someone else. It's not clever, it's lazy, and you will always be one step behind the original creators.

Particularly today, in this era of global connectivity and social media sharing, copy cats are quickly noticed. It takes only a second to lose your credibility if you are trying to pass off another person's work or ideas as your own. Just don't do it, okay? *Showcase YOUR unique thoughts, learnings and ideas.*

I have been copied a lot over the years, from my wacky hairstyles to brochure design and program content, to concepts shared at development phase that others have run with themselves. When you bravely stand out and are different, it naturally attracts some who 'want what she's got'.

Once again, I've learned I have no control over others' behaviours, only my response to it. I used to get angry. These days, I'm a tad more cautious with whom I share valuable IP I've created; there's a time to keep things close to my chest (challenging for an excited extrovert), and the right time and place to boldly showcase. Mostly, I try to see it as a compliment that someone wants to copy my style, or my branding, or the way I deliver my programs. As a leader of change, my mission is to inspire others to make changes, and clearly some decide to adopt my approach – exactly. So, in essence, it's confirmation that my influence is having a positive impact. *Gotta love a good mindset reframe.*

Of course, whenever I have the chance, and especially when I'm mentoring, I encourage others to take on board the learnings and ideas from other successful people, and then build on that by creatively adding their own individual style, thoughts and processes that will best showcase what THEY want to portray. That way, they are growing their individuality muscle and their own profile, not hanging onto someone else's ideas like a security blanket.

My point here is: when you do the deep work on your inner self, you will recognise that your values, beliefs, motivators and passions are quite different to other people's, even those you admire. Go deep to your core and narrow your focus: instead of a broad smattering of stuff copied from all over the place, find your clear, intentional, on-point purpose. *Your* life's purpose. No-one can copy that; it's original. *Uniquely yours.*

> **'Be yourself, because an original is always worth more than a copy.'**
>
> Original author unknown

Smash the expectation to CONFORM …

I learned from a very young age what conformity and cowering to fit in with others' needs does to your mind and soul. It sucks you dry. It depletes your passion, destroys your personal aspirations, and leaves you to constantly feel 'not good enough'. Actually, what I now know to be true is that many traditions, religions and systems (and some individuals) intentionally design rigid rules that way, for the purpose of ensuring you don't outgrow or outshine them, and so that you always need them. They encourage you to comply, play a smaller, submissive game, a manipulated game where they can continue to hold the control and power.

Of course, there are some things we need to conform to for our own good and protection in society, such as safety laws, human rights regulations, road rules, and health and safety practices; I'm not suggesting you ignore those things just to be different. But, by all means, question the things that are no longer relevant or have ceased to work effectively.

Dare I mention: our disintegrating two-party political system in Australia, the unethical way our major banks have been operating, the depraved acts committed against some children and the muted response from religious leaders, to name just a few things. Yes, of course – I dare. These things need to be addressed. Wrong is always wrong, even if people have been getting away with it for years.

That's where lobbying for change is a valid action. Most significant changes to outdated, irrelevant systems and processes have been achieved through collective activism (more on that later).

What I've observed in my coaching practice is that conforming becomes a mindless habit: you do it, but you don't know why. It's just the way it's always been, or perhaps the best way to not rock the boat. But, frankly, I don't know anyone who has made a significant difference in the world by following along like a blind sheep and being like everyone else. Leaders drive change, they don't conform to past ideals.

My point here is: please think about the things you are conforming to out of habit or the expectation of others that are no longer working for you. Especially the things that hold you back from being your full-arse version. I encourage you to stop conforming to others' ideals. Don't let others put the 'should' guilt on you. Bust out of that box. *Be YOU – the world has enough conformists.*

> '**To be yourself in a world that is constantly trying to make you something else is the greatest accomplishment.**'
>
> Ralph Waldo Emerson

DEEP DIVE – INNER CORE WORKOUT

Let's dive into it.

In my earlier years of leadership roles, being a leadership mentor and leadership program facilitator, I often referred to Simon Sinek's simple but powerful Golden Circle model. Simon Sinek is a contemporary leadership guru, a non-conformist in many ways, challenging leaders to change their focus, strategies and behaviours from traditional methods to more team-engaging and trust-building leadership approaches. If you are not familiar with Simon Sinek's work, Google him. Watch his popular video talks and read his bestselling books. His original *Golden Circle* model (2009 era) was all about getting clear on your purpose, believing in it, walking it, talking it, and inspiring others to do the same. The basic model looks like this:

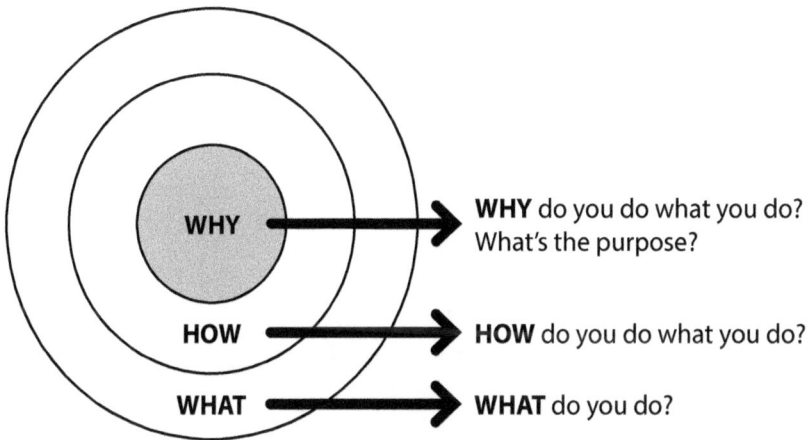

WHY

HOW

WHAT

WHY do you do what you do?
What's the purpose?

HOW do you do what you do?

WHAT do you do?

Simon's research into conventionally led organisations found that they approach this model from the outside in. People know WHAT they do and HOW to do it, but are less likely to understand WHY they do what they do. Robotic following of systems and processes may produce results, but it doesn't build strong passion and trust that comes from truly believing in why you do what you do. His challenge to leaders back then was to flip that: start from the inside out. Starting with the WHY builds greater trust and people are more motivated when they know, believe in, and are on board with the core purpose or mission of the organisation they work for.

While I agree in principle with this base model, from my decades of experience in leadership and life, I believe this circle has an important deeper core. Especially when it comes to leading and influencing others, and forming genuine connections.

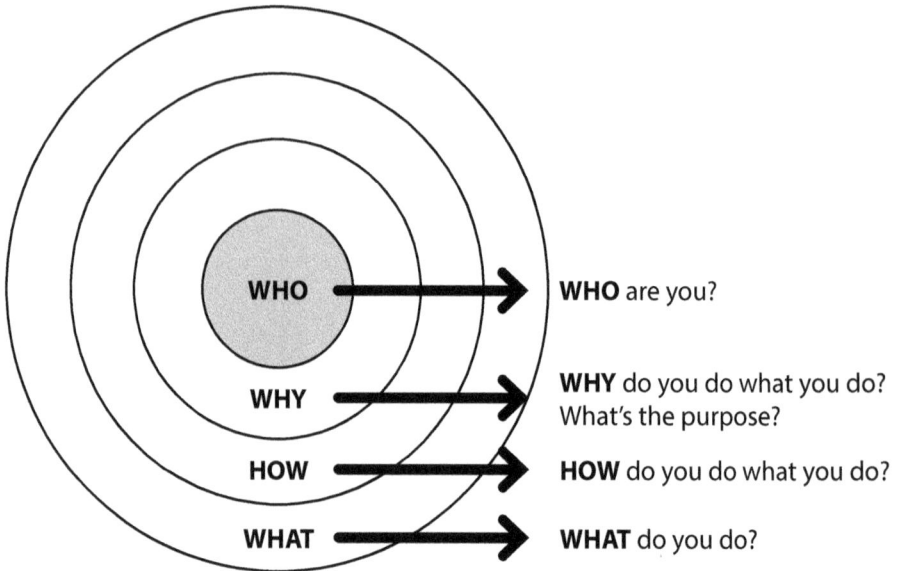

WHO are you?

WHY do you do what you do?
What's the purpose?

HOW do you do what you do?

WHAT do you do?

People want to know WHO you are, first … *then* why you do what you do and how.

They want to see the REAL YOU … the full, wholehearted, genuine version.

Your AUTHENTIC self.

Here's what I know for sure: whether you are in a lead role, or aspiring to leadership, or simply wanting to step up more bravely, stand out more boldly and speak up with more influence, YOU will need to have a clear understanding and strong belief in WHO you are and WHY you do what you do, before showcasing specifically WHAT you do, and HOW you do it – your unique way. You need to lead yourself first. Be the CEO of your own life, your own wholehearted purpose, your individual personal branding, and your career. Your reputation depends on it.

> *Leadership is an inside-out process.*
> *Do you need to get clearer on WHO*
> *you are and what makes you unique?*

DIVE A LITTLE DEEPER

Individuality comes from your inner core – your values, your beliefs, your passions, your experiences and learnings, your behaviour style, your choices, your actions … they are all unique to you.

It took me three decades to realise I needed to get clearer on WHO the real Jilinda was. Yes, I loved being a unique individual long before then, and my confidence and courage to stand up and speak out grew with each chapter, mainly through being a business owner and influencing change in community leadership roles, but some stuff in my life was not congruent with my values.

There was no one turning point where I suddenly realised some inner work on myself was needed; it was a gradual awakening. A rumbling that grew louder from deep within me. However, the chapter of increased momentum down that path was when I decided to leave my hairdressing career, knew I would leave my marriage (in time), and started a university degree. I wanted to understand why I felt the need to make those big, brave changes, so I could better explain it to those who would be impacted. Why this craving to be more? To be the REAL ME; to become who I was meant to be. My full-arse version, not some half-arse, half-strength version that was constantly being held back by others' neediness and ideals of who they thought I should be. *My turn, my time.*

I recall the immense dislike of the word 'should' that rose up strongly in me at that time. Like fingernails running down a blackboard, it grated on me. So, I decided to reframe it into:

I could, I can, I will and I am.

To this day, I still use that mantra during my beach meditation yoga. Keeping that inner core muscle strong. *Believe in yourself.*

So, I urge you not to wait any longer. Take the plunge and do the inner work on this. It will take a little reflective time and effort, but the benefits are absolutely huge. Remember: you must be able to understand and lead yourself, before you can successfully lead and influence others. *Inside-out process.*

Here's a starter self-awareness checklist, including some inner-strength assessment tools I have used and recommend to my coaching clients and women in our ElevateHER programs.

*	**Values self-assessment**	Values are powerful principles that underpin our decisions, our actions and our opinions of people and events. Sometimes referred to as 'critical needs', this exercise will help you form a 'must have' list that makes decision-making easier and more aligned. *Note:* Our values change significantly over the years, so getting clear on what that means to you in this chapter of your life is crucial.
*	**SEIP – Social + Emotional Intelligence (EQ) Profiling**	*SEIP* assesses strengths and vulnerabilities in 26 EQ competencies across four key areas: self-awareness, self-management, situational awareness, and relationship building. The comprehensive personalised report is full of useful development tips.
*	**DISC + Motivators – dual behavioural science assessment**	*DISC* assesses WHAT your behaviour preferences and patterns are across four types: Dominance (want results), Influence (want to be liked), Steadiness (want to be comfortable), and Compliance (want to be right). Motivators assesses WHY you respond that way – identifying your top core driving forces.
*	**LPI – Leadership Practices Inventory**	*LPI* can be used as a self-assessment of leadership strengths and weaknesses, or 360° tool where other observers rank your leadership behaviours into five key practice areas.
	HIGH 5 Strengths Test	https://high5test.com/ *Note:* Your strengths are not necessarily what you are good at. They are things that energise and strengthen you. You may be skilled at something that sucks your energy, that you would rather do less of (or not at all). That's not a strength, it is a weakness.
	Myers Briggs – MBTI	www.mbtionline.com Personality testing that identifies natural preferences in four key areas, sorted into one of 16 distinct personality types. It's a point-in-time assessment, as our preferences change.

* You can access these tools from my website – JilindaLee.com.au

STAND OUT – PRESENTATION MATTERS

Your style reflects your attitude,
your passion and your personality.

Once you get clear on WHO you are (your inner beliefs, values and drivers), WHY you do what you do, and HOW you do that (consistently), you are ready to rock all that uniqueness proudly on the outside.

Why is that important? Because others really do judge a book by its cover; it's human nature to immediately start forming a story from what is visually presented to us. But, don't be overly concerned about that. This is where individuality comes to the fore; an opportunity to present your personal brand. What you are known for. It's how you stand out from the rest and leave your authentic mark in this world.

Now, when it comes to the topic of individual style I could easily write a whole book (and perhaps I will). My passionate belief in the power of individual branding is such that I include it as one of the five intelligences (skill sets) in my signature leadership development program, as part of the *LQ – Leadership Intelligence Quotient framework*. I refer to it as IPQ – Individual Presentation Quotient. We spend a whole day on this topic at our women's retreats. And yes, this is just as important for men too.

I will briefly touch on these three areas to help you showcase your individuality on the outside, so you can start rocking more of your personal, unique style:

- style making
- hair matters
- colour magic.

Style making – unleash your individual style

I'm sure we would all like to present our best version to the world, to have an individual style that's comfortable (feels good for you), consistent (aligns to your values, beliefs and lifestyle), and portrays confidence (showcases who you are). You can.

Being known for your style is not about parading around in head-to-toe designer labels that have come straight off the runway. It's not about being the showiest, most vibrantly-clad person in the room. It's not about wearing the same style clothes every day like a uniform (my home office uniform is a sarong!). It's about presenting yourself in an original, independent way that oozes your inner confidence and sends a clear message about who you are, without having to speak.

> ### Fashion is about dressing according to what's fashionable at a point in time. Style is more about presenting your individual self to the world – consistently.

When we think of well-known, truly stylish women, they all have one thing in common – their own notably individual style. Remember Audrey Hepburn's famous style? Classy, elegant and understated. Known for her tailored sleeveless black dresses, she simply added quality necklaces, earrings, and often elbow-length black satin gloves. Oh, and lipstick; her richly coloured lips were always a stand-out feature. Outdoors, she was photographed generally wearing understated classic outfits with oversized, cat-eyed sunglasses, and a stunning broad-brim hat. She believed that personal style was timeless, famously saying: *'Everyone has their own style. When you have found it, you should stick to it.'* And this one:

'Elegance is the only beauty that never fades.'

Audrey Hepburn

Likewise, think about other women like actress Marilyn Munro (sexy, feminine style), singer Pink (bold, risqué with signature hair),

Princess Diana (sassy, elegant – once she could be the 'real' Diana), and – closer to home – Australian ex-MP Julie Bishop (corporate class, strong with a splash of feminine accessorising – earrings, shoes, colourful nails).

When you establish your own personal style, it doesn't change greatly with the fashion of the moment; you can generally work a few new-season pieces into YOUR style to keep it fresh. Likewise, you don't have to tone down your unique, individual style as you get older. Forget the 'mutton dressed up as lamb' judgements, the should-do or shouldn't-do rules around age-appropriate dressing. Personal style is ageless. *Keep on rocking your stripes.*

Since leaving politics, Julie Bishop has presented at numerous Australian women's network groups, sharing her personal style story about earlier parliamentary days, when she was given responsibility for the Aged Care portfolio. Apparently, some male political colleagues advised her she needed to swap her strong corporate-style outfits for softer pastel cardigans and pretty floral dresses. So she did, for a short time, but it felt wrong. Uncomfortable. Not congruent with who she was. She soon went back to HER style, adding a tad more feminine bling and eye-catching stylish heels. Who could forget the stunning red bling heels she wore with classic black corporate suiting for the 2018 press conference to announce her resignation from Deputy Leader and Foreign Minister positions? Do you think she just woke up that morning and grabbed the first pair of shoes in her wardrobe? Of course not. Her choice of style that day was deliberate, and the visual message was clear, that of a strong woman boldly walking away from a political debacle she didn't cause or want anything to do with. Those red heels spoke volumes, and it's no wonder the media pack honed in on them. They got the unspoken message loud and clear – even if her conservative male colleagues were clueless. *Stepping up bravely, standing out boldly, and speaking up brilliantly.*

I absolutely adore Iris Apfel's approach to life, her non-conformist attitude and famous sense of 'too muchness' style. Born in 1921, she has to be one of the world's funkiest older style icons, still rocking bright colours and big signature glasses well past her 90s. Google her if you're curious. She has a popular Facebook page and massive followers list.

Rock Your Stripes

I really hope I get to rock my unique, out-there, zebra-striped style into my 80s and beyond as well as she has.

Now, I know that defining your own personal style can be a little overwhelming in a world that markets to us constantly, especially if you are not sure what suits you. I'm not a trained personal stylist (except for hair), but I've learned a few things along a journey of embracing individuality all my life, trying to do the best with the body shape I've been given (height challenged, voluptuous inverted triangle turned post-menopause squishy apple-shape), and I enjoy helping others do the same (including men). When we cover this topic at our empowering women's retreats, I often bring in a style expert to help participants establish a base framework style guide. I highly recommend engaging a professional to help you do that.

Here's some exploration questions to get you started:

What three things do you like about your personality … what do you value most?

_____

_____

_____

_____

How do you want to feel when presenting YOUR style?

_____

_____

_____

_____

What personal branding message (about WHO you are) do you want to portray?

_____

_____

_____

_____

What's three things you like about your physical appearance ... what are your best assets?

_____

_____

_____

_____

What shapes and styles suit your height, face, body shape and bone structure?

_____

_____

_____

_____

What colours are you drawn to and suit your natural skin and hair tones?

_____

_____

_____

_____

What works easily and comfortably with your lifestyle?

_____

_____

_____

_____

Rock Your Stripes

Hair matters

Yes, I'm going there. After spending the first 20 years of my career in the hairdressing industry, I feel it would be remiss of me not to emphasise this valuable aspect of your personal profile presentation. Your hairstyle is one of the easiest and most beneficial ways to be noticed and remembered. No, not remembered JUST for your hair, but because your hairstyle is generally the second thing observed by the people you meet, and often the first thing they recall when trying to picture you or describe you to others.

Here's why. When you walk into a room, people will take in the whole vision. Your body language, your facial expression, your hair, your clothing and accessories like shoes, bag, meeting folder, and such – generally in that order (unless they are creepy peeps). The interesting and often overlooked fact is, when you meet with someone and have a conversation, it is your face they are focusing on (your eyes and expression), and what immediately frames that image is your hair.

YOUR HAIR – it does matter ... hair doesn't make the woman, but a good hairstyle definitely helps.

Think about it: when you try to describe a person you've met to another person, do you describe their face and the colour of their eyes? Generally not. I'll bet you start with their hair colour, length and style (for example, 'blonde, shoulder-length, wavy hair, like Jane's style but shorter'), and perhaps add something about glasses or earrings if they were also stand-out items framing the facial area. If none of that was remarkable, you would usually then add a description of height and body type (such as 'tall, slim, fit looking'). Am I right?

Sure, I know as women we are conditioned to observe (and judge) what others are wearing, so we might also remember the outfit, but that's a point-in-time observation. You had to be there at the time otherwise the outfit is irrelevant, and not everyone would have noticed who wore what anyway, especially the men in the room. Ever tried to describe someone to a man? Sometimes you wonder if they were in the same room, right?

My point here is: a stand-out, individual hairstyle can leave a lasting impression. I absolutely know that from my own personal experience. My unique hairstyle choice is deliberate. I don't want to be known for my hair, but if I'm noticed and remembered initially because of it, and it sparks curiosity – *'Who is that woman?'* and *'What's her story?'* – that's OKAY.

> **'A woman who cuts her hair is about to change her life.'**
>
> Coco Chanel

Building on the earlier story of discovering the power of being a unique individual (at age seven), it was no accident that I fell into a hairdressing career at 15. I was attracted to the idea of creating individual hairstyles equally as much as becoming financially independent. The company I trained with, and later managed salons for, was known for avant-garde styling. I had the privilege of learning the trade under one of Australia's top stylists who was known for his art, his dramatic expression, and his radical styles. It was such a creative environment; I soaked it up and loved it.

By far, the best thing he taught me was to break the rules. To not conform to the basic, conservatively structured TAFE theory training, but to creatively design individual styles for each client. Taking into account their face shape, personality, lifestyle, hair type and favourite colours, I learned the value of unique expression and the excitement of change. So many choices. Throughout my hairdressing days, I had a new hairstyle every season; the more 'out there', the better.

Even though women often brought in hairstyle pictures out of a magazine (Princess Diana and Jennifer Aniston pics drove me nuts!), we would create a style that was similar in concept but with notable individual difference as well. Or talk them out of it and into something more suitable. I learned how much individuality matters. No-one looked like an exact copy of someone else. I saw the positive effect it had on women as they walked out of the salon rocking their own unique look: *this is ME.*

During that career chapter, I also built a radar for identifying common patterns of behaviour and what motivates them. Like women who still hide behind long school-girl hair. Those who think wearing their hair like they did in their 20s will keep them looking young. Those who want change, but it has to be done in very small, subtle steps. Those who have entrenched limiting beliefs about what certain colours meant, like bleach-blonde babes or bold, brash redheads. Of course, I've been both of those colours (and many more) at one time or another, and while I definitely had more fun as a blonde, it's not been the hair colour that did that but my attitude and choices in life.

The short, gravity-defying, pink champagne–blonde hair that I rocked through my 50s, and similar style now as a 60s silver siren, has been my signature style for a while now; it reflects my attitude, personality, and core values. A little unexpected and bold. Definitely non-conforming. It suits my lifestyle and stage in life. Frankly, I can't be arsed to spend more than two to five minutes throwing some gravity-defying product into it with my fingers each morning (no brush or comb needed), washing it one or two times a week, and scheduling an afternoon of cut and colour toning every month to keep it edgy. That's it. My style without fuss or much effort. *Individually ME.*

Great hair doesn't have to take over your life, but it can be life changing.

My point here is: many women run with illogical stories in their heads that hold them back from experiencing the wonderful injection of confidence that comes from framing their most important and expressive asset – their face – with the second most notable feature – a flattering, signature hairstyle. *Just do it.*

TIPS FOR ROCKING YOUR OWN HAIRSTYLE

- Find a good hair stylist. One that will work with you to create your signature style.

- Research hairstyle designs online. Ones that take you outside your conservative comfort zone. It's never been easier to put together a collection of ideas.

- Think about the evolution of your personal brand and consider the message you want to convey.

- Focus on how you want to feel. Write it down (for example, funky, fun, cheeky, sexy, bold, confident, feminine, sassy, stylish, strong, sleek …).

- Consider your lifestyle and how much effort you are willing to spend on hair grooming.

- Just do it. It's just hair. It grows, it can be changed, and it's lots of fun experimenting.

The magic of colour

I discovered and embraced the magic of colour from early on. I grew up in a green house. No, not the type that grows plants (although we had lots of indoor plants). My parents had two favourite colours: lime green and emerald green. Apart from pops of bright orange features in the kitchen, bright orange lounge suite, and … *drum roll* … purple shag-pile carpet in the bedroom my sister and I shared (following a renovation that moved our bedroom to the back end of the house – an early non-conforming win), green was the overall theme.

It's fair to say my first introduction to understanding the full colour spectrum came with the start of my hairdressing career. I learned the magic of colour mixing, of adding bright highlight flashes to funky short styles and adding bright-coloured accessories to plain white salon uniforms. I remember clearly my bright red platform shoes, shiny red belt and red hoop earrings from week one.

Rock Your Stripes

Soon after commencing my apprenticeship, I was one of the key influencers in changing the policy on all-white uniforms (so boring, and impractical for a budding colourist) to one of new uniform styles each season (summer range and winter range). I say 'range' because it quickly became apparent that one style or one colour was not going to suit all, so we'd choose a new-season fabric pattern in several colour options, and staff could get a dress or skirt and top made in a style that suited them. *Individuality matters.*

Now, I was lucky to have a mother who could sew like anything, from any rough sketch I threw at her. Needless to say, my salon uniforms were always as different and out there as much as I could push the boundaries. Always one foot outside the uniform policy box (a carry-over habit from school days). *Dare to disrupt.*

Flipping forward a few decades, it's no surprise I'm still embracing individuality and am known for my unique, vibrantly coloured style; it is part of my personal branding. But, it's more than just clothes and accessory selection and knowing how to throw them together in a flattering way to suit my body shape. Colour plays a huge part in the way I present my personal branding. *Strong and consistent.*

You won't find pastel colours in my wardrobe. I just never wear pastel or neutral colours. For several seasons (2018–20) I bought no new shoes; nude-coloured shoes just don't do it for me, and that was almost the only offering in the shoe stores at the time – the standard black, tan, and five different shades of nude (read: boring beige). Then, I established a relationship with a local boutique shoe-shop owner, who had one of her suppliers make up a chunky-heeled sandal in bright orange leather, especially for me. Apparently, she also ordered six more pairs in the most common sizes, and they sold out immediately.

Yes, I know. Rocking bright colours is easy for me as a confident extrovert; my independent, vibrant streak is showing. I do understand that not everyone likes to be clad in bright colours from head to toe. I don't do that either. My go-to corporate presentation outfits are mainly black with white striping or zebra-print features, but I usually add a bright pop of colour somewhere (earrings, glasses, bangle, bag, shoes, lippy). I'm not a scarf wearer, but I know other ladies who absolutely rock brightly patterned scarves to add colour to a more neutral outfit. These days, I wear far less corporate-style clothing, especially since the increase of online presentations and more women-focused program facilitation; you're more likely to see me rock my full-arse, colourful style on screen and stages.

Likewise, the colours we surround ourselves with make a difference too. A house décor of beige walls and kitchen cabinets, neutral floors and beige blinded windows screams 'urgent makeover' to me. Yes, I've lived in units and houses like these for short periods as I moved around, but each time I immediately added 'my colour style' to the place, to make it feel like MY home. Colour evokes feelings and sets the tone in a home.

My point here is: we don't look at a beautiful bright-blue ocean and wish it was pale grey. We don't view those bright orange and yellow sunrises, or the spectacular winter sunsets of vibrant pink and orange, and think to ourselves, *'Geez, someone tone it down a bit, hey?'*

Why choose pale when you can be bright?

Why choose to be subdued when you could be bold?

Why choose to blend in when you can stand out and showcase your personal brand in all its brilliance?

Life is a great big canvas. Throw all the colourful paint on it you can.

Once again, I'm not the guru of everything colourful, nor do I have a degree in the psychological impact that colour has on people. I'll leave that to the experts. However, what I do know from personal experience is the power and benefits of knowing the colours that best suit your personality and how you want to feel, and importantly the message that colour imparts to others as part of your individual personal brand. *Colour congruence.*

Rock Your Stripes

Now's the time to get your coloured pencils out ...

While I've always been drawn to bright orange as my favourite pop feature colour, it's only in recent years that I have understood why. Since then, more of it features in my wardrobe, my house, my office, and in my personal and business branding.

Here's why: orange is made up from mixing the primary colours red and yellow. In my case: rich, bright red and vibrant, sunshine yellow. Never the diluted versions:

- **RED** – *rich, bright tone* ... is associated with strength, energy, determination, power, dominance (yes, I can be forthright), as well as passion, desire and love. It is the warmest and most dynamic of colours. It draws attention, represents courage and confidence, and encourages action.

- **YELLOW** – *vibrant, sunshiny tone* ... is associated with happiness, optimism, intellect, and innovation, as it inspires original thought and inquisitiveness. It is the most luminous of all colours, catching attention more than any other colour. It evokes increased mental activity and increased muscle energy, and encourages creative conversation.

So ... it's no wonder my favourite colour is the mix of red and yellow:

- **ORANGE** – *rich and vibrant tone* ... radiates warmth and happiness, combining the energy and stimulation of RED with the cheerfulness and optimism of YELLOW. It is the colour of adventure and extroverted social communication.

So me, right?

Well, here's the really spot-on association that resonates deeply within me: the colour ORANGE encourages gut reactions or gut instincts, as opposed to the physical reaction to RED (quick outburst or aggressive pushback), or the mental reaction to YELLOW (over-thinking or impulsiveness). It offers emotional strength in difficult times. It uplifts and rejuvenates our spirit. Those attracted to orange are forward thinking, outward thinking, and courageous enough to face consequences, take action and make changes, and are always ready to move onward and upward. *Yes, this is so me.*

In 2017, as we dug deeply and rose up from a major zag experience – that malicious, personal assault on our integrity (mentioned in the REACH section) – I had an overwhelming urge to refresh our business brand, to portray an even stronger message, more on point with our mission and passion for leadership development. During this rebranding process, the easiest decision was colour and style: rich, vibrant ORANGE would be the predominant colour, with black and white contrasts, and even more personalising – subtle hints of zebra print. Totally congruent with our message, target clientele and individual style.

A few years later, when launching ElevateHER Australia, we added a blended rainbow of colour (red > pink > orange > yellow), overlayed with zebra striping, and featured red, orange, and magenta pink to depict our networking, education and advocacy activities.

Then, as my speaker/author career evolved, for a more personal, individual Jilinda Lee brand, I added bright splashes of magenta pink to the bold orange and zebra print theme of my renowned signature branding (and in the clothing I wear). I feel the rich pink tones exudes a stronger, feminine wisdom that drives me forward with meaningful, legacy-leaving momentum.

Branding done well is personal, purposeful and professional. *Consistency matters. Colours add meaning.*

Your turn – Rock your own colours …
Explore and identify the colours that you are drawn to – and favourite shades of those.

_____

_____

_____

_____

Find out why … Google what those colours are associated with and the emotions they evoke.

_____

_____

_____

_____

Embrace the colours that make you feel the way you want to feel, and give off the visual messages you want to portray.

Discuss this with professional branding agencies and personal stylists, if you need help with that.

Showcase the colours that fit best with your personal branding message.

Do a colour makeover of your:

☐ wardrobe choices

☐ office spaces

☐ favourite home spaces

☐ business promotion collateral

☐ media communication platforms.

COLOURS ...	SOURCE ...	ATTRIBUTES ... INCREASES:	FEELINGS ... EVOKES:
RED	Primary colour	Physical energy Courage Confidence Stamina Attentive action	Power/Dominance Strength Passion Desire/Love Warmth
YELLOW	Primary colour	Attention Mental activity Energy Optimism Impulsiveness	Happiness Playfulness Creativity Conversation Connection
BLUE	Primary colour	Spaciousness Balance Tranquillity Loyalty Trust	Openness Calmness Coolness Sincerity Unity/Belonging
GREEN	Mix of ... blue + yellow	Harmony Stability Healing/Rebirth Comfort Self-control	Freshness Growth Hope Contentment Rest/Peacefulness
ORANGE	Mix of ... red + yellow	Gut instincts Emotional strength Vitality Agility/Change Innovation	Courageousness Enthusiasm Cheerful/Uplifting Forward thinking Social engagement
FUCHSIA – Pinkish purple – Similar to magenta	Mix of ... red + white (pink) red + blue (purple)	Emotional balance Free spirit Introspection Self-respect Transformation	Awareness Individuality Intuitive strength Deep love/Passion Aspirational change
TEAL – Blueish green	Mix of blue + green	Open mindedness Exploration Cautiousness Communication Thoughtful action	Objective thinking Wisdom Patience Contribution Social awareness

COLOUR IS A POWER THAT DIRECTLY AWAKENS AND INFLUENCES THE SOUL

'People are just as wonderful as sunsets,
if you let them be.

When I look at a sunset, I don't find myself saying:

"Soften the orange a bit on the right-hand corner."

I don't try to control a sunset.
I watch with awe as it unfolds.'

Carl R Rogers

SPEAK UP – BE WHOLEHEARTEDLY, CONSISTENTLY YOU

*When you own your voice ...
you own your power.*

When you have done the deep, inner core work and developed a clearer understanding of WHO you are and WHY you do WHAT you do, things that don't fit well with that or no longer feel right will increasingly become obvious to you. Staring you in the face. Lots of 'ah-haa' moments. It is highly likely you will want to make some changes, maybe quite substantial ones. You will want to bring the REAL you – the wholehearted you – into all you do. You will want to speak up. Make suggestions. Voice your opinion. *Courageously and confidently.*

There is good reason why I suggest you step up to the task of doing your inner core work first, and then secondly, stand out from the rest through building your IPQ (Individual Presentation Quotient) to align with that. Rocking your individual style with confidence on the outside requires an inside-out process. Inside work first, before you share it with the world.

In case you are wondering why I covered off on the external appearance stuff like personal style, hair and colour choices before getting to this important section on speaking up – here's why:

Style is the way you tell the world who you are without having to speak.

First impressions really do count. Within seconds of you walking into the room, others will have taken on a message about WHO you are from:

- **The way you dress** … how you present yourself:
  Do your clothes suit you? Are they a good fit?
  Are you rocking that individual style?
  Do the colours portray confidence?
  Or did you wear the usual beige, grey or navy to blend in?

- **The way you walk** … how you carry yourself:
  Did you walk with confidence? … Head up, walking wide and connecting with people as you move?
  Or did you sneak in quietly? … Skimming the walls and sticking to the outer edges?

- **The way you speak** … and how you respond:
  Was the tone of your voice showing enthusiasm, genuine interest and curiosity?
  Did you respond to questions confidently … passionately sharing your own opinion?
  Or did you hold back in fear of saying the wrong thing or jumbling your words?

Yes, impressions happen in that order. In fact, numerous studies have shown that the message others take is based on the following aspects:

- 55% visual (your presentation)

- 38% voice tone (how you say it)

- 7% words (what you actually say).

That's right. Your words are just 7% of the whole message. Why then do we spend so much time worrying about how to say something, or how to word it correctly, when the thoughts are clear in our heads and our gut has already formed an opinion? Why not trust your gut and share that – genuinely, openly and passionately? After all, it's *your* individual opinion, from *your* perspective, developed through *your* experiences. You have a right to voice it. Not everyone will agree, but that's OKAY. Lots of good decisions come from sharing left-of-centre ideas and debating opposing views.

Think about it. How many times have you been in a meeting and thought of a possible solution, but instead of offering your opinion, you held back (perhaps fearful of what others will think), only to hear the guy next to you put forward an idea that's exactly what you were thinking? So often, right? Kick yourself for stalling?

Sheryl Sandberg, founder of the Lean In global movement, shared her observations of most women entering a boardroom for a meeting. She noticed they often hang back and wait until others (mostly men) have taken the seats at the table, and then choose to sit off to the side, or the row behind along the wall. Her advice was: *'Sit at the table. Because no-one gets to the corner office by sitting on the sidelines.'*

My point here is: don't sit in the back row. Don't hold back because you haven't practised and honed your perfect response. Remember: there is no such thing as perfect. No-one wants to hear some rehearsed, robotic pitch. They want to hear what you genuinely think. Don't underestimate your unique capabilities. More people will connect with you at a deeper level when your words showcase your character (your WHO and WHY) and your competence (your WHAT and HOW) with conviction (your beliefs) and consistency (whole-heartedly, the full version of you). *Authentically YOU.*

Be an individual voice ...
not a conforming echo.

Speaking up doesn't have to always be verbal; remember, visuals and tone (voice or written) provide the strongest message. Posting videos, writing blogs and articles, and providing commentary via social and print media are great ways to share your individual thoughts and build your 'WHO and WHY' profile.

Have you ever done an online search on yourself? It's fascinating – and a surprise to some – what shows up. Mentions in print media (media releases, articles in newspapers and magazines), random comments made at board meetings where minutes are public record, videos (especially YouTube uploads), every personal photo ever posted online (and ones you've been tagged into on social media), member affiliations, and the usual links to your social media profile pages. Anyone can research your background. *Good to know. Scary for some.*

Just make sure that what you're putting out there is the real, authentic you. We are all bombarded with so much fake messaging and loud, 'look at me', ra-ra marketing with no substance or merit; it can take a while to sift through the big-noting BS to find what's real and true. Be sincere and focus on WHY you are sharing, WHO your message is targeted at, and HOW you can give value to your audience. Then let your individuality show through in the way you present that. *Be real.*

Yes, you sometimes have to deal with (read: ignore or block) the cyber-bullies or hecklers, and I can understand why some people avoid interactions on social media or even building a personal online profile. However, in a world of expected connectivity, constant chatter and quick information bites, silence or avoidance can also send an unintended message, especially to prospective employers or business partners.

No profile – *privacy*? No background – *secrecy*? What are they hiding? Could they be lacking confidence or competence in using social media? Stuck in the past? Do they really possess the 'people skills' and 'collaborative relationship building' approach outlined on their CV when they have no online presence or interactions? Are they really 'thought leaders' and 'influential change agents' when they haven't published so much as an inspirational post or blog or video or written a research paper or book? *Clarity and consistency matters.*

Of course, the global pandemic phase with periods of strict home isolation many of us in Australia experienced, brought to the fore the importance of connection, particularly online connectivity. Even my elderly mum (97+) learned to answer video calls on an iPad at that time, so her family could do online visiting. Frankly, if you don't have an online profile these days, you will be increasingly sidelined, irrelevant, or ignored.

My point here is: if you are going to be your full-arse version then you can't hide away or stay silent. Your individual opinions need to be voiced (verbal or written), especially as a lead expert, a leader of change, or emerging leader. Far better to have a noticeable presence that consistently showcases your personal character and competence levels and gives voice to your passions and purpose than no presence or no notable opinions at all.

It's more powerful to speak up than to silently resent.

Read on; I share more about speaking up and influencing as a thought leader in the *Influencer* chapter. Flip forward if you like, but don't miss the next chapter on growing your *Independent* muscle. It's the resilient supplement for rocking your full-arse version.

Tips for speaking up to showcase your INDIVIDUALITY

- Sit at the decision-making table, not on the sidelines. Don't wait until you are invited. Ask if you need to, otherwise – if seating is optional – don't hold back.

- Don't wait until you know it all or have an idea all worked out before you speak up and provide your input. Do it NOW.

- Don't wait until your 'who am I' marketing pitch is perfect. Let your passion and real character show. Speak up now, wholeheartedly, with genuine intent.

- Get clearer (and even a little obsessed) with things that you are passionate about, especially stuff that you want to help drive changes to for the greater good.

- Write down the three key things (content or points of view) that you want to share, with one short sentence for each:

  1. _____
     _____

  2. _____
     _____

  3. _____
     _____

- Go deeper … what are your unique thoughts or individual experiences you have about the three things that showcase WHO you are and your WHY – why this is important to you?

- Explore opportunities to speak up and showcase WHO you are … a confident individual who deserves to be heard.

- Do an online search of yourself. Make sure your online profile is portraying WHO you really are, confidently and consistently.

Rock your stripes

My mission in life
is not merely to
survive,
but to thrive ...
and to do so
with
PASSION,
COMPASSION,
HUMOUR,
and
STYLE.

Maya Angelou

CHAPTER 7

BE
INDEPENDENT

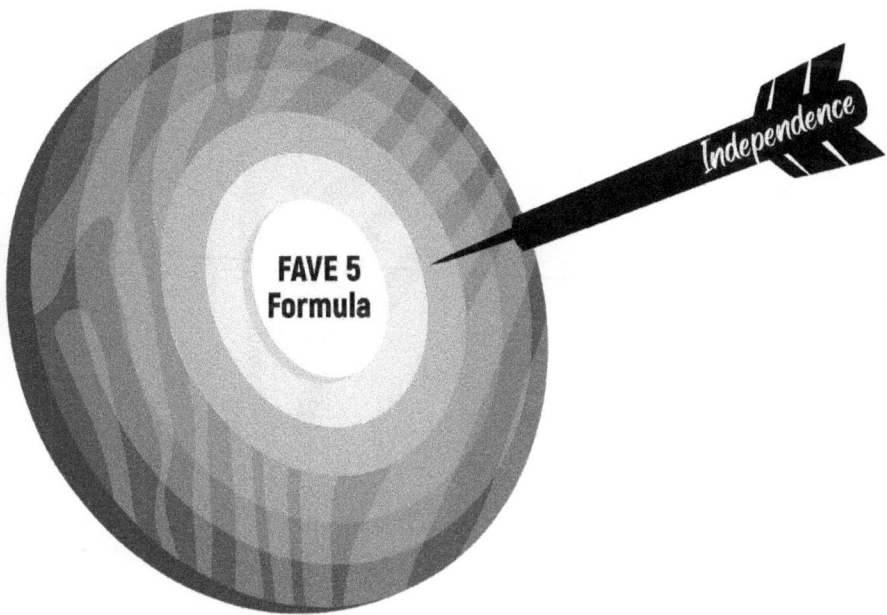

Independence

FAVE 5
Formula

Colour me RED ... or ... rock your own colours!

ZEBRAS LOVE BEING FREE AND WILD ...

Unlike horses, they have
refused to be domesticated.
To survive in the harsh
environment they share
with predators like lions,
cheetahs and hyenas,
they have evolved into a
particularly alert and
responsive animal that
quickly moves away from
potential danger.
If captured, the zebra
unleashes a powerful
self-preservation response.
One kick from a zebra can break
a lion's jaw. They also possess a
'ducking' reflex that helps them
avoid being caught by a lasso.
Domesticated, cornered, trapped
or stuck is not an option ...

INDEPENDENT STRENGTH!

> Believe in yourself ... you are BRAVER than
> you believe, STRONGER than you seem,
> and SMARTER than you think.
>
> Author unknown

STEP UP – RESPONSIBLE YOU

I kicked off my school-girl panties and bobby socks to put on big-girl knickers and platform heels at age 15. You may recall the story from the DISRUPT section, about how I deliberately forged out a career as a hairdresser, knowing that would provide a springboard leap into a level of independence I was craving.

By 17, I had amassed a wooden chest (traditionally called a 'glory box') full of household items, mostly bought at sales or on lay-by payments from a meagre apprenticeship wage. I remember it took me six months to pay off two thick, queen-size blankets and a fluffy bed spread with a big striped tiger on it – grrroar! Perhaps it was the Helen Reddy influence: *'I am woman – hear me roar'*. Clearly this was prior to the $25 Kmart doona era.

Just weeks after turning 18, I moved into a two-bedroom flat on my own, on the opposite side of Toowoomba to my parents' home, with no phone connection (pre-mobile era). There was a phone box around the corner if I needed to call someone. Oh – the absolute bliss of independence. The start of a new chapter of life on my own terms.

A year later, having just completed my apprenticeship, I was promoted to Salon Manager in a busy salon of five staff (several of them older than me) and awarded a company car (first one ever provided by my employer, who owned a chain of salons at the time). On reflection, I am amazed and grateful that my employer saw leadership qualities in me at such an early age. Perhaps early signs of the FAVE 5 Formula; or at least these 3C's Influencer attributes ...

Confidence + Courage + Can-do attitude

Several months later, I ended a long-term relationship with my boyfriend, who I'd simply out-grown. His idea of the obligatory birthday and Christmas gift was useful stuff like cutlery sets, formal dinner sets, and stainless-steel cooking pots. Well, clearly that was not going to end well for an independent, budding feminist like me. As I mentioned in earlier chapters, I had no intention of being a kitchen-bitch; frankly, that urge has never surfaced in me. I was getting ready to branch out and explore the world in my 20s ... do some broader 'adulting', or so I thought.

Those early independent exploration years took me on a couple of under-30s bus tours; one to Northern Territory (Alice Springs, Darwin, Katherine Gorge), and another around Tasmania; and a 'get wrecked', rather risqué holiday on Great Keppel Island. Let's just say: what happened on 'Keppel' stayed on 'Keppel'. And that was it.

I got engaged at 20, married at 21, mother at 24. Shackled.

Why, Jilinda?

I hear you. I know ... I ask myself the same thing. Those disempowering, illogical fears I've already mentioned; clearly, I hadn't learned to smash them yet. I no doubt buckled to the pressure of the 'should' expectations of society; most of my colleagues and friends were getting married. All that, and my strict, god-fearing upbringing;

good girls don't sleep around or 'live in sin' with seasonal boyfriends. I was yet to discover the joy of *zigzagging*.

One thing that is very clear when I reflect on decisions I've made over the decades since: I have always treasured my independence. Guarded it. It became one of my 'must have' top values. I would not let anyone take that away from me. Not parents, not husbands, not babies, not opportunistic boyfriends, not crappy financial circumstances, not politically driven career-ending decisions; I know I will always make independent choices, while I'm mentally capable of doing so.

> **I was born an independent woman, and refuse to become dependent or be the victim of circumstances.**

Just to be upfront, I'm not anti-marriage (although I do prefer to use 'partner' over husband or wife labels), or against motherhood (as long as it's a choice, not an expectation), or joint mortgages and bank accounts (as long as there is trust and transparency), or communal independent living arrangements (I enjoy townhouse-complex, shared-community living). I'm all for those things, as long as the arrangements are fair and equal, and no party feels like they have lost their freedom, or have to give up their dreams, or feels manipulated or stuck – without choice. *Rock your own independent stripes.*

NAVIGATING THE MUMSY STUFF

Now, while I may have been charmed into marrying at a young age, talking me into motherhood required much stronger negotiation. You see, marriage hadn't reduced my individuality or independence. I still rocked my own style, had my career, my own bank account (read: spending money), my own car, and my own social life. My husband (of that era) didn't drink alcohol, so no need for a taxi after a night out with the girls. Having been a bachelor for many years, he knew how to wash clothes, iron them, and loved cooking. I saw no reason to disrupt that routine. *Winner. Winner. Chicken dinner.*

So, here's how the somewhat-older-husband-initiated *'let's have kids'* conversation took place. After a mild panic on my part – mostly about the thought of losing my independence, my entire 20s, and being stuck at home – I asked one of the most important questions of my life:

How are WE going to manage that, because I'm not giving up my career?

What I know now is the real driver of that question came from a deeper place than just the impact on my career goals: it was: *'I'm not giving up my independence'*.

The negotiated solution: he left a mind-numbing, repetitive manufacturing job of 20-plus years and went off to college to become a high school teacher. We had two kids in 20 months; one of each sex, so the use of my womb was over and done with in two short years. Soon after, we engaged a day-care Mum until the kids were school age, and then they all had the same out-of-home hours and holiday breaks. I took over on weekends, and did all the household organising, bill paying, and set the procedural boundaries, while running my own hairdressing business six days a week. As it turned out, I did mostly Mr Mum duties (finances, decision-making and discipline), while he did mostly Mrs Mum duties (cooking, washing and children chasing). Cleaning was another matter altogether; that incompatibility issue of their untidiness nearly drove me insane. But, for the most part, the arrangement suited both of us. We raised two children into level-headed, highly independent, intelligent, hard-working, non-needy, responsible adults. One minimalist, metrosexual neat freak; one slightly messy, spontaneous socialite. Both of them living authentic, successful lives, currently at opposite ends of the world. Both rocking their own stripes, their own way.

But back to that important 'WE' pre-parenting question; here's what I don't understand. If 30-plus years ago I'd figured out that one-sided parenting (read: women lumbered with all the child-raising responsibilities) was unfair and unacceptable, and refused to conform

221

to the norm, WHY are so many young women today seemingly not having the same family-planning conversation? Or the same expectations of equal, shared parenting? Perhaps they are, but their men are not taking on half the parenting responsibility? Or maybe it's because of the entrenched systems in society and workplaces that make equal parenting more difficult (read: inflexibility)?

My point is: it's not that hard to fix this. *Challenging – maybe. Impossible – no.*

Why is this important? Well, apart from a significant drop in freedom of choice and hours in the day to rock your own independent goals and aspirations (yes, I concede – motherhood may be one of them), a stalled career, reduced income or no individual earning capacity leads to Jill having a dull life and ends with much less financial security later; especially if Jill outlives Jack (which the stats show is significantly more likely than Jack outliving Jill), or Jack takes off with Julie. That's a huge and very real issue, with increasingly dire outcomes.

It's a concerning fact that single women over 55 are our fastest growing poverty sector in Australia. Learn from those women who have walked before you. We all need to be individually responsible and financially independent. The days of women marrying for economic security reasons over compatibility and love are long past – surely? A husband is NOT a financial security plan.

Here's the thing: build, treasure and guard your independence. Don't reduce it to please others or conform to stereotypical gender 'shoulding'. Discuss and agree on your parenting plan beforehand.

And it's never too late to speak up and say: *this isn't working for me.* Don't assume all the parenting responsibility. Don't put your own needs last. Do accept individual financial responsibility. And most importantly, don't give up on your dream goals.

> **'If you want to fly, you have to give up
> the shit that weighs you down.'**
>
> Toni Morrison

FORGET THE FAIRY TALES

There's a young man I mentored over several years; mainly career progression coaching, but like all self-development, every aspect of life impacts on opportunities, decisions and growth. This young man is level headed, kind, responsible and career-minded, with high levels of emotional intelligence. I really admire the maturity and depth of his thinking. However, the one thing he has struggled with is finding a partner who is equally all those things. He's gone through two significant relationship break-ups that he initiated because, in both cases, these young women (in their 20s) had not learned to be strong individuals in their own right. These decisions were in no way flippant or driven by commitment phobia; it was gut-wrenchingly hard for him to have to be 'the grown up' and make the tough call to end it, but deep down he came to realise they were not the type of life partner he wanted.

Why? This young man wants a partner who is independently responsible, emotionally stable, career minded, self-confident, financially responsible; not someone who shirks on rental payments, continually needs bailing out of credit card debt, or needs constant reassurance that they are 'pretty' or 'hot'. He doesn't want a woman who needs rescuing, or still relies on parents to prop them up. He wants an equal partner; a strong, capable woman who can stand in her own power, confidently and courageously rocking her own stripes. No, I'm not seeking enquiries on his behalf. But I am calling out to all the young women out there. Grow up – FFS! Drop the neediness. Don't be looking for a knight in shining armour to ride in on his white horse and rescue you. Drop the fairy-tale dreams, throw away the princess tutu, and pull on your big-girl panties. Get your shit together and take responsibility for your own life. Be an adult.

Harsh words – yes. I feel strongly about this because I know there are those who still play the precious princess on a pedestal game, and don't realise (or don't care) about the negative ramifications that has on the way society views and treats women. It just continues to feed the narrative that women are the weaker species. It makes it that much harder for all the rest of us strong-minded, independent women to be considered capable enough to stand on our own feet and be given equal opportunities. And it's such a 'yesteryear' mindset.

My point is: as we are teaching our men (especially next-gen young men) about the importance and mutual benefits of equal partnerships – of women having the same choices, the same opportunities, the same pay, and being treated equally all round – there will be increasingly fewer options for needy, precious princesses. Time's running out, girls. Step up to be a real woman. Grow your independence muscle.

Here's the thing: you are a complete person on your own. You don't need someone else to complete you ('*you complete me*' is a romanticised phrase I particularly dislike). The ideal partner is someone who complements your unique self, whose values are similar, who stands beside you (not propping you up), who encourages you to reach for your goals and be your full-arse version. A partner who, when you are with them, makes you feel energised and stronger (like a dynamic duo); not a relationship that sucks the life out of you, or you suck the life out of them (while draining their pockets). Equality means equal responsibility.

Step up. Be a strong individual. Be independent of mind, own your personal goals and take responsibility for your own life. Don't choose to live life at half-strength and expect others to top you up. Don't be one of those fragile, needy good girls or princesses wanting to be rescued by prince charming.

Invigorating independence is way more attractive than draining dependence.

HOW TO BECOME A STRONG, INDEPENDENT WOMAN

These tips may seem scary to some, I know. It takes confidence and courage for women to go out on their own and establish their independence, and many are held back by two of the biggest blockages:

fear of what others will think and *fear of failure.* By now you know what I think about those …

Learn how to successfully and happily live on your own

Living alone is the best way to learn WHO you are, what YOU want, what works for you, what doesn't, what motivates you, what simple routines make boring survival stuff like grocery shopping, cooking, washing and cleaning up so much easier. You become better at system-ising and scheduling all the little things that keep your life in order. *CEO of your life.*

I've had several significant periods of living on my own; early adult years, between partners, and periodically when my partner's study or work has involved living away from home for weeks at a time. What's interesting these days is that, even though my partner is like this 'fairy' who just miraculously does most of the mundane housework stuff before I even think about it (also known as Mr Routine), when he is away, my single-life routine kicks right back in. Like I just flick the independent woman switch back on, light up and relish my own time and space. I even remember to feed the dog.

Learn how to budget your money and plan your financial independence

By budget, I mean learning how to live within your means; not how to juggle multiple credit card payments. Work out what's important to you – your *'must have'* list and your *'nice if I can afford that too'* list. I know shopping for shoes, handbags, makeup and that new season dress can be fun, but are those things really necessary or your top three to five priority budget items? A good question to ask yourself is: what will that give me – short term, and longer term?

Oh, and if the part of the brain that loves figures and finance detail has never been lit up or is unlikely to burn brightly in you, engage a financial advisor (preferably an independent one – not a product sales person), and a good accountant. Find support agents who can digest the detail and spit it out into easily understood chunks. *Delegate detail. Know the necessities. Plan to progress. Own your money story.*

Rock Your Stripes

Moving into a flat on my own, at age 18 on third-year apprenticeship wages, taught me how to budget for weekly and monthly expenses. Rent, groceries, power, fuel for car; then I'd juggle what was left over on occasional fashion items. As a budding individualist, I bought cheap clothing items and cleverly modified them into 'my own style'. During those frugal early days, I established some budget priorities that I still use today: stick to an essentials-only weekly grocery list (no extras, no waste), invest in my-style clothing (not seasonal fashion flipping), and keep a separate stash account for holidays, spontaneous adventures or freedom dashes. *Freedom is one of my top three 'must have' values.*

Learn how to holiday and go to a restaurant or a movie on your own

Start by going to a movie or show on your own; that's easy once you're there, blending with other individuals doing the same thing. Take your Kindle or book or favourite magazine to a restaurant; lots of people eat out alone. Learning to do stuff on your own will help you to stop caring what others think. Don't just sit there mindlessly scrolling on your phone; drink in the beauty of your surroundings. Enjoy your alone time. *Rock your own space.*

Interestingly, I built confidence to go out on my own and do my own thing in my late 20s and throughout my 30s – yes, during my first marriage. Gosh, when I reflect back further, it started on our honeymoon. He played golf every other day, I amused myself by shopping and going to the beach. In later years, what became obvious was I needed social stimulation, he didn't. I travelled away to conferences, enjoyed music gigs, and loved taking off to the beach by myself with a good book. Yes, it was a survival tactic. After that chapter ended, I moved to the tropical north, and spent many long weekends exploring the local beachside holiday spots on my own. By far my most memorable holiday was four weeks in Italy; yes, on my own. I even drove a hire car around Tuscany and Umbria, exploring the beautiful countryside villages for two weeks, on my own. Stopping wherever I wanted, eating in small cafes, trying out a little Italian language. *Would do it again in a heartbeat.*

Learn how to break the rules, or at least question them

Most women I know seem to have been raised with a set of rules or guidelines about what is expected of them. How to behave (read: good-girl rules). How to dress (read: understated, not too showy). How to speak (read: submissively, not assertively; no or limited swearing). How to mother (rather than how to co-parent). Forget all that. I smashed those crappy restrictive rules out of the park years ago. As long as you are not breaking any laws of the land or deliberately hurting others, dive in to life fully and work it out as you go. Just do it YOUR way.

You have probably seen several variations of the inspirational quote: *'All the magic happens outside your comfort zone'*. Well, my independent-focused version pushes that notion out a tad further:

All your independent growth happens outside other people's comfort zone.

STAND OUT – ROLE MODEL YOU

I admire author Brené Brown's research work and her challenging yet inspiring personal development books. I have gained gold nuggets of wisdom from every one of her books, and I consider her to be an influential personal mentor. Not because we have any official arrangement; it's just that her words of wisdom and advice in each new book seem to always come at a time when I need to receive that exact message.

Her book *Braving the Wilderness* was released in 2017, just after my partner and I had been uprooted by a shocking shit storm (that unexpected, malicious zag incident I mentioned in the REACH section). Her uplifting messages of standing in your own power could not have been more on-point or beneficial. The core theme of the book is the pursuit of belonging; a basic human desire to belong or be part of something bigger, and the realisation that true belonging is NOT about fitting in with a partner, or group, or being part of an organisation or community; it's about belonging to yourself so fully that you are willing to brave the wilderness on your own. Willing to drop the self-preservation security blanket and choose courage and conviction over comfort. *Tough gig.*

Courageously step into the arena ...

Why would you want to do that? Because true belonging to your own values and beliefs is where courageous strength is derived; the courage to embrace your authentic self and seriously guard your independent ownership of that. Yes, that requires us to be vulnerable, get uncomfortable, and sometimes walk into the arena alone to stand up for what you believe in, rather than selling out because that's easier or safer. *Integrity matters.*

Both my partner and I know what that's like. We're strong individuals, with independent thinking and highly valued integrity; we won't conform to dodgy practices, won't put up with bullshit leadership, and are not afraid to challenge the unacceptable status quo. We can also get pushback, and sometimes the end result is not favourable towards us; but each time that happens, we become stronger for the experience and even more courageous to stand out from the rest. More determined to speak up about the need for REAL leadership. Leadership is not about turning a blind eye and quietly conforming to a crap status quo; it is about speaking truth to your independent convictions. It's about being true to YOU first, then not being afraid to show your full-arse version; not some cowardly, diluted version.

> True belonging requires you to
> BE who you are, not CHANGE
> who you are to suit others.

WOMEN IN THE LEADERSHIP ARENA

While writing this book, I was elated to see a growing number of courageous elected women leaders distancing themselves from conservative political parties with entrenched misogynistic and bullying practices, moving to the cross benches to stand alone in the arena as independent representatives. These women are strong, intelligent, confident communicators, passionate about making a difference for the greater good of our Australian society, in line with their own values (firstly), and the values of those they represent. Woo-hoo! I have been spruiking for years that our country would be better led by a diverse team of independents (including more women), rather than what we have had for way too many decades: teams of political-party puppets.

I have met many strong-minded, self-aware alpha females who would be great political leaders and community representatives, but who will not put their hands up for pre-selection of any political party. Frankly, they don't want to get down and dirty in that pit. They don't want to play those dog-eat-dog political games. They want to LEAD, to engage, inspire, encourage and influence positive change. *It's time for more women-wise independents!*

Lead like a WOMAN, not a manette.

We've all seen or met those strong, confident, independent women. They are the ones who command a presence in a room, noticeably assertive and perhaps a little domineering. Sometimes referred to as alpha women, they can also be described as bossy, opinionated, and perceived as manipulative or condescending. That may be true in some cases; not everyone uses their strong traits in a positive way.

An alpha woman may have a strong personality, but that alone doesn't make her a good role model or a great leader. I know a few who are certainly not leadership material; not by their observable behaviours (narcissistic and power-driven). As an avid people watcher, I've been curiously observing and researching women who create circles of influence and inspire positive action. Women like Oprah Winfrey, Sheryl Sandberg, Melinda Gates, and in Australia, Ita Buttrose,

Rock Your Stripes

Rosie Batty, Jane Caro, Kate Jenkins, Sam Mostyn, and yes – elected representatives like Julia Gillard, Penny Wong, Linda Burney and Larissa Waters; not specifically for their political persuasions, but for their passionate contribution to causes they personally care about. If you're not familiar with some of these women, I encourage you to be curious, explore more broadly than your own backyard.

Through my research, I've collated a list of traits and attributes I believe independent alpha women leaders possess. I use the term 'leader' as one who influences and inspires, not in terms of a position held. This list is not everything, but it does provide a substantial starting base; one that I personally strive to live up to every day. You might like to use it as a checklist, to see which ones you could build more independent muscle in.

Stand out attributes of an independent alpha woman:
- ☐ She is authentic – genuine to her core.
- ☐ She invests in herself.
- ☐ She is optimistic.
- ☐ She is confident.
- ☐ She cultivates a life she enjoys.
- ☐ She is courageous.
- ☐ She stands up for her values and beliefs.
- ☐ She knows her strengths and builds on those.
- ☐ She embraces vulnerability as a strength, not a weakness.
- ☐ She is pro-woman and pro-equality.
- ☐ She is capable and comfortable to be alone.
- ☐ She takes responsibility for her own decisions.
- ☐ She desires a partner, not a saviour.
- ☐ She makes her move.
- ☐ She creates her reality.
- ☐ She doesn't hold back or push herself down.
- ☐ She doesn't compete for attention.

- ☐ She knows her purpose and intentional goals.
- ☐ She dares to go for it – wholeheartedly.
- ☐ She uses her strong, powerful voice to influence and inspire.
- ☐ She uses her power for the greater good.
- ☐ She seeks support and encourages people to come together.
- ☐ She inspires, coaches and mentors others.
- ☐ She calls out people's bad behaviour.
- ☐ She knows when to walk away.
- ☐ She never gives up on her purpose.
- ☐ She is resilient.
- ☐ She knows the life she lives may be intimidating to some, but she lives it anyway.

SPEAKING UP – RESILIENT, INDEPENDENT YOU

In this section, I want you to take the time to sit and reflect; to build resilience around your independence muscle. Believe me, if you are going to embrace your wholehearted, authentic self and showcase your full-arse version to the world, you are going to need it.

Listen to your internal voice

Before you go rushing out and speaking up about your newly found, independent alpha-woman-inspired identity, take the time to find and listen to your internal voice. Tell the negative voices to shut up. Call them out. Ask: *really?* Smash any rising fears. You don't need to listen to them. It's important to clear the way for the real independent you to rise up and speak out; but not until you know who that unique animal is and you are ready to unleash it.

Why is it important to keep reflecting back on your core purpose and keep strengthening your resolve; your independence muscle? Because there will be times when your independence is challenged to the core; and your core needs to be a well of rich, resourceful rejuvenation, not a murky, dark hole.

Independence reality check

As a fiercely independent, proud alpha woman, with independence being one of my top five values and a 'must have' driver of many decisions I've made since my mid-teens, you would think that this chapter was the easiest to write out of all the FAVE 5 Formula chapters. Actually, no; it was the most difficult. I procrastinated, sat with it for a while, and had to work out what was causing the blockage to write about independence, and then work through that.

Here's what I discovered: there have been two really significant times in my life when I have plummeted down to a point of having to seriously question my inner values and the strength of my conviction to those. Both times, my core need for independence was challenged. The first time was like a sudden jolt, when I had serious shoulder surgery that ended my hairdressing career and prevented me from working and moving forward with my 'next chapter' plans, during the nine-month recovery. The second time was more like a slow, silent dissention that I didn't recognise until I hit the bottom, when I had around 60% of this book writing completed. Both times evoked two big energy suckers for me: not earning my own income, and being 'stuck' at home.

Having to rely on the financial support of a partner flies in the face of my core need for independence. We met as two strong individuals, melding into a dynamic duo – neither of us needing the other, but wanting to be together as a couple of likeminded equals. Gradually I became aware of just how far left I'd allowed the pendulum to swing from the equal centre. I felt a level of shame and vulnerability like never before. *Unequal, underperforming, undeserving.*

Granted, the book writing took longer than I'd anticipated, so what I thought would be a few short months focused on writing with no client work distraction ended up being six months of virtually no income.

During the same time, shutting myself off from all unnecessary social distractions and sitting in my home office day after day, week after week slowly became my self-imposed prison. There were days when I didn't get out of my night T-shirt, wash my face, do my hair, or step outside for some fresh air, or even a walk. *Unbalanced, unfulfilled, un-Jilinda.*

Yes, I've learned that's what many writers do. Lock themselves away in an attic and insanely do nothing but write, finally emerging looking like a bedraggled beast. *An extrovert's hell.*

So, the sticking point in writing about the importance of maintaining one's independence became obvious: incongruence. I wasn't walking my talk, which is another of my core values: authenticity. I was a 'kept woman', something I never, ever wanted to be. Something that had crept up on me and took me down a spiral of guilt, despair and panic. That was one huge blockage.

Now, like all blockages, the first thing you have to do is find out the core cause. Tick that box. Nailed that one the moment I recognised and named it. The second thing is to sit with it, rumble around a bit and question why I'm choosing to respond in that way. Because we each choose how to feel, think and respond to situations, right? The third thing is to find another way around that; choose a different response. Clearly my mindset at the time was not working for me. It needed a radical reframe, from a blockage issue to a determined driver.

And that's what I did. I reduced the negative focus on how it felt at that moment in time, except for the panic bit; I used that to ignite a stronger drive in me to finish writing the damn book and smash that 2018 goal. I heaped more emphasis on how good it will feel when the writing phase is completed, and I can get back to being a kick-arse independent working woman – resiliently rocking my own stripes.

That said, I'm very grateful for the support of my understanding partner who endured this first-time writer's roller-coaster journey with me. He fully understands my need for independence. Actually, he loves it; he values his independence too. The beautiful thing about equal partnerships is we don't need each other; we choose to be together and support each other's journey. *Thankful beyond words.*

Here's the thing: discover and build on the core needs and strengths that will keep your independence muscle strong and resilient enough to cope with the challenges. Independence doesn't mean you have to go it alone; it means you are capable of doing that and comfortable in your own skin. Likewise, what I've learned through personal experience is that accepting someone's help or support doesn't have to make you any less independent. You set the boundaries. You choose how

Be INDEPENDENT

you respond to that. Be grateful that others believe in your journey and want to see you rock your own stripes. And, remember, it's a journey. Growing and evolving is life-long work. None of us are 'there' yet.

There has never been a better time for strong, independent women to support other women's journeys to independence.

Do you need an independence reality check?

If all this talk about independence has rocked you, or triggered a sense of vulnerability, and you feel the need to build greater personal resilience and strengthen your independence muscle, you may find the following exercise a useful starting point.

Building your independent resilience exercise

Your top five values are:

_____

_____

_____

_____

_____

What are three things that empower and strengthen your independence?

_____

_____

_____

Do more of these!

What are three things that suck your energy and deplete your independence?

_____

_____

_____

Get rid of those or reframe your response to them.

What is your internal negative voice saying?

_____

_____

_____

_____

Question it: REALLY? Smash its credibility or reframe to something more realistic.

Review the *'Stand out attributes of an independent alpha woman'* list in this chapter. Write down three to five things you need to build more independence muscle in. Think about how you could do that.

_____
_____
_____
_____
_____

Who would benefit from you sharing this section with them?

_____
_____
_____
_____
_____

Rock your
stripes

Here's to
**STRONG, INDEPENDENT
WOMEN .**
May we
KNOW THEM.
May we
BE THEM.
May we
RAISE THEM.
May we
SUPPORT THEM.
May we
LIFT THEM HIGHER.

CHAPTER 8

BE AN
INITIATOR

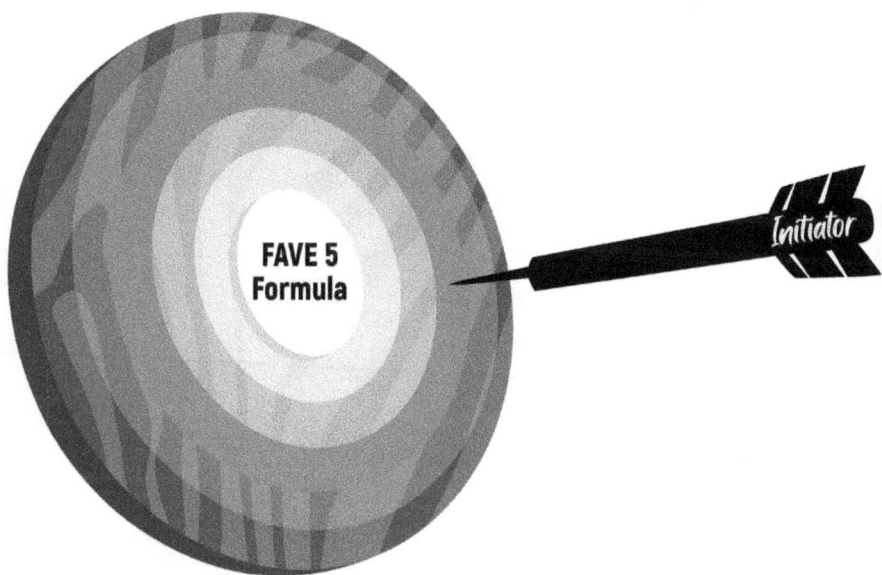

FAVE 5
Formula

Initiator

ZEBRAS ARE
ALERT, AGILE AND ADAPTIVE ...

Constantly watchful of
their environment,
they know that
awareness, agility
and adaptability
are the only way to
survive and flourish
in a land full of predators
and harsh seasonal changes.
Resourceful and ready to
quickly change paths,
the zebra knows that there are
always other choices to make,
other chances to take,
many changes to initiate,
and opportunities to
lead the way forward ...

INITIATE CHANGE!

'You can't spell

CHA<small>lle</small>NGE

without

CHANGE ...

**If you're going to rise to the challenge,
you have to be willing to change.'**

Author unknown

STEP UP – CHOICES, CHANCES, CHANGES

Unless you've just opened the book at this section (totally okay to do that), you've probably read this many times already: I've built a personal reputation as a Change Champion. Yes, I freakin' love change; initiating it, creating it, driving it, leading it and influencing others to make positive changes. In essence, encouraging people like you to make changes is an intentional theme throughout this book for good reason. *Stuck is not an option.*

So, in this 'how to' part of the book, I'm not going to bore you by continually banging on about why it's important to be open to change, embrace change, continually explore choices, and jump on those new chances as they come along. I'm quite sure I've done enough of that in previous chapters. Instead, I'm going to start with the premise that you already know there are probably some things in your life that need to change. Little things that need tweaking, medium-size things you may be already working through, and possibly some big ones you've been avoiding. Right? Let's take that as a given. *Initiating change is now required.*

242

As I mentioned in the earlier EVOLVE chapter, we need to have a heightened awareness about the stuff that is rapidly changing around us (like technology and career options), potentially requiring us to make quick decisions and to be more agile and willing to leap onto the exciting zigzag path I keep promoting. Alternatively, some change happens at snail pace: *W A Y   T O O   S L O W!* That may be frustrating for you if you are waiting for others to change. Or perhaps you're the one who is slow to make decisions and initiate the actions required. Be aware how frustrating that may be for others. *Like me!*

Do you have lots of ideas, lots of 'gonna do', 'maybe later' talk, but little action? It's a common problem.

Let's change that …

Here are THREE key things I know for sure … from years of experience in initiating change:

- Changes that don't work out well are most likely because the change happened too slowly or too late. Changes that are proactive or occur in rapid response to shifting circumstances are more likely to succeed. *Agility matters.*

- People overcomplicate decision-making (often with all the 'what if', fear-based scenarios). *Decisive process equals desired progress.*

- Women often don't ask or are reluctant to negotiate for desired changes (especially around shared responsibilities, flexible working hours, equal opportunities and equal or fair pay). *Speak up.*

I'm on a mission to change all that. Come on board the change train …

AGILITY MATTERS

'The pessimist complains about the wind. The optimist expects it to change. The leader adjusts the sails.'

John Maxwell

Personal agility is increasingly becoming an important self-management skill to maintain currency and relevance, to keep growing and successfully reach your goals, and to build your resilience muscle that enhances your survival in a rapidly changing world. The global pandemic (from 2020) was a catalyst for rapid change in many of our lives; somewhat forced, somewhat embraced. I hope one positive outcome from all that disruption was the growth of your personal agility strength.

In fact, agility skills are so important that it's included as a key EQ self-management competence in the globally renowned *Social + Emotional Intelligence Profiling* (SEIP) framework I use with my coaching clients, is a core module in our leadership programs, and one of my most popular keynote topics.

The *Institute of Social + Emotional Intelligence* describes personal agility as:

> ' ... the ability to anticipate and respond rapidly to changing conditions; acknowledging we live in an era of global change, agility means taking a proactive approach to change, anticipating challenges and opportunities, a willingness to rethink past assumptions, and readily, willingly, rapidly and effectively adapting to change.'

Yes, all that is easier said than done, I know. It's natural for humans to experience an initial pushback response to changes, especially the ones we were not expecting. Our thought process takes us along neural pathways in our brain, often straight to the amygdala – the part that immediately senses a threat and initiates the fight, flight or freeze response. After the initial shock to unforeseen change subsides and panic responses settle, we then traverse through these phases of the change process:

Denial > Resistance > Exploration > Acceptance > Commitment to the change

The agility variance is in how long it takes to get to the commitment outcome. How long do you stay in denial or resistance mode? How long do you procrastinate by half-heartedly exploring options but not deciding or committing to any of them? Does that sound like you? Or someone you know?

HOW AGILE ARE YOU?

Action/Behaviour	1 Never	2 Almost never	3 Some-times	4 Almost always	5 Always
1. I find it easy to operate outside of my comfort zone.					
2. I'm okay when things are 'up in the air'.					
3. I readily embrace new ideas and concepts.					
4. I quickly make decisions and solve problems, even when I don't have all the information.					
5. I don't go around cursing change or let change put me in a bad mood.					
6. I like to learn new skills and new ways of doing things.					
7. I anticipate change and plan my response in readiness.					
8. I tend to be an early adopter (of technology, new ideas, and new procedures).					
9. I am comfortable working with people who have different thinking and problem-solving approaches.					
10. I happily rearrange my schedule to fit with changed priorities and new deadlines.					

Total score _____

Obviously, total scores of 40 to 50 show your personal agility is high, and at the opposite end of the scale, scores of 10 to 15 indicate you need to do some serious work on this. But don't get too hung up on the scores. Simply note which behaviours need the most work, and then dig deeper to find the cause and cure.

People with low agility generally have a strong need to control outcomes (certainty), and a desire for things to be comfortable and easy (security blanket). REMEMBER: There is no such thing as certainty and security. Nobody can guarantee that. The sooner you step out of that fairy-tale world, the more resilient you will be.

Here's a few development tips:

- Acknowledge that there are some things you have no control over, and that's okay.

- Identify what fears are holding you back and explore where they originated. Sometimes we run old stories or unrelated cases in our head that are not relevant to current circumstances.

- Separate fact (actuals) from fiction (assumptions). Differentiate between what is actually happening and what you think or fear will happen.

- Seek out people who can provide you with support during transitions.

- Ask questions to gain more clarity and understanding about the need for change.

- Be willing to try out new ideas, even in 10% increments.

- Better still, proactively initiate the changes YOU want to see.

RESILIENCE MATTERS

Agility + Realism + Self-care = RESILIENCE

Let's talk about plans, goals, schedules and task lists. Whether in your business, or job, or personal life, the general advice from coaches and mentors is to plan your year out into goals, prioritise them, develop schedules and strict timelines, and create monthly, weekly and daily task lists. While I agree with the benefits of having a clear vision and direction, and goals to work towards, those long, never-ending task lists just do my head in.

Years ago, I learned (the hard way) that filling a diary up with daily back-to-back tasks and meetings is a recipe for constant disappointment and overwhelm disaster. Other unplanned stuff always comes up that requires flexible thinking and agile action to address something more urgent than what's on my list. Since then, I've adopted a more feasible approach of simply choosing two or three things each day that I'm realistically going to achieve, leaving enough breathing space for whatever else pops up needing immediate, quick action. Oh, and I've learned to say 'NO' – without the guilt. *Winner.*

Generally, I plan my day using a '4D' decision framework:

- **DO IT** – now, if it's urgent and important – or schedule it by priority level (today > this week > this month).

- **DEFER IT** – for later, if it's important but not urgent – schedule by importance into a realistic timeframe.

- **DELEGATE IT** – to someone else – YEAH! Seriously question whether YOU need to do this, now or *ever*.

- **DELETE IT** – be ruthless. Is it urgent, important, interesting, educational or enjoyable AND will it assist you to reach your goals? If not – dump it.

Now, while I'm aware 'bucket lists' of personal goals are an increasingly popular thing to create, I don't have one of those either. Well, not a written down checklist, as such. You know – that bucket list of 'must do before you die' things to achieve and cross off in the race towards an undefined finish line. That's way too planned, prescriptive, and procedural (read: inflexible) for me. I'd rather keep scanning the changing horizons for the next opportunities with an open mindset. Life changes quickly, as do our circumstances and priorities. Besides, who needs the added pressure of staring at yet another list of unmet (and often unrealistic) expectations. That's a recipe for disappointment and regret. I've found life is less stressful when you aim to enjoy each day, acknowledge the one to three small goals completed, or chunks achieved towards bigger goals, and stay agile; ready to shift gears, jump into action on new opportunities and challenges. Say YES, and work out 'how' along the way. *Spontaneity rocks.*

Of course, to remain capable of doing that, I've learned a few other things along the way about agility and resilience. Self-care is absolutely crucial; physical and mental wellbeing. Having a fit, strong body; a healthy, enquiring mind; and a centred, fulfilled soul – these things have been important priorities of mine for decades. Increasingly so in recent years.

Specifically; I've learned that I need to:

- start my day with a morning self-care ritual – greet the sunrise, gentle beach stroll, meditation, journalling, setting intentions.

- keep exercising my muscle groups (walk, swim and stretch daily, and regular gym workouts)

- eat nutritionally balanced, healthy food (smaller portions, more regularly).

With a busy mind that's always full of creative thoughts, I give my brain a regular declutter by strolling the beach, incorporating a gentle yoga and meditation routine (bare feet grounded under the palm trees, in my courtyard tropical sanctuary). That works for me. It's my way of staying agile and ready to respond to whatever life throws my way. Unsurprisingly, beachside living has also become one of my 'must haves'.

Again, I'm not perfect and sometimes that healthy balance is disrupted. Rigid routines are not my forte, so I mix it up a bit, depending on work and social commitments, but that's what agility is all about. Being able to stay flexible, in mind and body. Being able to rise up from the knocks, and rejuvenate your soul with the things that strengthen your resilience. *Self-awareness is key.*

Here's the thing: becoming your full-arse version does NOT mean trying to do everything or cramming as much as you can into each day. It doesn't mean crossing off more things from your lists than others, like you are in a race against time. You won't achieve your higher purpose, aspirational goals and drive desired change if you run out of oxygen or burn out. Self-care is important to fuel your energy, to enable you to be more agile, and to ensure you have the resilience to keep reaching, growing and evolving. Put your own oxygen mask on first. Be an initiator of positive change in your own life.

Oh, and learn to say 'NO'.

> **'*No* is a complete sentence. It does not require justification or explanation.'**
>
> Author unknown

DECISIONS, DECISIONS

Through my coaching practice and facilitating corporate leadership programs, I have met many people who agonise over making decisions. They really struggle to make the final call, sign the approval, or choose between several options. I've seen this in all levels of government, recruitment selection panels, personal career decisions, and even simple everyday transactions and mundane approvals.

I understand the need for in-depth consideration and caution when making major life-changing decisions, but those things are not everyday occurrences. It is frustrating when people (particularly those in lead roles) waste so much time and energy over-analysing, over-contemplating and over-complicating what, in reality, is a straightforward decision: yes or no. This one or that one. It meets essential criteria or it doesn't.

Generally, the underlining cause is *fear of failure* (fear of making a mistake), which drives a self-protecting need for certainty and accuracy, and causes a whole lot of meticulous box-ticking before deciding. When we dig a bit deeper, the root cause is often lack of confidence in their abilities and trust in their own gut instincts.

My point here is: don't be like that. If you want to be a game-changing woman, you are going to need to make game-changing decisions before the game is over. *Competently, confidently and courageously.*

What do YOU need to know to be confidently ready to make a game-changing decision? To review ALL the options, read ALL the detail, do LOTS of research? To collect LOTS of recommendations and MANY opinions from others? To trial VARIOUS options over SEVERAL months, and rate the 'best of the bunch' as the winner?

Here's the thing: great change leaders, dynamic people managers, and successful people in general know how to make quick, decisive decisions. HOW? They are clear on their values and intent, their 'non-negotiables', their bonus point 'desirables', and the minimum number of ticked boxes that will result in a YES decision. By minimum number, I mean they either have a small number of boxes to tick (ideally three to five), or they only need to tick their top three to five boxes in a longer checklist that some risk-averse analyser developed to seemingly overcomplicate the process. *Oops, my public sector experience is showing.*

I developed a succinct approach many years ago when hunting for an investment property as a single, newly divorced woman, during a fast and frantic favourable buyers' market. I learned to be decisive and pounce, or miss out. Because many open houses were listed at the same time, I developed this template so I could tell at one glance if a place had the 'must have' essentials. If not, I walked away immediately (two-minute turnaround) and was off to the next option. If deciding between two houses that had the essential elements, I'd then compare the 'nice if it also had' – the bonus list. This worked so well, I have since used it for all types of decisions, from furniture, to cars, to job options, to fashion purchases … yes, even for choosing a life partner.

NOTE: Be concise … generally your MUST HAVE list will be short (three to five essentials – no more than seven), to the point, and only include those things that, if missing, will result in a definite NO. The NICE TO HAVE list may be longer and include any extra things that add more weight to making a confident YES decision. They are variables, not essentials, and may be prioritised or rated by importance; for example, *five must haves + top five desirables = a confident YES.*

A TEMPLATE FOR WEIGHING THINGS UP

MUST HAVE ... ✔	NICE if it also has ... ✔
✓ Essential needs – links to your values, beliefs, intent and purpose in making this decision ✓ Non-negotiables ✓ Critical elements ✓ Must-have items ... or it's a NO	✓ Desirable points ✓ Nice if it had these additional bonuses ✓ Adds more weight to a YES vote ✓ Provides some quick comparison with alternative options

INTUITION MATTERS

There's one other important factor I need to mention when it comes to making decisions, especially when initiating change: intuition. We all have a sense of intuition at some level. Think about those times when you got 'a strong feeling' about a situation, or a person you met, or a decision you were about to make. Did you listen to it, and explore why you felt that? Or did you dismiss it and go looking for facts to prove it wrong or eliminate it as a 'nonsense' over-reaction?

Over many years of questioning my gut-feel about things, I have learned to absolutely trust it. Honestly, almost every time a major decision I made didn't work out, my intuition (voice from deep within my gut) was screaming at me, and I chose to ignore it. One of those was walking down the aisle to be married at 21. It could have so easily been a 'runaway bride' incident (like the famous movie starring Julia Roberts). I initially ignored my inner turmoil as just nerves, then my head told my gut it was too late to change my mind, and my heart said: *you've got this. You'll be okay, no matter the outcome. You'll always have choices.*

More recently, my intuition was again spot on in sending out alarm signals. I had a strong gut feel that my partner was in an unsafe working environment, and that several others in powerful positions felt threatened by his leadership strengths and the success of his program outcomes. Specifically, the behaviour I observed from the CEO was far from normal. In fact, he displayed quite disturbing psychopathic, anti-social tendencies, with a noticeable disregard for the rights of others, a lack of empathy or consciousness of his impact on others, some quite reckless decision-making, and then deceitful coverups. While we both had growing concern about the situation, my partner's approach was to downplay it and keep working around it – in his words: *'take the higher moral ground and rise above'*. But my gut told me things would only get worse, as psychopaths in lead roles who feel cornered (or 'found out') delight in seeing others squirm and reduced to insignificance (or forced to leave).

My gut was right. Ignoring it resulted in the CEO turning his destructive dial up even further, inflicting a malicious and vexatious attack on the thing we value most – our integrity. This forced us out of the small community where we were both making a significant positive impact at the time.

My point is: intuition is a strong and valuable force that, if accessed and understood, can provide a clear and accurate guidance system to assist you in making decisions that are right for you, and prepare you for inevitable, even unexpected change – change that your intuition often already knows about.

Here's the thing: when it comes to decision-making, and your essential 'must-have' boxes are ticked, together with a couple of bonus desirable points, and you are ready to pounce – sit with it for a moment. Check in on how congruent the option is with your values. Take a broader glance around the surrounding environment, the people, and anything else you immediately notice from a visual perspective that may impact the successful outcome of that decision. How does it feel, deep down? What is your gut-feel telling you? What I've discovered every time I do that is my gut already knows the answer; like having that extra sense – the centre of all knowing.

Truly successful decision-making relies on a balance of knowledge, experience and intuition.

Note: Intuition is a huge subject that I can only comment on from my own personal experiences and those shared by my coaching clients. If you want to go deeper and understand how to access and make better use of your intuition, I highly recommend reading Australian author and intuition guru Craigh Wilson's book *Intuitive*.

STAND OUT – KNOWLEDGE + CREATIVE THINKING

Initiate your knowledge growth

Accredited in a range of human behaviour analysis tools which I regularly use to identify behaviour preferences in coaching clients, I know that one of my top three motivators is *theoretical*, which means I have a strong passion to search for knowledge, discover, analyse, and make sense of the world we live in. In short: I constantly need to know and understand the WHY, WHAT and HOW of lots of interesting stuff, so I continue to become WHO I am meant to be. *A wise, whacky, full-arse woman with lots of stripes to rock.*

Knowledge provides the clarity and personal power to make better, more informed decisions and initiate positive change. So, I read lots of books and articles and continually search for more inspiration. I value knowledge. It is one of the best ways to stand out from the rest. I don't mean that in an elitist way, but in a way that showcases real credibility in a world full of fakeness and ra-ra marketing spiels.

Consider the importance you place on knowledge ...

Knowledge is IMPORTANT ...

- **Education:** to seek knowledge, to learn, to expand content – technical and theoretical understanding (school, TAFE, workshops, courses, uni).

- **Meritorious recruitment:** top-rated selection criteria: '*High-level knowledge of ...*', '*Demonstrated good comprehension of [content or technical skill] ...*', '*Ability to quickly gain knowledge of ...*'

- **Continual learning:** expanded knowledge through practical experience, exploring new ways, challenging processes, researching and innovation.

Knowledge is VALUED …

- **By others:** it's an attractive 'must have' for some relationships, most employment, society acceptance in general, credibility levels, and global competitiveness.

- **By YOU:** a core motivator or driver, feeding an internal thirst for knowing *'why it is so'* … *'the evolution of stuff'* … *'the purpose'* … to explore *'what's next'*.

- **Are YOU:** an avid reader, documentary watcher, researcher, questioner, creator?

Knowledge is POWER …

- **Personal power:** knowing stuff equals confidence, self-worth, personal value and achievement, and supports goals and aspirations.

- **Advantage over others:** knowing more than others equals competitiveness on credibility, respect, and rewards like meritorious promotions.

- **Power over situations:** identifying and anticipating potential answers or solutions to issues; wisdom; clarity; decisiveness; control; vision; thought-leadership; and inspiration to others.

Here's the thing: knowledge makes decision-making easier and provides valuable credibility. If you are going to initiate change and inspire others to get on board with your creative ideas, you need to know why, what, how, and where to jump next. In this age of so much readily available information, ignorance is a poor choice.

> *Passion and motivation alone are not enough. If you take a passionate idiot and you motivate him, you now have a passionately motivated idiot.*

Creative thinking

Your ideas matter. Your creativity is the most valuable resource you have when it comes to initiating change. Creativity improves your life. It increases your capabilities. You can't use up your creativity; the more you use, the more you have. Sadly, too often it is smothered rather than nurtured. It is buried and under-utilised. It is an undervalued intelligence. *Unlock your creative potential.*

Creativity is intelligence (IQ) having fun. People admire intelligence, and they are attracted to fun, so the combination is awesome! People (and employers) are drawn to creative people.

Creativity helps you learn more. It is the joyful play of NOT knowing it all, NOT having all the answers. It is seeing problems as opportunities to explore options. Those who actively seek new ideas will always learn more.

Creative thinking challenges the status quo. Actually, the status quo and creativity are incompatible. Creativity and innovation walk hand in hand.

What areas in your life need a boost of creative thinking?

Here's five ways to discover the creativity within you …

1. Remove the creativity killers
Which of the following phrases do you hear often … or say … or think?

☐ *I'm not a creative person.*

☐ *Don't ask questions.*

☐ *Don't be different.*

☐ *Follow the rules … stick to policy.*

☐ *This is the way we do it around here.*

☐ *We've/I've always done it this way.*

☐ *We've/I've tried something like that before.*

- ☐ *We/I can't risk making a mistake.*

- ☐ *We/I don't have time to try something new.*

- ☐ *Yes, but ...*

2. Ask the right questions

Wrong questions shut down the process of creative thinking, directing you down the same old path. To stimulate creative thinking, ask:

- ■ *Why must it be done THIS way?*

- ■ *What is the root problem?*

- ■ *Why is it important? ... What is its purpose?*

- ■ *What would happen if we/I don't do it this way?*

3. Develop a creative environment

Negative environments kill millions of great ideas every day. Give your creative thinking space a makeover. Give yourself permission to explore, innovate, create ... fail, and learn from it.

4. Spend time with other creative people

Creativity is contagious. When was the last time you participated in a good brainstorming session, where one person throws out an idea and others keep adding to it, taking it to a whole new level?

5. Get out of your box

Creative thinkers know that they must regularly break out of the box that contains their own history, habits and personal limitations. Many limitations that hinder us are self-imposed. Travel to new places, change your routines, and read about new topics.

SPEAK UP – BE THE CHANGE

When it comes to asking for a fairer or more favourable outcome (at home and at work), we don't do it enough, and when we do, the outcomes are often undesirable or not worth the repercussions. We often end up settling for less.

Ask great questions – negotiate

I'm going to dive right in and say it: women have a serious negotiating deficit. This is driven in part by other chronic genetic conditions: the 'giving' disorder and the 'give-in' disorder. If these disorders are prevalent, our capacity to negotiate is seriously reduced. *Smash those disorders.*

We must get more skilful at this, especially when it comes to salary negotiations.

Harvard Business Review 2018 research suggests that 20% of women never negotiate their pay level on commencement of a new job. They've calculated that women graduates who don't negotiate their starting salary package will earn on average $7,000 less in the first year than those who do (predominately male graduates), and stand to lose between $650,000 and $1 million over the course of a 45-year career. Wow! That's a very compelling reason to start asking questions and hone your negotiation skills. But women tend to view the negotiation as an uncomfortable chore, whereas men play it like a game.

Negotiation is a tricky business for women. Here's why …

Regular studies and data updates on the gender pay gap issue, together with stories shared within our ElevateHER Australia communities and in panels and presentations at women's conferences, reveal that men and women face quite different outcomes when they enter salary negotiations. Women who choose to negotiate are commonly perceived as too pushy, selfish or overly ambitious, and often face resistance, but men can negotiate aggressively without any fear of repercussions.

Sheryl Sandberg – founder of the Lean In global movement – put it this way:

'If you are negotiating for a raise and you are a man, you can walk in and say: "I deserve this." That will not backfire on you. We know the data says it will backfire on a woman.'

Why is that?

Well, it starts with the entrenched social stereotypes, what society expects of women and men, and how that governs certain assumed behaviour. Men are thought to have more agentic traits: they are expected to be confident individuals, independent, assertive and competent. Boys are taught to be more aggressive and take on a warrior stance. Women are taught to be more communal in their approach; they are expected to be nurturing and relationship focused, friendly, kind, giving, unselfish and expressive. Girls are taught to be more conciliatory. That's what makes us 'likeable' – apparently.

What utter crap this is, but these biased expectations still exist. As unfair as that is, until this antiquated gendered societal model is significantly disrupted, it pains me to say this but women need to negotiate differently to men for the outcome to be successful.

Four steps to achieving a successful negotiation:[2]

1. **Assess.** Do the benefits of engaging in this negotiation outweigh the costs? Can you have influence in this situation? What will it cost you if you avoid negotiating?

2. **Prepare.** What are your interests in this negotiation? What are the interests of your colleague/s, team and organisation?

3. **Ask.** Engage with your colleagues. You have unique information they need to consider. Your conversations with your colleagues will give you the opportunity to share this information as well as listen to their perspective. If you don't ask, you won't achieve any resolution.

4. **Package.** Make proposals that package together issues and solutions. Start with the results you can deliver to your colleagues, your team, or your organisation. Do not get bogged down negotiating issue by issue. Use 'if/then' statements as a tool to present your 'ask'. Use 'we' rather than 'I'. For example: *'If we did this [proposal] then [this outcome].'*

Sheryl Sandberg's advice to women is to learn how to leverage themselves more as assets to the company or organisation as a whole,

---

2   Adapted from 'Negotiation', Stanford University Institute for Gender Research.

instead of focusing solely on their own performance and accomplishments. While she admits that this approach plays into the sexist mindset that women are caretakers and conciliatory within a work group, and that they are expected to care about a company as a whole rather than seeking recognition for their own accomplishments, in our current environment a communal approach to negotiating increases the chance of a successful outcome for women.

I agree – reluctantly … but as a starting point only, and to encourage more women to build their negotiation skills and confidence.

Here's how: instead of approaching negotiations as a win/lose situation, go into it with the intent to come to an agreement that improves the outcome for both parties. It won't go well if you start with a demand or ultimatum. Think of negotiation as problem solving, an opportunity to explore an alternative solution that can benefit both parties. Frame it in such a way that the focus of negotiation is on the benefits it will bring to your colleagues, team or organisation as a whole. Go for the greater-good stuff.

Negotiation is a popular and robustly discussed topic in the ElevateHER Australia Masterclasses and peer circles. Many circle members have shared stories about not negotiating salaries at the time of accepting their job offers, only to find out later that their colleagues (mostly male) were on higher pay rates or had more favourable packages. After our sessions on how to negotiate, what I love most is hearing the successful outcomes. It certainly pays to prepare, ask, and be flexible in negotiating a fairer deal.

Here are two such stories:

One public sector manager had accepted her salaried role without negotiation. At her level, she was not bound by the public sector award, a 36.5-hour working week and employment conditions like the other staff. In fact, it was an 'unwritten rule' that her position required her to work whatever hours were needed, including being on call on weekends. Furthermore, she was not entitled to monthly rostered days off like her team members. She soon realised that, overall, her hourly rate worked out to be less than her direct reports, who also enjoyed the benefits of rostered days off, weekends off, paid overtime or additional time off in lieu of overtime. So, she negotiated a better deal, took control of the hours she worked, learned to say 'NO', and a short time later she moved on to a new job with better conditions and more realistic expectations. *Winner.*

One other young manager who is ambitious and a high achiever in her industry discovered something similar. Her male colleague at the same level (but with substantially less client caseload) was receiving more favourable treatment in the workplace regarding hours of work, client allocation and commissions. In her peer circle of supportive women, they helped her prepare for a meeting with her boss (also male) the very next day. We were all elated to hear how she responded to resistance, held her position around fairness, and negotiated a packaged deal that benefited her boss, the organisation and – importantly – herself. *Win/win.*

This is why it's so important that women support each other and stand together to collaboratively push for positive change towards a fairer society, more equal opportunities and equal treatment.

Each time WOMEN gather to support each other the world HEALS a little more.

INITIATE ACTION ON EQUALITY

I believe the strongest way to initiate and drive positive action on gender equality will come from changing entrenched, often unconscious biases towards women. Like gender-specific roles, the impact of social conditioning from childhood leaves a lasting impact. In fact, we all carry biases, conscious and unconscious.

Consciously, courageously, consistently, collaboratively

Sometimes phrases just roll out of my mouth, and when I think about the meaning others may take from hearing them, I realise the potential bias I may have inadvertently implied. Because my visual, aesthetic driver is another one of my top three motivators, observing how people present themselves (the total package) and then forming an opinion in a nanosecond is an entrenched habit that I've become more conscious about. Why? Because, like all gender biases, I was inclined to assess female presentation more harshly than male presentation.

My partner made me aware some years ago that I was commenting on (read: critiquing) what a female newsreader or weather girl was wearing, and made no comment (read: show of interest) in her male counterpart's appearance. I recall my partner's comment was: *'What about his tie; does that suit his skin and hair colour?'* Hmmm. Point taken.

> **'There is no force equal to a woman DETERMINED TO RISE.'**
>
> Author WEB DuBois

Yes, most of us have become more aware of this in recent years and are trying to reprogram our thinking and entrenched habits (even in our homes). Parents are now more conscious of their responsibility as role models to their daughters and sons regarding the message their children are taking from observing who does what around the house, their career choices and priorities.

I acknowledge there are some times when it feels like political correctness has gone nuts. But we need to be careful that media-hyped extreme cases or exaggerated fear campaigns don't take away from the positive momentum that is currently happening towards creating a more gender-equal society.

Jump on board and ride this gender equality wave. Let's all be INITIATORS and supporters of improving gender equality by:

- **consciously** noticing when there is an imbalance (take the blinkers off; don't ignore)

- **courageously** calling out the behaviour (name the issue as something that requires change)

- **consistently** questioning the process (speak up; don't accept it as *'just the way it is'*)

- **collaboratively** working together to seek solutions (drive momentum, initiate resolutions).

Be an initiator of the changes you want to see in the world, now and for future generations.

Your plan to initiate action

Ask yourself ...

If I could initiate changes to the things or situations that are currently not working for me, what would I action first? What is ONE thing that would make a big, positive difference?

_____
_____
_____
_____
_____

Can I do that? What would it take?

_____
_____
_____
_____
_____

When will I do that? If not now, then when? What's one thing I could start exploring choices for, take a chance on, or change – RIGHT NOW?

_____
_____
_____
_____
_____

Remember: *now is the only time you have. Yesterday is gone – forget that. Don't waste time looking back. Tomorrow is not a given, it's a gift. Don't wait for later. Use the time you have, RIGHT NOW.*

Visualise …

So, when I do [this action] …

_____
_____
_____
_____
_____

… then it will feel like …

_____
_____
_____
_____
_____

… and I will be able to …

_____
_____
_____
_____
_____

… and then I will have [the result you want].

_____
_____
_____
_____
_____

Focus ...

Now focus on how awesome it will be when you make those changes and you have the result you want. What else will it give you? What will be some of the flow-on positive effects? How will you feel?

_____

_____

_____

_____

_____

Commit ...

On [date] _____

... I will initiate this action ...

_____

_____

_____

_____

_____

... and change ...

_____

_____

_____

_____

_____

Rock your stripes

I CHOOSE
... to live by choice
not by chance,
to make changes
not excuses, to be
useful not used, to
be motivated not
manipulated, to
excel not compete,
self-esteem not
self-pity,
I CHOOSE ... to
listen to my inner
voice not the
random opinions of
others.

CHAPTER 9

BE AN
INFLUENCER

FAVE 5
Formula

InFluencer

Colour me ORANGE ... or
... rock your own colours!

ZEBRAS ARE SITUATIONALLY AWARE AND SOCIALLY CONSCIOUS ...

Always scanning the horizon,
they are first to notice slight
situational changes and
potential threats.
It is said that when
the zebra stops,
raises its head and
starts twitching,
all the surrounding
animals take note ...
when it starts to move,
the others follow.
Whether the need requires
an urgent change response or
slow, deliberate movement
towards more
sustainable conditions,
Zebras are known to
influence other animals
to make necessary changes
for the greater good
of their society ...

INFLUENCE MATTERS!

> You will never INFLUENCE the WORLD
> by trying to be like it.
>
> Author unknown

STEP UP – INFLUENTIAL LEADERSHIP

Influential leadership featured strongly in my childhood, largely due to relentless exposure to religious fundamentalism and persuasive beseeching of evangelistic preaching styles, intentionally designed to instil fear into followers. By my mid-teens I had observed enough to understand that influence, like many behaviours, can be used resourcefully (for good) and unresourcefully (for manipulative purposes). It's fair to say that by the time I was a young adult I could spot a manipulator a mile away, especially those who prey on the vulnerable and needy by making them feel even more helpless and undeserving, with the intent to command unquestioning devotion. By my mid-20s I had no time or energy for that life-limiting shit. I was ready to discover new influencers.

> 'There are only two ways to influence human behaviour:
> you can manipulate it, or you can inspire it.'
>
> Simon Sinek

While preparing to write this chapter, I reflected back to identify and make a list of the people who had a strong, positive influence in my life. Those who believed in me and lifted me up. Those who have encouraged me along the way to give it my all, to have a good hard crack at life, and to be my unique, colourful, individual self – my full-arse version.

What surprised me (like a slap in the face) was how few there were.

I don't mean to be disrespectful to the many others who stirred me into action and motivated me in short bursts throughout my zigzag chapters; every experience influences our decisions in some way. But I do want to acknowledge and thank those really extraordinary few whose influence and guidance has had a profound positive impact on who I am becoming (yes – still evolving) and how I now influence others.

Please join me in raising a glass to these inspirational leaders and influential mentors:

■ **#1: My first employer during my hairdressing chapter – E.**
From age 15 to my mid-20s, he unleashed my creative mind, taught me to think outside the box, to experiment and take risks, to break the rules, and most of all – the power of expressive individuality. He's still cheering me on from the social media sidelines. *You rock, E.*

■ **#2: My best friend from teenage years and still to this day – V.**
Brought up in similar restrictive circles, we were both breaking barriers in our late teens and sharing combat stories. She always gets me, and has understood and accepted every zigzag turn I've taken without judgement. Her strongest influence on me was the power of education and independence. Life-long friends. *Rock on, V.*

- **#3: A very wise and insightful elderly country lady and client – Mrs P.**
  Her influence was short in time but had such a profound impact at just the right time, that I've never forgotten. We spoke every week during my Western Queensland chapter (seven years), a period of massive personal change, discovery and growth. She had her own style and grace, and a genuine interest in encouraging women into community lead roles. Her wise advice was: don't change to fit in with the locals; be your unique, vibrant self. Stand out, be the change. Women-wise influencer. *RIP, Mrs P.*

Then, there's this huge gap of about 10 years, when I was building my own influential leadership skills in public sector roles. I distinctly recall a growing awareness of the lack of what I considered to be inspirational or influential leaders within the public sector at that time. No wonder I decided to start my own leadership development consultancy after leaving this sector, and now coach and mentor many in similar situations. The need to develop more purposeful and positive influential leaders became obvious.

- **#4: My partner in this life chapter, referred to in this book as – Mr G.**
  A genuine, generous, caring and considerate man among men. He has shown me a breadth of love I had not experienced before, and to trust in my own ability and 'enoughness'. An influential leader and change driver in his own right, together we make a pretty formidable dynamic duo. Like a doubleshot espresso, he fuels my drive to keep reaching for those big aspirational, personally fulfilling goals. *Deep appreciation, G.*

- **#5: My other best friend and unofficial personal coach – L.**
  Drawn together as coaching buddies in 2012, we both had the same intuitive alarm bells ringing over the same manipulative situation at the same time. Since then, an amazing connection of mutual encouragement and pooled intuition has formed. She has taught me the power of core emotions and to trust my gut – absolutely. *You rock, L.*

- **#6: My mentor in all things authoring and speaking – AG.** Such a privilege to build connection with this genuine and generous man who inspires me to be my full-arse version and rock it at 100%, through personally modelling the FAVE 5 approach himself. We had similar blank canvas starts in life, and I swear he's my brother from another mother. He gets me. He pushes my buttons. *Respect bro, AG.*

On review of the collective outstanding traits these six influential leaders possess, what immediately comes to mind is: integrity, inner drive, intentionality, generosity, and trust. Each of them values integrity (as I do), does things with purposeful intent (as I do), enjoys giving of themselves to enable others (as I do), and connects on a deeper level that builds trust in the relationship (which I now do, but struggled with in my earlier years).

TRUST MATTERS

Trust is a biggy for me. I have developed a strong BS radar for picking up on things that are not congruent (read: inconsistent behaviours) or are surface-level behaviours (such as insincerity, fake friendliness or incessant questioning) that mask true intent. I, too, lived on the surface for many years, fully aware of the inconsistencies surrounding me.

Here's what I know for sure from experience: if you want to be an influential leader then building trusted relationships is crucial. Trust in the leader is the glue that holds workplace cultures together. Leaders will not inspire others, ignite action or influence positive outcomes if the people they lead don't trust them.

> **'Trust is the glue of life. It's the foundational principle that holds all relationships.'**
>
> Stephen Covey

In my leadership development practice I have developed a 5C Trust Formula that underpins the leadership programs I facilitate, and I regularly refer to when coaching leaders to be more engaging, inspirational and influential. It is:

Character + Capability + Courage
+ Commitment + Connection

Let's take a look at each of these:

■ **Character** is about WHO you are and WHAT you stand for. Traits like integrity, authenticity, genuine caring, ethics, beliefs, strengths … these are observable behaviours that come from one's core values.

REMEMBER: People want to connect with the real you. The wholehearted version.

- **Capability** refers to your knowledge, skills, experience and competence. The substance that underpins your behaviour, choices and actions, and most importantly – your credibility.

  REMEMBER: Knowledge also helps you make decisions – concisely and confidently.

- **Courage** to step into the arena to inspire and influence change. Courage to provide honest feedback or call out bad behaviour. Courage to show your vulnerabilities and be the real you.

  REMEMBER: When you have to dig deeper, you'll find the strength you need at your core values.

- **Commitment** to the longer-term, big-picture vision, the direction, those strategic goals, and the development of others to reach the desired outcomes. Following through on promises. Consistently walking your talk.

  REMEMBER: Take the time to genuinely engage and build trusted relationships.

- **Connection** is about the importance of relationship building, collaboration, networking, influencing others, and building influential and supportive circles – at all levels. Trust is built through genuine and intentional engagement.

  REMEMBER: Together we will always achieve more.

INFLUENTIAL READING

Probably the most referred to book on the topic of influence is Dale Carnegie's *How to Win Friends and Influence People*. I first read this in my late 20s, as a first-time business owner and starting to get involved in community groups. Several years ago I picked up a revised version written for the digital age. When I picked it out of my bookshelf again while writing this chapter, it fell open on a highlighted section that reads:

'The two highest levels of influence are achieved when:

(1) people follow you because of what you've done for them, and ...

(2) people follow you because of who you are.
In other words, the highest levels of influence are reached when generosity and trustworthiness surround your behaviour.'

It's no coincidence that the six people who have had the most positive impact on me personally are all generous in spirit and giving of their time, and absolutely trustworthy. I can tick off all five of the Leadership Trust Formula Cs for each of them, and I endeavour to consistently be like that, role modelling this formula as an influential leader of others.

My challenge to you is: would others consider you to be a positive influencer? Or an influential leader? Do you have positive influencers in your life? Or do you need to look more broadly to find them?

Perhaps you are in a situation where there are no obvious influential leaders you aspire to be like. That's okay. I've been there. During that significant gap in my life was when I did the most self-driven self-development, mostly through formal study and lots of reading.

Here's the thing: be open to being influenced by others you admire, respect and trust. Be open to being challenged, to change your mind and expand your thinking. If you want to be more influential, you have to be clear on what you stand for and be able to back that up with WHY (your purpose and intent) and WHAT (your knowledge and understanding that supports your actions). Keep learning. Keep growing. Actively search for and engage a variety of mentors. Keep updating. Keep it fresh and relevant. Use your full-arse version for influencing positive change.

Here's a list of my top 10 most influential books (not in order of importance – in order of growth stages from my 20s till now), and what key learnings I took from them at the time.

AUTHOR/S	TITLE	LEARNINGS
Dale Carnegie and Associates	*How to Win Friends and Influence People in the Digital Age*	Commonsense, timeless advice on how to successfully engage with others, revised from original version to be even more relevant.
Anthony Robbins	*Awaken the Giant Within*	Read at a time when I was ready to take charge of my own life, it inspired me to focus on my core values and build personal power. (I am not a fan of the author's evangelistic, manipulative stage presence.)
Susan Jeffers	*Feel the Fear and Do It Anyway*	I learned to identify the fears, smash them, and make decisions that were right for me. To feel deserving.
Daniel Goleman	*Working with Emotional Intelligence*	I gained a deeper understanding of the importance of EQ and how to use that as an influential leader.
John C Maxwell	*How Successful People Think*	I learned how to change my thinking, reprogram unresourceful thoughts into good thoughts, and stay focused.
Louise Hay	*You Can Heal Your Life*	I learned about self-love, forgiveness, attracting love, mental health, how the mind and body connect, and to listen to my gut.
Brené Brown	*Daring Greatly*	I learned about the courage to be vulnerable, to stop caring what others think, to trust my gut, and to drop the need for perfectionism.
Sheryl Sandberg	*Lean In: Women, work and the will to lead*	So many 'yes, yes' moments. Her thoughts aligned with my thinking and experiences at the time the book was launched, and ignited my passion to lean in and create women's peer circles.
Brené Brown	*Rising Strong*	Released and read at exactly the right time for me. Failing is how we learn and build courage to rise back up. This book reinforced my belief in the power of integrity.
Brené Brown	*Braving the Wilderness*	Gained a deeper understanding about my thoughts on belonging, and boosted my strength to walk into the arena, stand alone and speak my truth.

Go to my website, JilindaLee.com.au, to access a regularly updated list of recommended influential books.

STAND OUT – THE WOMEN-WISE ROLE MODEL

Reflecting on her personal experiences working alongside some of the most powerful men and women in the world, ex-MP Julie Bishop has since stated her agreement with the research that indicates women leaders are more inclined to build teams, emotionally engage with individuals, and be empathetic and sympathetic to the needs of people than male leaders, saying:

> *'Men are more likely to be driven empirically to set team goals, they're less likely to focus on the individual and it's much more punitive and less sensitive. They set goals and judge the team and call them to account at every step.'*

The research concludes, and I agree in general, that women's leadership style is more transformative (people focused), and men's leadership style is more transactional (measurable-goals focused). The key point she made, while presenting to a group of aspiring women leaders, that I strongly applauded was:

> *'Of course, there are strengths and weaknesses in both. But it leads me to conclude: if you're trying to be a man, it's a waste of a woman.'*

Bravo! Spot on. Years ago, I coined the label 'manette' to describe women in leadership roles who appeared to have dropped their natural womanly, engaging, collaborative approach, to be more like the male peers they were predominantly surrounded by. Perhaps it was their way of feeling accepted – part of the boys' club – or maybe it was a case of emulating those boss-leaders who walked before them (mostly males).

Two such manettes had a significant influence on my creation of that label. One was a direct supervisor, the other a director, both in the early years of my public sector chapter.

Supervisor C was a gruff, barking bully, who liked to pick on weak subordinates, especially unsure, nervous women. She seemingly enjoyed the cat and mouse game of toying with them as they asked for her advice on tricky issues. While I stood my ground, and even wrote a university assignment on workplace culture featuring a peer survey I had conducted with that team, her behaviour factored strongly in my decision to leap across to a better opportunity in another division within 12 months.

Director A was a pompous leader who flaunted around in designer clothes looking all important, but her engagement with others was superficial. After working with the division she led for 12 months, we happened to ride the same lift to the carpark together on my last day (picture: me holding a box of personal items), after I had accepted a promotional opportunity in another region. I will never forget her words: *'Oh, you're Jiliandra, aren't you ... '* She struggled with the pro-nunciation. *'I never did get to know you, but I believe congratulations are in order. Where is it you are going again? A remote posting, isn't it?'* All said with a dismissive, unimpressed, elitist, detached tone.

Eighteen months and two promotion levels later, having just com-pleted a departmental leadership program, the other participants and I were each giving a 20-minute presentation on what we learned to a group of senior departmental leaders. Sitting right in the front row was Ms Director A. My talk was scheduled for after morning tea break, and during the morning I had a growing urge that I wanted my pre-sentation to send a clear message to those in the front row about what leadership IS, and what it IS NOT. I wanted to inspire and influence change. So, I spent the morning tea break tucked away in another room, changing my presentation, and amazingly, what came up for me was SO clear. A motto, an acronym outlining what would become my personal leadership creed, that I still use to this day.

Rock Your Stripes

It is:

D – Deliver

A – Authentic

R – Responses

E – Every time

T – Truthfully

O – Openly

with

B – Bold

E – Enthusiasm

M – Model the way

E – Encourage the heart

The last two phrases 'Model the way' and 'Encourage the heart' are two of the *Five Practices of Exemplary Leadership*, the globally renowned framework developed by Kouzes and Posner that our leadership program had been based around. I concluded my presentation that day by touting what I believed to be my biggest learning, the courage to *challenge the process*. I challenged the senior leaders in the front row to be role models of exemplary, heart-fuelled leadership.

Contrary to what you might be thinking, it was not a career limiting move. Rather, it was the launch pad from which I built a reputation as an influential leader in the public sector, unafraid to challenge the status quo.

You will never influence the world by trying to be just like it.

I have told that story many times in presentations, as sadly it still resonates across various sectors. However, I believe it will become less of an issue the more REAL women we have in leadership roles, as women-wise leaders, not manettes.

After many years of writing this personal motto at the top of my whiteboard in every office I've occupied, several years ago I had it tattooed on my forearm. Now, that puts a whole new dimension to the saying 'wearing your heart on your sleeve'. *Influential inking.*

'The difference between those who change
the world and those who don't is that
those who do believe they can.'

Simon Sinek

YOUR BRAND – YOUR INFLUENTIAL MARK

If you want to leave a lasting, deeper impression, there's a few more things you can do to leave your influential mark on the world by strengthening your personal brand.

> ### Your brand is what others feel and say about you after you've left the room.

Personal branding is the process of developing, honing and being known for your unique 'mark' that makes you easily recognised and well remembered after you've left the meeting, the building, or moved on to the next challenge. Obviously, we all want that to be a positive mark.

In today's disposable economy and the fast-changing career market, building your personal brand has never been more important. It's vital to showcase who you are, what you stand for, what you have to offer, and the level of positive influence you can bring to an organisation, or indeed any situation where you want to leave your mark. Frankly, if you don't develop your own personal brand, others will do it for you. Do you really want to risk your brand to other people's assumptions?

Of course, these days the easiest way to present your authentic self is on social media platforms (the main ones being Facebook, LinkedIn, X and Instagram), and on your own website. That way anyone can check out who you are, your consistency of character (across all media), your capabilities (LinkedIn profile) and your passionate commitment (social causes, latest research, industry interests). Becoming 'world famous', a 'thought leader' or 'global influencer' has never been so easy, but just make sure the world is receiving your intended message.

In my consulting role, when I'm about to meet with a new client company, I check their website for the names of the CEO and executive teams, then check out their career history and experience on LinkedIn. If that triggers more questions, I do a further Google search for articles or media in relation to that person. It's not hard to piece together a picture of WHO they are and WHAT they do, and the journey that got them there. It's also a bonus if they've published articles or blog posts, as I may gain deeper insight into their thought processes and passions (a glimpse of their WHY or drivers).

On the flipside, the notable issue with social media research is incongruent messaging. Inconsistencies in what you portray or post across media platforms lead to questions around genuineness and trustworthiness. *Credibility matters.*

Let's rock your stripes to the point of proactively ensuring that 'brand YOU' is what you want to be known for.

Seven tips to help you create your own personal brand:

1. **Identify your values and set your priorities.** It's important to have a clear picture of your personal and professional goals, both short and long term. Focus on the things that move you closer to those goals. Don't get caught up in the white noise. Stay narrow and deeply focused on your core values.

2. **Identify your uniqueness and your strengths.** Think about the characteristics and strengths you've built across all aspects of your life. What's the 'one thing' that everyone says you rock at? If stuck, ask others for ideas … it's often more obvious to others than ourselves.

3. **Own your space.** Once you've identified your unique strength – perfect it. Learn all you can – become the expert in that area. Read, absorb, share and teach it.

4. **Build your platform.** Get into social media to build your virtual platform, so that your brand is visibly represented and you have a place to share your voice more broadly. LinkedIn is the most credible platform for professional influencers.

5. **Share your knowledge.** It's not enough to learn it or just showcase it. Influencers share their knowledge to help others. Do videos, social media, write both online and offline, and conduct presentations. This is where you prove that you know your stuff, build trust in your credibility, and gain exposure as a thought leader.

6. **Be yourself.** Find your own presentation style that works for you. Don't do what everyone else is doing; create your own style and leave some unique footprints for others to want to step into and follow your lead.

7. **Craft your unique personal brand persona.** Your brand persona can be created by identifying three things:

   – *Your emotional appeal.* What are your personality and behaviour features? This can be as easy as saying you have a crazy sense of humour or that you are obsessively organised. Take a moment: why do you think people are or will be attracted to the brand of you? What appeals to their emotions?

   _____

   _____

   _____

   – *Describe yourself.* When it comes to your brand, who are you and why do people enjoy working with you?

   _____

   _____

   _____

   – *Identify your specialty.* What do you do, and what do people want you to do for them?

   _____

   _____

   _____

Use these tips to create a strong brand identity that you can refer back to when it comes to creating materials that support your brand (such as CVs, social media pages, covers on presented work, PowerPoint style guides, websites). *Consistency matters.*

Building a personal brand takes time and effort, but it's worth it. The need for a personal brand will continue to increase. It's the one thing that no-one can take away from you and follows you throughout your zigzag journey. In fact, I believe it is a credibility requirement for influential leaders to have a strong, consistent personal brand. A brand that leaves the impression and feeling you are intending others to take away from interacting with you.

Real leaders don't hide behind doors.

One word of caution I feel the need to add: keep your ego in check. Don't allow your ego to grow bigger than your influence as you build your personal brand. Ego is not a dirty word. We all have it; in its pure sense, it simply refers to your self-worth, which is important to have. In fact, I'm intentionally encouraging you to build your internal personal power and self-worth, because that's where the courage to be your full-arse version comes from. BUT ... how you use that or portray that to the world matters greatly.

Everyone has an EGO ... it just doesn't have to be in the form of a strutting peacock.

It is not about popularity or chasing shallow measures like how many followers you have on social media, or 'likes' you have on a particular article you posted, or being Ms Popular Party Girl. Stay focused on the bigger goal, the greater-good outcome: influential leadership. Influence – like trust – has to be earned.

Flick back to the **Trust Formula** earlier in this chapter and review each one of the Cs. Make sure your brand is showcasing each of those.

Are you consistently marketing a personal brand that leaves the influential mark you want to be remembered by?

Checklist: how's your personal brand currently looking?

☐ Is your CV up to date?

☐ Does your CV style stand out from the pile?

☐ Do you have a current professional photo?

☐ Do you have a current LinkedIn profile?

- ☐ Do you actively research, interact and contribute on LinkedIn?

- ☐ Do you have a Facebook page? If so, is it consistent with your personal and professional branding?

- ☐ Do you have a website 'about you' page?

- ☐ Do you have a blog, YouTube channel, or other online presence?

- ☐ Does it showcase what you want prospective employers, mentors, colleagues or clients to see?

- ☐ If your name was Googled, would your profile come up? If so, would your influential media contributions (videos, articles, website, social media profiles) and other involvements fill the first page?

- ☐ Does it mention your active engagement with industry or business networks?

- ☐ Do you have a consistent branding or style that makes your work easily recognised and remembered?

SPEAK UP – OPPORTUNITIES TO INFLUENCE

> **'Surround yourself with only people who are going to lift you higher.'**
>
> Oprah Winfrey

While that popular quote is great advice, it's not always an easy thing to do, especially if your zigzagging leaps to take up new opportunities mean regular shifts to new regions. In the past decade, as we've moved three times to different regional locations, I've discovered just how limited the surrounding choices can be and how long it takes to build trusted relationships. At times, I have had to stand alone in the arena and speak up to inspire and influence positive change, sometimes a tad too much for the locals' liking. As tough as that can be, it has also been wonderful to see many women embrace the mentoring opportunities I have offered, such as the ElevateHER (Lean In) Circles facilitated in each region I've lived in since 2014.

While living in a remote location for two years, I saw a need to help the women in town find their voice and the courage to use it. When I first floated the idea of starting up a women's Circle, one female councillor told me it would never work: *'This is not the city, you know.'* But, true to form, I don't always do as I'm told, so I offered it anyway. The 12 circle places filled within 36 hours of opening registrations. By the end of that first year, I had enough on the wait list to start a second circle. *Win/win.*

During the second year, I discovered the community organisation that had run International Women's Day (IWD) events previously had decided not to do it that year due to missing out on some government funding. As an avid supporter of IWD celebrations and having presented at several over the years, I was keen to ensure IWD was celebrated in this small community. So, with only 10 days' notice and no budget, I decided to coordinate an IWD dinner, booked out a local restaurant, organised a guest speaker, planned the internationally themed program, and offered tickets online. It was a gamble, but thankfully all 40 tickets sold out in three days. It was a great success for the community and the attendees. I had run an event that inspired 40 other women (and several others who missed out) to jump on board, celebrate and support each other to 'be bold, be brave, be the change', which was the 2017 IWD theme. How could I NOT do something with a theme like that, right? Such a good match with my personal, influential leader brand.

If you can't surround yourself with positive influencers, be the inspirational leader others need.

These days, now settled (read: feet firmly grounded) on the coastal fringes of a large regional city with lots of networking and social events, and plenty of community groups to join, it's easier to pick and choose the things that match my values and where I can learn from others and potentially form mutually influential relationships. That said, I tend to think bigger and broader than just influencing local mindsets or community change-making, and find I'm continually drawn to raise the bar and join forces with national and global partners, those who have BRAGs (big, radical, aspirational goals), who want to not only improve their communities ... their aim is to change the world.

Since first writing and publishing this book (2019), the opportunities to influence at a broader global level have become increasingly available and easier to access during and post the global pandemic, evoking a heightened need to connect, build deeper relationships with colleagues to support each other, establish circles of influencers and game-changers, and collectively create meaningful, positive impact. Forming and being involved in movements that influence and create change has never been easier. Now is the time for more of that ... *ripples of impact.*

My point is: look for the opportunities to positively influence others. Ask if you can be part of an event or change movement. Jump on board if you can, or do your own thing. Life is too short to stand in the corner and wait for someone to notice your wisdom and potential influence.

RECRUIT YOUR OWN BOARD ...

As Chief Executive Operator of your own life's choices, Director of your career leap decisions, and Chief Planner of how you will influence and leave your mark on the world, it's a good idea to look at WHO's influencing YOU. Yes, the reality is you need more than one or two people as your 'go-to' mentors. You need a circle of influencers. A Board of Directors.

Who are your influential Board of Directors?

BOARD POSITIONS	YOU GO TO WHEN ...	NAME/S
Trusted advisor	*You have a problem ...*	
Teacher/mentor/coach	*You want to learn new things ...*	
Cheerleaders	*You want support and encouragement ...*	
Elder/role model	*You want wise counselling and good sound advice...*	
Creative inspirer	*You want to explore new ideas ...*	
Industry expert	*You want to gain knowledge and insight ...*	
Sponsor	*You want support to turn your ideas into actions ...*	
Wellbeing coach	*You want to stay balanced, healthy and resilient ...*	
	You want ...	
	You want ...	

If you have vacancies on your Board, think about how you could identify and engage the right individuals to join 'TEAM YOU'. You may also consider how YOU can offer your services in similar support roles to others.

I've learned that people will forget what you **SAID,** people will forget what you **DID,** but ... people will never forget how you made them **FEEL.**

Maya Angelou

CHAPTER 10

BE INVOLVED

FAVE 5
Formula

Involved

Colour me TEAL ... or ... rock your own colours!

ZEBRAS KNOW THE POWER OF SOLIDARITY IN NUMBERS ...

Just like their bold,
contrasting stripes,
zebras are both
independent and interdependent.
Community - belonging
to a herd and
sticking together to
support each other –
is an important aspect
of their survival.
While individually they can be
feisty and strongly defensive,
they've learned the dangers
of being ostracised,
and the vulnerability of
standing alone in the wilderness.
They know that working together
strategically and combining
their strengths and smarts
potentially outwits their
opponents, producing
greater survival rates, sustainability
and progress that comes
from communal effort ...

INVOLVEMENT COUNTS!

'GET INVOLVED ... the world is run
by those who show up.'

Author unknown

STEP UP – INTO THE ARENA

So, you made it. You've arrived at number five of my FAVE 5 Formula, hopefully with an ignited passion and strengthened resolve, ready to unleash your full-arse version and become one of the game-changing, influential leading women our world is crying out for. Are you ready to step into the arena?

While writing Part I, I most certainly felt like I was standing in the arena, right in the middle – alone and vulnerable, almost stripped bare, to openly share my personal stories and zigzag experiences, in the hope that it would challenge and inspire you to:

- dare to DISRUPT the status quo ... *get out of your comfort zone and drive positive change*

- dare to ASPIRE to those BRAGs ... *those big, radical, aspirational goals you deserve to achieve*

- dare to REACH higher … *to rise up from the knocks, learn, and keep reaching upwards*

- dare to EVOLVE … *to keep going, keep growing, and become your full-arse version.*

Not wanting to leave you hanging, all fired up but without some practical advice and suggestions on how to not only DARE but to take action and DO, I included Part II to encourage and hopefully enable you further to:

- embrace your unique INDIVIDUALITY … *own it to the core, and rock it*

- grow your INDEPENDENT strengths … *stand tall in your personal completeness*

- bravely INITIATE changes … *for yourself and others*

- build your INFLUENTIAL leadership strengths … *your personal brand and reputation.*

And NOW … if you are still holding back and not yet using all that to make a bigger difference … it's time to come out from behind the door, step out of your comfort zone, and step into the arena.

Please don't sit and wait for success to fall into your lap. Don't wait until you are invited to the decision-making table. Don't just strut your newly boosted FAVE self in front of your mirror or video camera.

I urge you to go out there; get INVOLVED. Use your newfound (or rejuvenated) confidence and courage to proactively contribute for the greater good of society. Be one of the game-changing women, find others to connect and collaborate with, and join in with them.

Why?

Here's the thing: the only game you can realistically change on your own is the one that plays inside your head. By all means, start there. Do the inner core work, build your personal power and identity, your independence and resilience muscle, negotiate better outcomes for yourself, create your personal brand, and be the CEO of your own life. But don't stop there. Every other game in life needs at least two to tango, and many more to move those massive mountains (read: entrenched BS status quo).

It sucks to sit on the sidelines. It's nuts to complain about the status quo or blame others – and choose to do nothing. It's lonely being at the top of your game on your own. Get involved. Contribute.

> '**When we choose contribution over criticism and courage over comfort, we can do anything.**'
>
> Brené Brown

INVOLVED AT ANY AGE, STAGE OR PHASE

I often hear comments (and excuses) on 'ideal' ages, stages or phases in life for certain levels of involvement or 'appropriate' levels of experience and wisdom for leadership roles. That's crap. I have seen community committees, business women's groups and corporate business sectors boosted greatly by the injection of young, relatively inexperienced women, or women from diverse backgrounds with limited experience in similar industries. I also know the benefits some of those younger women receive from being mentored from wised-up, whacky older women (yes, like me).

Sure, many of us took a few decades to find our stripes, before we got to the point of fully rocking them. But it's my belief that through mentoring and enabling our younger women with greater opportunities and choices than past generations had, their confidence will soar from early involvement in lead roles, and they will become tomorrow's women-wise leaders (not those 'manettes'). *YEAH! Bring it on.*

That said, of course the more experiences we go through the wiser we become, and women's wisdom needs to be valued and utilised more; hence my encouragement throughout this book for women of all ages, stages and phases to leap towards new opportunities and ride the exciting zigzag path. Experience (broad and varied) trumps textbook learning or a job-for-life mentality. *Nothing grows in the comfort zone.*

Encouraging the early involvement of young women is not the only answer in driving change to the status quo. I'm mindful of the difficulty many mid-life ladies have in getting past the recruitment gatekeepers to even get an interview to be considered for a higher level position. And it is a national shame that, while listed as 'employed' on census counts, when you dig deeper into the data many women are grossly under-employed or casually engaged in low-paying roles. We have to change that, too.

There's also something about turning 40 that seems to spark a level of urgency in people (especially in women) to make significant changes in their lives, like it's now or never. I know – I felt that too. As I approached 40, I remember surveying my situation, feeling the heaviness of it, and thinking to myself: if I don't get out and make changes now, I will end up being a bitter, angry 55 year old who feels like she's wasted her best years in an unhappy personal situation. So I jumped out of that energy-sucking box, and have never regretted it. Not even for a second. *Say NO to half-arsed living.*

I came across this Oprah published comment that made me laugh, then agree, then look forward to my next phase with excited anticipation:

'In your 40s you're just coming into it, you're intellectualising things, and you kind of know it and you feel it. But there's a deepening and a broadening and quickening of the knowing that happens in your 50s. Maya Angelou used to say to me "the 50s are everything you've been meaning to be". By the time you hit 60, there's just no damn apologies left. You got no time for that. You know who you are, what you stand for, what's important, what's not ... and life becomes a whole lot simpler. And peaceful. I have no angst, no regret, no fear.'

Rock Your Stripes

Bring on the 60s chapter, I say. My articles, columns and presentations are bound to get even more colourful! Although, if you've read through most of this book before landing here, you would realise I like to encourage all women to know who they are, what they stand for, what's important and what's not, and to not feel they ever have to apologise for any of that. How awesome would it feel to be like that in your 20s and 30s?

OMG. What I would now tell my 20-year-old self is:

RUN! Explore the world.
Experience lots of stuff.

Find out and embrace WHO I AM.
Fall in love with ME first.

Rock my unique stripes. Keep adding
more colourful stripes.

BE me – in all my full-arse version glory.

Don't let anyone or anything stop me from
being fully engaged, fully involved in life.

On reflection, I have been standing in the arena and INVOLVED in influencing, driving and leading change since my 20s. For me, it was always about 'what's next' and making a bigger difference:

- **Testing Teens:** asked lots of questions, tried out different stuff, embraced independence.

- **Triumphant Twenties:** first taste of successes, failures, learnings and achievements, major milestones, setting career direction.

- **Thoughtful Thirties:** working out what matters, what doesn't, honing WHO I am, and planning the next chapter.

- **Frantic Forties:** big changes, mid-life panic, realigning WHO I am with WHAT I will or won't accept, new beginnings.

- **Fabulous Fifties:** living life on my own terms, high-point achievements, more BRAGs, life balance, embracing choice, more zigzags, more influential phase.

- **Sensational Sixties:** I'll let you know in my next book … planning lots of writing, speaking, and influencing impactful change.

- **Satisfying Seventies:** hopefully, I'll still be writing, speaking and creating an impactful legacy.

- **Endearing Eighties:** if I get to enjoy them, it will be because I'm still agile, still reading and learning, still pushing the envelope, still asking questions, and still able to share some whacky wisdom with those who will listen.

Interestingly, the written reference my first employer gave me when I was in my late 20s outlines an extraordinary path that I couldn't see at the time, but he did. He wrote:

> '**Her creative talents are many and only matched by her management acumen and the presentation of an outstanding personality. It would not be out of place to recommend Jilinda to any position that requires a woman of the highest integrity and dedication. The position of first female Prime Minister is not beyond her grasp should it be chosen on talent rather than political preparedness … '**

Don't get hung up on the flowery words. At the time, I considered it to be creatively exaggerated as I had no interest in politics. Yet, I now understand that what he saw was a young woman whose observable personal brand and capability was such that nothing was beyond her reach, and whose contribution at high-level leadership roles would be considered a valuable asset. That, and a gutsy determination to change the world (yes, even in my twenties). The thing is, my career path DID indeed take me into government regional leadership roles, some 15 years later, although it was certainly not part of my career plan at the time that reference was written.

Oh, and Julia Gillard pipped me at the post at being the first female prime minister.

Joking of course; that political leadership role was never on my aspirational radar. Although I'm quite sure some public sector colleagues at that time were suspicious of my motives and enthusiastic ambition. That said, I am now a proactive advocate and mentor for women stepping up into political representative roles and believe in the power of women supporting women; particularly through formal mentoring program arrangements. As I mentioned in an earlier section, I'm excited to see strong, intelligent women stepping up as independent community leaders, not party puppets. *Igniting a spark of curious interest.*

My reason for sharing this story is: I see women of all ages, stages and phases oozing similar levels of leadership capability and potential, but with little inclination to step into the arena and start contributing. I'm on a mission to change that, because I see the benefits coaching and mentoring support provides, something I didn't have access to in my early years.

Facilitating ElevateHER (Lean In) Circles and mentoring Circle Leaders is one way I contribute to my mission of encouraging and enabling more women to step up into lead roles and change the game. I've also mentored for the Institute of Managers and Leaders national mentoring program, developed and facilitated an eight-month leadership program for Local Government women Councillors (90 participants) across Queensland, and provide ongoing mentoring and support for many of them. In recent years I've become involved in board roles with the Australian Local Government Women's Association (ALGWA), Australian Gender Equality Council (AGEC), and actively support Women for Election (WFE) and Pathways to Politics (P2P) programs and initiatives. *Contribution matters.*

Here's the thing: it doesn't matter what age, stage or phase you are at in life. It doesn't matter what your background is, or even what your current position is. Leadership is never about position; it is a set of behaviours and actions. I encourage you to use your passion for whatever causes you believe in, or changes you'd like to see, and find opportunities to contribute. To be INVOLVED in making that happen.

> **'Success is not a function of the size of your title but the richness of your contribution.'**
>
> Robin Sharma

STAND OUT – MAKE YOUR MARK

From 2017, my ElevateHER programs (run as a separate community development initiative of after-hours women's coaching circles) was initially run under the banner of our leadership consulting company – Vital LEADERS. Our intention was deliberate in ensuring that clients were aware of our passion for equality and fairness, and to showcase consistency of alignment between our personal passions and our professional brand. A wholehearted approach. *And yes, the recognisable zebra striping theme runs through all our program branding.*

So, when the national network *Women & Leadership Australia* (WLA) announced their #100daysforchange initiative from 1 July 2018, and invited organisations to join with them by pledging an action that supported improved gender equality, I jumped at the opportunity. ElevateHER, supported by Vital LEADERS, stood proudly to support this, not only in words but in actions. We pledged and followed through on our commitment to:

- post 100 inspirational quotes (one per day from 1 July) on our ElevateHER Leadership Community Facebook page
- roll out another ElevateHER Circle for Cairns women.

Towards the end of the 100 days, I realised that while the daily inspirational quotes (encouraging gender equality) were popular, we were kind of preaching to the converted. Our ElevateHER community page following is mainly women who have been on our programs or who follow us because they already support the ElevateHER equality mission. Basically, it was 'nice', but not challenging the right people to make a big enough difference. So, I decided to post these same quotes on my broader LinkedIn network for another 100 days. The difference in engagement and debate was notable. Not only did the quotes now attract a wider audience, they enticed some great comments and even a little 'pushback' debating (which I welcomed). Driving change requires that the status quo be challenged. *Stepping into the arena.*

Of course, what was really exciting was the combined impact. Many organisations across Australia also jumped on board that WLA #100daysforchange initiative, with an estimated 200 pledges for specific changes to be actioned and – according to subsequent WLA reporting – a staggering 200,000 people impacted in 2018, and imagine how many more changes were instigated in the flow-on effect since. It was great to be a supporting partner of such a great initiative.

In the years since, ElevateHER Australia (under my leadership) has continued to partner with other women's equality and empowerment organisations and movements, including AGLWA, AGEC, IWD, UNwomen, Lean In, and other national initiatives.

My point is: I truly believe in our ElevateHER Australia motto:

TOGETHER – we are stronger

TOGETHER – we can drive change

TOGETHER – we will make a greater difference.

One woman can make a difference, but together we can rock the world.

WISE AND INTENTIONAL INVOLVEMENT

Most of us would like to have more time in our lives, to be involved in more things and go to more events. While we all have the same 24 hours, seven days a week, we don't all have the same options and choices in how we use that to make a bigger difference, or the same priorities. That's okay. Whatever stage you are at in life, you need to be realistic and choose wisely the things you are going to be involved in.

I know lots of women who struggle to say NO to random additional roles, like secretary of their partner's soccer club (because none of the blokes will do it), or time keeper at a school swim race (because the other mums work full time), or bookkeeper for a community charity (because their best friend – the charity president – asked for help). You need to ruthlessly question what the best use of your limited time is. Will any of that bring you closer to YOUR aspirational goals? Or is it depleting your time bank and sucking your energy? What are you passionate about? What energises you and fills your satisfaction bucket? What legacy are you wanting to leave? Then – do more of that.

Passion drives motivation > Drives energy > Drives commitment > Drives action

After many years of regional, rural and remote location career hopping, we now choose to live within the outer coastal boundaries of a vibrant regional city where there are many and varied proactive groups and networks to join, and always lots of community and cultural events to go to. As an extrovert, I was often tempted to go to as many of these as I could fit in. Yes, it was probably driven by some FOMO thinking (fear of missing out). But, I learned to ask myself these questions before committing to local networking functions or business or community group involvement, to ensure that I use my time wisely and my involvement is valued (by me and others):

Checklist: Perhaps you need to ask yourself these same questions:

☐ Is this something I'm passionate about and that fits well with my values and current goals?

☐ Will I learn anything new, be challenged, or grow from my involvement?

☐ Would my involvement in this bring me closer to or assist me in achieving my priority goals?

☐ Are the others involved in this potentially my business or program target market?

- ☐ Will involvement provide opportunity to actively engage with likeminded peeps?

- ☐ Do I feel my contribution or presence would be valued, or even welcome?

- ☐ Is the group proactively making a difference, or floundering to survive?

- ☐ Will there be opportunity to help drive change for a greater-good outcome?

- ☐ How much time will it take up, and what are the potential impacts on my other projects or tasks?

- ☐ If it's a longer-term involvement, what are the commitment level options? How flexible is it?

- ☐ Have I assessed and discussed the potential impact on my significant other? Does it fit with OUR plans?

Now, you might think that being so strategic and intentional (read: picky) is not the way to proactively showcase my full-arse version. But what I've found is it's better to have more impact for time spent by choosing to be involved with only those things where I can make a big difference, rather than being one of the ra-ra socialites who turns up to every ribbon cutting, awards night or networking event. Politicians aside, no-one takes people like that seriously. It gives off the message of craving attention, needing to be popular and liked.

Here's the thing: be known for who you are and why you do what you do, not for how often you are seen or how many boards, committees or groups you are involved with. It is far better to dive deeply into the few things you are passionate about than have shallow involvement in a whole lot of random things just to be noticed.

'Life is not accumulation, it is about contribution.'

Stephen R Covey

SPEAK OUT – WITH UNITED VOICE

Surprisingly, I've never really considered myself as an activist – you know … one of those placard-waving, chanting, angry marching brigade. That's never been my scene. Perhaps it's because I grew up in the '70s during what is referred to as 'the second wave of feminism', watching the hippy protests and seeing them dragged away by police (on TV, not from standing on the sidelines). However, I have a new appreciation of what being an activist really means, since more recent campaigns such as the #metoo and #timesup movements. Women are angry (read: frustrated and fed up), and rising up in numbers 'too big to ignore'. Our online connected world has made activism and collective involvement much easier, and perhaps more enlightened and civilised in approach.

Activists and advocates

A quick Google search will tell you that an activist is a person who believes strongly in political or social change and takes part in activities such as public protests or campaigns, or supports strong actions to try to make this happen. An advocate is one who supports or promotes the interests of a cause or group.

So, turns out I AM an activist, or at least a strong advocate for gender equality, for individualism, for independence, for initiating and being involved with change. One of those revolutionary 'accidental feminists', like Australian author Jane Caro, who writes about pushing boundaries and making changes as more opportunities opened up for us than our mothers ever dreamed of, in her 2019 book of the same name.

With my larger-than-life face on the Institute of Managers and Leaders 2018 banners and posters as a national ambassador for their Chartered Managers program, I was certainly not hiding behind the door when it comes to advocating for raising the bar on leadership competence levels. Many of my social media posts, blogs and video messages also have a strong activism and advocating tone to them. *Full-arse passion.*

When you passionately believe in the need for changing the status quo and encouraging others to get on board, to get involved and help drive that change, you can't keep all that to yourself. Frankly, I think I'd spontaneously combust if I didn't get out there and join with others to help change the world.

So, I encourage you to explore opportunities to connect with like-minded people across the world. It is amazing how many doors this may open for you. Imagine how exciting and satisfying being involved in something far bigger, far broader reaching than you can ever achieve on your own, could be. Imagine the legacy your involvement could contribute to.

Here's the thing: one activist can bang her own drum, wave her own placard, post her own social media rant, and make a loud noise, but a whole group can turn an even bigger noise into actioning positive change. Be an advocate for change. Find your activist circle or group. Support each other and please help change the world.

Never doubt that a small circle of women can change the world. Indeed, it is the very thing that is proven to work.

I've chosen to finish this chapter – and indeed, end this book – with my adaptation of a famous inspirational quote. Like bestselling author and research psychologist Brené Brown, and many other influencers and advocators for courageous, game-changing leadership, I too have been moved and motivated by Theodore Roosevelt's quote, referred to as 'The Man in the Arena'. That said, when thinking of including it as the last inspirational quote in my book – a deliberately frank, fierce, full-arse femoir, written to inspire and urge women to step into the arena and courageously lead change, I was moved to adapt the wording to be more meaningful and motivating for women.

What can you contribute to actioning positive change?

WHAT are you so passionate about that you feel you'll burst if you don't say or do something?

_____

_____

_____

WHAT changes in your community or the wider world would you love to help drive?

_____

_____

_____

WHAT strong message would you like to send to others, and if you did it collectively it would have a bigger impact?

_____

_____

_____

WHERE will you do that?

_____

_____

_____

HOW will you do that?

_____

_____

_____

WHO do you need to connect with?

_____

_____

_____

IT IS NOT THE CRITIC WHO COUNTS;

NOT THE PERSON WHO POINTS OUT HOW THE BRAVE WOMAN STUMBLES, OR WHERE SHE COULD HAVE DONE DIFFERENT OR BETTER DEEDS.

THE CREDIT BELONGS TO THE WOMAN WHO IS

ACTUALLY IN THE ARENA,

WHOSE FACE IS SMEARED BY GREASE, SWEAT AND TEARS, WHO STRIVES VALIANTLY, WHO STUMBLES, WHO COMES UP SHORT

AGAIN AND AGAIN,

BECAUSE THERE IS NO EFFORT WITHOUT ERROR AND SHORTCOMING;

BUT SHE WHO ACTUALLY STRIVES
TO DO THE DEEDS,
WHO KNOWS GREAT ENTHUSIASMS,

THE GREAT
DEVOTIONS;

WHO COMMITS HERSELF TO
A WORTHY CAUSE;
WHO AT THE BEST KNOWS IN
THE END THE TRIUMPH
OF HIGH ACHIEVEMENT, AND
WHO AT THE WORST,

IF SHE FAILS, AT LEAST
FAILS WHILE

DARING
GREATLY,

SO THAT HER PLACE SHALL NEVER BE
WITH THOSE SMALL AND TIMID SOULS WHO
NEITHER KNOW VICTORY
NOR DEFEAT.

Adapted from Theodore Roosevelt's 'The Man in the Arena'

ACKNOWLEDGMENTS

Despite this book being part personal memoir, and proudly baring my life-long feminist thinking and advocacy for urging more women to step up into lead roles, it was certainly not a solo effort. Like most successful achievements in life, it takes a team of supporters, advisors, coaches and cheer-peers to ensure you reach the end goal.

My deepest thanks is for the unwavering support and encouragement from my partner – Gary Kerr. He's been my in-house manager (carrying way more than half the household maintenance load), back-of-house office manager (picking up the dropped balls), and wellness coach (meals, exercise, balance ... although I failed the eight-hour sleep regime) throughout this longer-than-anticipated authoring journey. Living with a creative person who constantly has too many tabs open at once is a full-on wild ride. Much gratitude. Deep love.

A huge bear-hug thank you (and that's significant because I'm not a hugger) to the most genuine and generous man I know in the professional world – Andrew Griffiths, my mentor in all things authoring and speaking. Not only do his author and speaker programs hit the mark, his ongoing support is second to none. I doubt this book would have ever been completed without his 'how to' guidance, proven frameworks, shared experience in smashing all the blockages, and occasional whipping (figuratively speaking). We did it! Massive thanks. Deep respect.

A special thanks goes to my very dear friend and intuitive coach – Leonie Lomax. She felt the power of my back-story from the day we met and knew that the journey to extract it from the back shelves of my consciousness would be a long, bumpy and emotionally charged one. Her listening ears and quiet whispers of encouragement were ever present, and often used. Heartfelt thanks. Deep bond.

The quality look and feel of this book – while ensuring it captured my unique individual quirky style and all the elements I wanted to include – was no small feat. Many thanks goes to Michael Hanrahan Publishing for the understanding, patience and persistence it took to manage the process from woe to go. Thanks for getting me. Let's play again.

Finally, I want to acknowledge all the awesome women who have cheered me on from the sidelines. Those I know well – my besties, and long-term friends. Those I've coached in women's circles. Those I've connected with through our ElevateHER Australia community. Those I've met and had enriching discussions with through gender equality partnerships and initiatives, facilitating programs, speaking at forums, and all those online Zoom interactions in recent years. How wonderful it has been to hear your stories, gain your input and feedback, and feel your encouragement to keep doing what I do. And those I'm yet to meet, but who have followed this journey and continuously liked and shared the related blurbs I've posted. Thanks for cheering me on.

Together we will always make a bigger difference.

WANT MORE?

Connect with Jilinda

If you've been inspired by this book to step up bravely,
stand out boldly, and speak up brilliantly,
to courageously make changes and lead change,
there are a number of ways you can keep that
game-changing momentum going.

Check out how to connect and work with Jilinda
in the following pages or visit her website at
www.JilindaLee.com.au.

You can also follow Jilinda's regularly shared
insights on these platforms.

WANT TO DIVE DEEPER?

Sign up for the *FAVulous YOU* online program

If you're ready to build more confidence, capability and courage to become your full version, and use that to make a bigger difference, then consider diving deeper into the FAVE 5 formula by enrolling in the full program.

Discover your unique **INDIVIDUALITY** and how to rock that – boldly.
Develop your **INDEPENDENT** strength and security – boldly.
Delve into your choices to **INITIATE** changes and take chances – bravely.
Define your passions and areas of **INFLUENCE** to drive change – bravely.
Determine where you can become **INVOLVED** and contribute – brilliantly.

To find out more about doing this program individually, or as a group, go to **www.JilindaLee.com.au/programs**.

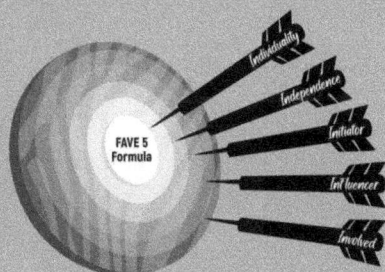

WANT COACHING SUPPORT?

Making changes can be challenging, and often needs a boost of courage, someone to explore options with you, and provide those little pushes and prods to take the next step.

Jilinda is a highly credentialled and experienced coach, internationally accredited in a range of coaching disciplines and behavioural science frameworks, and known for her genuineness and generosity in helping others make positive changes in their lives.

As a Change Champion coach, Jilinda is a lifelong learner and dedicated to continual professional development, to ensure she can provide current and credible mentoring support in her chosen areas of expertise:

- Leadership – character, capability, courage
- Women-wise leadership
- Understanding behaviour types and motives
- Social + emotional intelligence
- Gender equality
- Individuality – personal branding
- Independence – personal power
- Authentic living – positive aging.

To find out more about coaching programs, individually or group coaching, go to **www.JilindaLee.com.au/coaching.**

NEED AN ENGAGING SPEAKER?

Engage Jilinda to inspire your audiences to think differently, initiate change, and influence positive action.

Jilinda is an experienced and engaging presenter, having delivered workshops, programs, webinars, keynotes, and interactive forum sessions for a range of industry groups, leadership organisations, and women's events. She is a sought-after speaker for International Women's Day events and gender equality summits and panels – globally.

Jilinda enjoys inspiring others by sharing her wisdom gained from zigzagging through six decades of life and over three decades of leadership experiences. She weaves personal stories, latest research, and thought-provoking messages into her presentations, challenging audiences to make changes and take action to become game-changers.

Expect bucket loads of passion, straight talk, and a playful splash of individual quirky style as she authentically rocks her own colourful stripes, to inspire others to unleash their full potential.

To find out more about engaging Jilinda to speak at your next event, either in person or virtually, and check out her latest speaking topics – go to **www.JilindaLee.com.au/speaker**.

WANT TO INTERVIEW JILINDA?

Panels, Podcasts, Publications

Jilinda brings a unique mix of lived experience, research, and wisdom gained from decades of advocating and driving changes, to speak with authority and passion on the following topics:

- The future of leadership – authentic, agile, accommodating
- The need for more diversity at decision-making tables
- Women-wise leadership – game-changing characteristics
- Gender equality matters – disrupting societal norms and systemic barriers
- Women's rights (human rights) – choices, chances, changes, opportunities
- International Women's Day themes
- Individuality – the power of creating and owning your personal style
- Authenticity – the importance of building a rock-solid inner core
- Ageism – bias awareness, positive aging, being impactful at any age, stage or phase
- All things to do with changing the narrative for women in life, leadership and legacy.

To enquire about interviewing Jilinda or inviting her to your next panel discussion, go to: **www.JilindaLee.com.au/contact**.

Record your thoughts, ideas and actions in these pages

www.ingramcontent.com/pod-product-compliance
Lightning Source LLC
Chambersburg PA
CBHW052108030426
42335CB00025B/2890